FORESTS, POWER AND POLICY

FORESTS, POWER AND POLICY
The Legacy of Ray Williston

Eileen Williston
and
Betty Keller

Caitlin Press Inc.
Box 2387
Station B
Prince George BC
V2N 2S6

Forests, Power and Policy
Copyright © 1997 Eileen Williston and Betty Keller

Caitlin Press
Box 2387
Station B
Prince George, BC
V2N 2S6

All rights reserved. No part of this book may be reproduced in any form by any means without the written permission of the publisher, except by a reviewer, who may quote passages in a review.

The Caitlin Press grately acknowledges the financial support of the Canada Council for the Arts for our publishing program. Similarly, we acknowledge the support of the Arts Council of British Columbia.

Layout and Design by Vancouver Desktop Publishing
Cover design by Warren Clark Graphic Design
Indexing by Katherine Plett

All photos are from Ray Williston's private collection.

Canadian Cataloguing in Publication Data

Williston, Eileen, 1920-1996
   Forests, power and policy

   Includes index
   ISBN 0-920576-69-9

   1. Williston, Ray. 2. British Columbia—Politics and government—1952-1972.* 3. Cabinet ministers—British Columbia—Biography.* 4. Politicians —British Columbia—Biography. 5. British Columbia. Dept. of Lands and Forests—Biography. I. Keller, Betty. II. Title
FC3827.1.W54W54 1997   971.1'04'092   C97-910615-X
F1088.W54 1997

Table of Contents

Author's Note / 7

Foreword / 8

Acknowledgements / 9

CHAPTER ONE:
The Reluctant Politician / 11

CHAPTER TWO:
A Start in Life / 23

CHAPTER THREE:
A Career in Education / 53

CHAPTER FOUR:
Minister of Education / 73

CHAPTER FIVE:
The Member for Fort George / 97

CHAPTER SIX:
British Columbia's Forestry Revolution / 115

CHAPTER SEVEN:
The Two Rivers Policy / 169

CHAPTER EIGHT:
Minister of Lands / 223

CHAPTER NINE:
Life After Politics / 247

CHAPTER TEN:
Retirement / 287

Index / 296

Author's Note

ON A SPRING DAY IN 1947 MY HUSBAND, *Walter Dolf Thumm, came home from classes at UBC and said, "How'd you like to move to Prince George?"*

Principals and school board officials from various parts of the province had come to Vancouver to recruit teachers, and Walt had been interviewed by a number of them. Because there was a teacher shortage, qualified people could pick and choose where they would teach. But Prince George! To me it seemed as remote as Mongolia.

"Why Prince George?" I wanted to know.

"The principal. . . I liked the cut of his jib."

"What's his name?"

"Ray Williston, and I think he's the sort of guy who'll delegate responsibility then let you go to it."

On that assessment, we went to Prince George. For two years Walt taught physics in the high school, then became principal of the newly-opened Connaught Elementary school. We lived in the dorm in its opening year, then in Pine Manor in its initial years.

We remained in Prince George for three years—a significant period of our lives, for our first son was born there and lifelong friendships were made.

Time went by, intersecting circles tracing the patterns of all our lives, then 38 years after Walt and I had taken the fork in the road which led us to Prince George, Ray Williston and I, both widowed by then, were married.

Eileen Williston/1995

Foreword

EILEEN WILLISTON BEGAN THIS BOOK as a series of short articles based on anecdotes that her husband, Ray Williston, had told her about his early life and his adventures in politics. Encouraged by the members of the writers group to which she belonged to make them into a book, she was in the midst of revising and organizing them when she died on April 3, 1996.

Having promised her that this work would be completed and published, I began work on the manuscript a few months later, interviewing Ray at great length to complete the story of his years in government, his adventures as an international forestry consultant, and his extremely busy retirement. With the aid of old newspaper files and other published and unpublished sources, together Ray and I were able to round out his story by placing his memories in the context of the events occurring on the provincial, national and international scene.

The result, although technically a biography, is also an intimate portrait of the inner workings of B.C.'s government in the turbulent 1950s and 1960s when the whole face of this province was changed by the Forestry Revolution and the Two Rivers Policy. Ray Williston, although always a reluctant politician, was an intimate part of both of these upheavals—both as a catalyst and a policy maker. Governments have come and gone since his terms in office, policies have changed radically, resources have become threatened, and industries have evolved, but much of what he accomplished in those years still stands as a valuable legacy for future generations.

Betty Keller/ August 1997

Acknowledgements

RAY WILLISTON AND BETTY KELLER ARE INDEBTED to the following persons for providing information: Mauri Skogster; Neil Swainson; Donna Lloyd of B.C. Hydro; Garth Decker and Sally Murdoch of Canadian Forest Products; and Yoshio Hayashi of Oji Paper; and to the members of the Quintessential Writers Group for their encouragement and critiques.

CHAPTER ONE:
A Reluctant Politician

IN EARLY 1952, WHEN 38-YEAR-OLD RAY GILLIS WILLISTON had been employed for almost two years by the British Columbia Department of Education to inspect schools in the Prince George/Peace River area, three Prince George businessmen—Elmer Nelson, Alex Floen and Chuck Gabrielle—called on him to ask whether he'd ever thought of going into politics.

"No."

"How about letting your name stand for nomination?"

"No, thank you. . . . What party are you talking about anyway?"

"Social Credit."

"Social Credit? I know next to nothing about it."

Not many other people in British Columbia knew much about it either. At the time the three businessmen called on Ray, the province was governed by a shaky coalition of Liberals and Conservatives under Premier Bjorne or Byron "Boss" Johnson, but an election was looming and the fledgling Social Credit party was running a number of candidates. The party's leader was W.A.C. Bennett who had left the Conservative party in 1951, dramatically crossing the floor of the legislature to sit as an independent. Later that year, having decided to design a party of his own, he had toured the provinces to investigate other political parties. The one that appealed to him most was Alberta's Social Credit government, although it was by then Social Credit in name only, having moved a long way from the doctrines of the movement's founder, Major C.H.

Douglas, a Scottish engineer who was obsessed with rebuilding the world's financial systems. What Bennett saw was a government which emphasized sound fiscal policy, and this is what he was looking for. "It had balanced budgets every year," he later explained to Ray (and anyone else who asked), "and it was getting out of debt long before they found oil. They were on their way, and they were really a non-partisan type of government." British Columbians, however, had been taking little interest in what was going on in Alberta.

"Look," Ray told the three businessmen, "I'm flattered but I can't do it. I have dozens of inspections to finish so teachers can qualify for permanent certificates. I just can't drop everything." More to the point was the fact that Ray Williston was not a political animal. There had been no discussion of politics in the family home. He was aware that his grandfather had always voted Liberal because of his mother's comment that "If a horse was running with a Liberal ticket on it, your grandfather would vote for it." She put her own vote on the man rather than the party. Ray grew up uninterested in politics, aware only that one never voted CCF because socialists believed "the world owed them a living," and his family had never subscribed to this view. He had, in fact, gone out to work at age 14, just a month after his father's death, in response to his mother's announcement that "No one's going to look after us now. We'll have to look after ourselves." And they did.

But Ray was puzzled why the three businessmen had sought him out. "Why me?" he wanted to know.

"Remember that business about financing for schools?" Gabrielle asked.

Ray could hardly forget "that business." The previous January he had been invited to address the Junior Chamber of Commerce on education financing. There had been a large turnout in the banquet room of the Prince George Cafe, so as he stood up to speak he did not notice Nestor Izowski, mechanical superintendent of the *Prince George Citizen*, pulling out a notebook.

After the meeting, Izowski dropped his notes on the editor's desk in the *Citizen*'s deserted office. The next morning, editor Terry Hammond used the notes to write an account of the talk, and since he was a staunch Liberal supporter and Izowski's notes seemed to indicate that Ray had been attacking the policies of the Liberal education minister in Victoria, Hammond attacked Ray. Headlining his story INSPECTOR R.G. WILLISTON FLAYS SCHOOL COST POLICY, he accused Ray of announcing an imminent increase in Prince George's share of school costs while rural assessments remained low. He went on to say that Ray had taken "a roundhouse swing" at the calibre of local teachers.

Although Ray protested the inaccuracies in the article, Hammond refused to retract the story and even refused to print Ray's letter-to-the-editor correcting it. Finally Ray was forced to take out an ad in the paper explaining what he had really said. In it he denied forecasting higher school costs and local assessments, and said that he had only been explaining that since the rural area served by the Prince George School District paid a flat rate for school operation, future increases for the district's overall needs were going to fall on the shoulders of the town's taxpayers. He had no means of predicting what this would actually mean in tax increases. As for remarks about local teachers, he said that rather than "a round-house swing" at them, he would prefer to give them a hug of appreciation. "There are more temporarily certified teachers at work in my inspectorate than there has been since the war... because the supply of fully certified teachers is not sufficient to meet the demand." Then he added, "But what may be lost to experience is gained by the added energy, interest and enthusiasm these people bring to their work."

While this flurry was taking place in Prince George, worse squalls were blowing in Victoria. The news services had picked up the original story, and the Liberal organizer for B.C., a man called Bridgeman, demanded that Ray be fired on the grounds that as a civil servant he had no right to air his views on government policy.

Dr. Francis T. (Frank) Fairey, deputy minister of Education, reacting to the outcry, phoned Ray and summoned him to the capital. Ray swears that Fairey's voice was so loud that he could have heard it all the way from Victoria by just opening his window. An Englishman, Fairey had served with the Canadian army in World War I and still held the rank of colonel in the militia, and he tended to take the military approach to his subordinates in the Department of Education. But Fairey was not only reacting to the educational issues involved in the fuss over what Ray had said or not said; he had his own political axe to grind in the dispute because he was prominent in the Liberal Party and would, in fact, become the party's candidate for the Victoria riding in the 1953 federal election. Ray had provided him with fodder for the campaign trail.

"What the blazes do you think you're doing, Williston?" he demanded as Ray entered his office. "You're supposed to be a civil servant!"

After trying unsuccessfully to get in a few words in his own defence, Ray decided there was no use arguing with the man and walked towards the door.

"Where do you think you're going?" Fairey demanded. "We're not through with you yet. The minister wants to see you. You'd better get in there!"

The atmosphere in the office of Education Minister W.T. Straith (Liberal MLA for Victoria) was by contrast calm and friendly. He shook Ray's hand and motioned him to a chair. "What's this all about?" he asked.

Ray produced the newspaper clippings. "Here, these tell the story."

"I can see you're frustrated," Straith said after reading them, "and maybe with good reason. I'll tell you what: before the next budget, I'll call a meeting of inspectors and you can have a go at us then. In the meantime, how about keeping a low profile? Just tell people you have received a very, very, very severe reprimand and let it go at that."

Understandably, this whole "business about school financing" was very fresh in Ray's mind when he was approached by the three Prince George businessmen, but when they persisted in trying to persuade him to run for the Social Credit nomination, he just laughed. "No. N.O. No!" he said and saw them out the door.

Later that year a Social Credit minority government was elected, but the following spring Bennett, sensing a swing toward his "new broom" party, engineered a defeat on a budget vote. A new election was called for June 9, 1953, and at the end of March the same three men came back to Ray. "What about it this year?"

This time he could not plead too much to do. He had been one of four B.C. educators chosen to attend a University of Alberta Kellogg Foundation seminar on administration in education and had finished his inspections early in order to be in Edmonton in April. He gave the nomination offer some thought and decided it was just possible that he could do more to resolve educational problems if he was in Victoria than if he stayed in Prince George. Of course, if he was elected, he would have to give up his inspector's job, but perhaps it would be possible to keep up with his profession by taking a course or two at the University of Washington. (At the time it was not uncommon for Victoria teachers to commute to classes in Seattle.)

"Look," he told his visitors, "how does this sound? I'll let my name stand, but I won't push for it. That's your job. Then, if I do get nominated, I'll pitch in and go to work on it. Okay?" And they agreed.

His decision promised trouble because there was already a Social Credit sitting member for Fort George—an area that took in everything from Prince George to the Alberta border, south to Quesnel and north to the Peace. Ray would have to run against him for the nomination, and he knew nothing about the riding's back-room politics. In 1952, when he had declined to run, the competition for the nomination had been between Lou King of Prince George and lumberman Bert Leboe of Crescent Spur in the McBride area, the "east end of the rail line." As there was no road connecting McBride and Prince George, the Leboe supporters had rented a CNR sleeping car to take them to Prince George for the convention and provide them with accommodation while they were there. But just before the date for the nomination meeting, the Lou King supporters had done some arithmetic, and realizing they did not have enough committed votes to get their man in, they postponed the meeting for a week. Leboe and his supporters were not informed of the change and took their sleeping car to Prince George on the original date. They were furious when they learned of the postponement, especially since they could not raise the money to make the trip a second time. The official meeting took place the following week without them, and Lou King was duly nominated.

The McBride people did not have a candidate in 1953 because Leboe had refused to go through the charade again, but they showed up in force anyway on nomination night, April 25, ready for battle. In the turbulent meeting that followed they threw their support behind Ray and clinched his nomination. It was Lou King's supporters' turn to be furious—so furious that they phoned W.A.C. Bennett in Victoria to insist that he help them.

"Lou King is our member and we want to keep him!"

"And what do you expect me to do about it?" Bennett asked calmly.

"Refuse to accept this guy's nomination!"

"No, I won't do that," said Bennett. "If Williston was chosen, then he's your candidate." No amount of pleading would budge him.

Meanwhile, as soon as Ray's nomination in Fort George had become official, he was fired by the Ministry of Education. This came as no surprise since Dr. Fairey had been on a campaign to keep teachers out of politics. Speaking to the Greater Victoria Teachers'

Association on March 8, he had declared that "One of the occupational hazards of teaching is that you, like a civil servant, are not a complete citizen. The teacher has no business in politics. I know a lot of you won't agree with me... but the teacher's place is in the classroom and that is where he should stay." Fairey sent two assistant inspectors to replace Ray in the Prince George inspector's position, but this did not end Ray's job. In order to make sure that the teachers in his district all received their inspection reports, he remained at his post without pay, supervising his new assistants until the end of the school year.

As a result of these public battles, before the election hoopla got off the block in the rest of the province, it was already in full bloom in Prince George with letters-to-the-editor, street corner stumping and coffee club arguments. In Victoria, Premier Bennett, who thrived on controversy, decided that Prince George would be the ideal place to kick off the Social Credit campaign. When he arrived in town on May 11 for the opening rally, he immediately sent Ron Worley, his executive assistant, to tell Ray to show up early so that Bennett could give him his orders in person.

The CCF Hall, the biggest room in town, had been chosen for the rally. There was an air of lively anticipation in the community, and long before the show was due to start, the place was so packed that loudspeakers had to be installed outside for the 400 people who could not get into the hall.

Backstage, Bennett buttonholed Ray. "You get up there," he said, "tell them who you are, then sit down. I'll handle the meeting after that."

As Bennett rose to speak, there was a stamping of feet from the first ten rows, then the shouting began.

"We want Lou King!"

"Make Williston resign!"

The premier laughed and said, "I am pleased at your enthusiasm and know you will show it equally for others in the future."

But the King supporters persisted. "King's our man! We want King! We want King!"

Bennett waited, undaunted by the clamour. Finally he said, "I don't dictate who the candidate will be. You decide and I'll take him. Ray Williston got the most votes, so he's your choice. If there is any doubt about your nomination meeting, call another. But who you choose is your business, not mine, and I have no intention of asking Williston to step aside."

Bennett knew, and the Lou King supporters knew, that there was no time to go through the nominating process all over again. And so the members of the Fort George Social Credit Association settled down to work for their candidate, declaring—on an unexpected note of solidarity—that Lou King would be Ray's campaign manager. The job turned out to be in name only, however; Ray's real campaign manager was his friend Harold Moffat who, as school board chairman, was used to being drawn into wrangles.

Their partnership, however, was nearly cancelled before it began after Ray dropped into the Moffat family's Northern Hardware to discuss an upcoming trip to McBride and found Harold and his father shouting at each other. Harold had just had a run-in with a man named John Toney about the one-room school near the airport. "Who do you work for anyway?" roared Alex Moffat. "Does the school board pay your salary? No! You get your paycheque from the Northern! So why don't you work for the Northern instead of running around the country getting into fights over one-room schools?" He took a breath for the final thrust. "And now you're into this damned election thing, we won't see hide nor hair of you around here!"

Ray ducked out of the store, convinced he was on his own, but as soon as he got home the phone rang. It was Alex Moffat. "I hear you're going to McBride," he said. "You'd better take Harold along. He knows everybody along the line."

After that Harold accompanied Ray to most of his political meetings, the two men sharing a hotel room in each town. One morning just as they were about to leave their room, Harold took his wallet and loose change from the dresser and shoved the coins into his pocket, only to hear them jingle to the floor.

"What-the-hell!" he muttered. "I didn't have holes in my pockets when I took my pants off last night!" Then he looked at the suit Ray was wearing. "Hey, Williston!" he said. "That's my suit you've got on!" And he turned out his pockets to show him the holes. The two men were so much alike in height and build and in their taste in clothes that Ray had not noticed he was wearing Harold's suit.

Ray campaigned mainly on education, particularly on better teacher training and better school financing, but he also spoke about the need for roads and for access to power in northern British Columbia. His wife, Gladys, and Harold's wife, Helen, sometimes went along to his rallies while he was still getting his baptism into public speaking, and standing at the back of the hall with Harold, they realized that Ray would fasten onto a particular word and unwittingly repeat it . . . and repeat it . . . and repeat it. The more nervous he was, the more he was afflicted. To cure him, whenever he became enamoured of a particular word, one of them would hold up a finger each time the word was used. If they ran out of fingers on one hand, they started on the other. Sooner or later Ray would see the array of fingers and have to figure out which word he was abusing. Although he never entirely conquered the habit of over-embracing some words, by the time the campaign was over, speech-making was coming easier to him and he was becoming comfortable in the public forum.

One night, however, he suddenly found himself out of his depth in front of an audience in Dunster, a tiny village east of McBride. He had successfully handled a barrage of lightweight questions, but when those questions began to dwindle, a high-profile CCFer rose to his feet clutching a prepared list of questions that he knew Ray was too green to handle. Before getting to his first question, however, the man read a long eulogy on socialist policy and seemed about to launch into a campaign speech himself when the chairman finally banged his gavel. "Do you have a question?" he asked.

The CCFer had just opened his mouth to reply when the hall was pitched into total darkness. When the lights failed to come on again, the chairman declared the meeting over and the people filed out of the hall. Later Ray learned that the owner of the power plant which lit the hall was a strong Williston supporter; switching off the power had been his contribution to the campaign.

Ray had waited until after his nomination to tell his family in Vancouver that he was entering politics. His sister Rosabelle's husband, Johnny Fisher, was at the time a patient in Vancouver General. Two years earlier, doctors had operated to permanently collapse one of his lungs because abdominal fluid had leaked into the lung tissue after the pleural lining had deteriorated. The method was drastic: the ribs over the lung were removed, then allowed to grow back under weights to force the lung to remain deflated. Johnny, who was only in his forties, had remained immobilized in hospital all this time, then just when he was happily contemplating discharge, the doctor told him the ribs had grown back improperly and the operation would have to be repeated. With this news, Johnny's optimism vanished, his health deteriorated, and the operation was put on hold until he was in better shape.

It was at this point that he learned of Ray's nomination, and he began following the election campaign as closely as a bettor follows the horses, forgetting about his own condition. He even organized a polling station in the hospital, but on the morning of the election he was wheeled off to the OR, protesting vigorously. His first question as he fought his way out of the anaesthetic after the successful operation was "Did he win?"

He was never able to return to his job as chief engineer with

Union Steamships, but he got work as an engineer at Weldwood's plywood plant. And he remained one of Ray's greatest supporters.

During the campaign, Ray noticed that lawn posters in Prince George were vanishing quicker than they could be replaced. The mystery wasn't solved until a mortified mother phoned Ray to confess that she had found a cache of VOTE FOR WILLISTON signs in her basement. She was the wife of Ray's friend, Mayor Garvin Dezell of Prince George, who just happened to be the Liberal candidate in the election. The two Dezell children, Cliff and Denise, had been secretly doing their bit for their father.

Camaraderie between Ray and his Fort George opponents persisted throughout his career. Before one election Spike Enemark, who was the Liberal candidate for that particular round, stopped Ray on the street to tell him he hadn't a hope in hell of winning.

Ray laughed. "If you beat me at the polls I'll shine your shoes right here on Third Avenue at high noon."

"It's a deal! If you win, I'll shine yours," Enemark said.

The day after the election a photo appeared in the *Citizen* of Enemark shining Ray's shoes on the main street of Prince George. (Eventually when Spike retired from the political ring, his son Tex took on the Liberal candidacy. Many years later when the author met Tex at a Prince George reunion, he referred to Ray's long run as MLA for Fort George. "Yes," he said wistfully, "we all had a whack at him.")

In the election of June 12, 1953, the complicated multiple-choice voting system, which had been introduced by the old Liberal-Conservative coalition, gave the Social Credit party 28 seats in the 48-seat house. One of those seats was filled by Ray Williston, although he did not have a clear majority in the first count. On June 11 when all polls had been heard from and all first choices counted, he had the edge with 2,893 votes, Dezell for the Liberals had 1,654, and Bond for the CCF had 1,525. However, on the second count, which included all absentee ballots and the second choices on the ballots on which the CCF had been first choice, he was clearly the winner—3,509 votes against Dezell with 2,173. (In McBride, which had formerly been a Liberal stronghold, a determined campaign by Leboe's group gave Ray 183 votes, the CCF 79 and Liberals 71.)

Ray Williston was now launched on the political career which would keep him in the legislature for the next nineteen years.

CHAPTER TWO:
A Start in Life

ALTHOUGH RAY GILLIS WILLISTON WAS BORN IN VICTORIA, British Columbia, the Willistons are an old New Brunswick family. In 1784 John Bailey Williston, a 27-year-old carpenter, had deserted the American army and made his way to New Brunswick as a United Empire Loyalist. He was granted property near Saint John but, dissatisfied with the rough land assigned to him, moved north to Bay du Vin on the Miramichi. In 1788 he married Phoebe Stymiest, daughter of another Loyalist, and they had ten children—eight sons and two daughters. Very few descendents of John Bailey Williston strayed from the Miramichi, but Ray's father Hubert broke with family tradition, going first to Hull, Quebec, where he worked for the E.B. Eddy Company, then further west to Winnipeg and a job at Swift Canadian Company.

It was in Winnipeg that Hubert met Islay (*Eye'lah*) McCalman. In 1884 her father, Peter McCalman, working his way west building water towers for the Canadian Pacific Railway, quit his job when the rail line reached the boom town of Winnipeg and went into the construction business. He boarded there with a relative, Lizzy Gibb, who acted as matchmaker between Peter and her friend Elizabeth Anne Gabriel, an English girl who worked at the Mint in Washington, D.C. Peter and Elizabeth married, built a home in boom town Winnipeg—the property is now occupied by the Elmwood Cemetery—and in due course they had one daughter, Islay.

When Hubert Williston began his courtship of Islay McCalman, he was 32 and she just 20. Peter McCalman was not at all pleased, and not only about the age difference; Hubert was an Anglican, the McCalmans staunch Presbyterians. (Peter had conveniently forgotten that Elizabeth had been Anglican before marrying him.) Determined that Islay would not marry Hubert, Peter sent his wife and daughter off to search out the McCalman family roots on the Isle of Islay in the Inner Hebrides. However, the six-month separation only confirmed the old adage about absence and the heart, and the McCalmans finally agreed to the marriage, but only if Hubert became a Presbyterian. He and Islay were married in a proper Presbyterian ceremony in Winnipeg. Their first child, Norman, arrived in 1910. By this time Hubert had moved up the ladder at Swift's and was in the running for a manager's job when the company decided to open branches in British Columbia and Fiji. The toss of a coin decided that Hubert's close friend Jack Gillis would go to Fiji and Hubert would move to B.C. In Maillardville in 1911, he opened Swift's first British Columbia plant.

Peter and Elizabeth McCalman retired to Victoria, and in 1913 Hubert quit his job at Swift's and moved his family to Victoria too. There he opened the Victoria Feed Company which included a livery barn and feed store located in a sheet-metal building on Government Street, next door to Labatt's Brewery. Their first home was in Victoria West and it was there that their second son, Ray Gillis Williston, was born in 1914. (The name Gillis honoured Hubert's old friend who had been sent to Fiji.) Four years later Ray's sister Verna arrived.

Meanwhile, Hubert's business had been slowly failing as trucks replaced horses and wagons on the streets of Victoria. In 1920 he was offered a job in Ladner with Charles Idians & Sons, a brokerage business dealing in feeds and potatoes, and once more the family moved. It was in Ladner that Ray's sister Rosabelle was born and there that Ray began school. A year later Hubert was transferred to the Idians branch in Vancouver, and the Willistons moved into a suite over a store at the foot of Sasamat Street in Point Grey. As part of the move from Ladner, eleven-year-old Norman and seven-year-old Ray were assigned the job of getting the family cow to the city; Norman led it with Ray trotting behind urging it along. After crossing the Fraser River on the ferry, they walked the cow across Lulu Island, some five miles past peat bogs and fields of wild blueberries and finally across the Marpole Bridge. The tired pair then sat on the steps of a hotel in Marpole to wait for their father who arrived later in a truck to transport his sons and the cow to their new home. The Vancouver location meant a new school for Ray—Queen Mary Elementary.

The family's future began to look brighter in 1922 when Hubert landed a job as manager of the Salmon Arm Farmers' Exchange. Launched as a small fruit-shipping cooperative in 1907, the Exchange had grown to include vegetable handling in its operation as well as cold storage, retail flour and feed, hardware and building supplies, a sawmill and wholesale lumber. But it was best known for the enormous volume of apples packed and shipped every year.

While Hubert tested the waters of this new job, Islay and the four children moved back to Victoria to stay with her parents. There Ray attended Craigflower, the oldest school in the province and his third school in two years. He was in Grade Four when the family joined Hubert in Salmon Arm. Their first home there was rented, but shortly after they were established in it, Islay's mother died and Peter McCalman traded his Victoria house for one in Salmon Arm big enough for his daughter's family and himself, with an apple orchard in the backyard. (The Salmon Arm United Church now stands on that property.)

The next five years were contented ones for the Williston family, but just before Christmas 1927, Hubert was killed in a fall down the elevator shaft at the fruit exchange. In the process of winding up her husband's estate, Islay learned that he had left an enormous outstanding debt. It seems that while working at Idians, Hubert had done some brokerage business on his own, and in 1921 had borrowed money to buy Lulu Island potatoes to fill a very large order. The purchasers, however, had wanted dry-belt potatoes from Ashcroft or Wenatchee. To accommodate them, he bought the dry-belt kind to fill the order, hoping to sell the Lulu Island potatoes to another purchaser; when a recession developed later that year, he was forced to sell them well below cost. To cover his losses, he had borrowed again without telling his wife.

Islay also learned that earlier in the year Hubert had switched his insurance from Great West Life to another company. Ironically, his Great West coverage had expired at the beginning of December, and the new policy was not scheduled to take effect until the beginning of 1928, so there was no insurance whatever.

Islay now faced bringing up her children and paying off the potato debt on a compensation of just $56 a month. By giving his age as 18, 16-year-old Norman soon landed a job with the local CPR, but his wages were too meagre to make much difference to the family income, and Islay decided to take in boarders. It was the first of these boarders—Agnes Blackburn, a bookkeeper at the local SAFE store—who suggested at supper one evening, just a month after Hubert's death, that 14-year-old Ray should apply for a job at the store for after school and weekends. Ray was hired.

At the SAFE, a cooperative store which at one time had been affiliated with the Salmon Arm Farmers' Exchange, Ray began work stocking shelves and keeping the dust off the merchandise in the Fancy Goods department. A few months later he was transferred to Groceries. In those days before the invention of the shopping cart, customers did not make their own selections from the shelves but went to the counter to dictate their requirements to a clerk. Their orders tended to be large because most people shopped no more than once a week, and since most groceries came in bulk, it took some time for the clerk to weigh and package each item. The department manager, a one-legged war veteran named Andy Collier, taught Ray and the other young helper, Walt Tennant, how to cut cheese, measure flour and take the customers' orders. Cheese came in cylindrical wooden boxes about the size of a hassock—in fact, the empty boxes were prized by customers for making into hassocks—and the boys learned how to peel off the cheesecloth and wax encasing it, cut it horizontally into three big rounds, then place a round on the block ready for cutting into wedges. Whenever business was slack, they would weigh out sugar in 10- and 20-pound paper bags or chop huge blocks of dried dates into smaller chunks. They unloaded the SAFE's groceries which arrived by the boxcar-load from Vancouver and were picked up at the railway station by drayman Spike LeClair and later by his replacement, Phil Calvert. The same draymen made the store's deliveries as well.

Grandfather Peter McCalman died in September 1928. He had been picking apples that hot afternoon when he entered the kitchen announcing, "I think I'm going to die." After getting her father to lie down on the couch in the dining room, Islay pushed Ray out the kitchen door to run for one of the Doctors Beech—brothers Alan and Stuart. It was Dr. Alan who answered the call and after checking Peter's chest with his stethoscope, he proclaimed him "sound as a nut." After he left, the Reverend Campbell, who had dropped by for a visit, sat beside the old man and said, "Don't worry, Peter. You'll live to be as old as Dad Quick." (He was referring to a recent item in the Vancouver *Province* about a man known as Dad Quick who had celebrated his 105th birthday.)

Ray's grandfather closed his eyes. "Oh, no I won't," he said wearily. Then there was a rattling sound, heard even in the kitchen where Islay was sterilizing canning jars. She shouted, "Ray! Quick! Get Dr. Alan back here!" The doctor, who had just reached the other side of the street when Ray caught up with him, hurried back to the Williston house, but this time there was no need to get out his stethoscope. "I guess he just wore out," he said. Granddad McCalman was 84.

Islay was left the mortgage-free house and the small apple

orchard that surrounded it, but Granddad McCalman had accumulated little savings, so the family economics were unchanged with his death. As Norman now worked full-time for the CPR, Ray took over the management of the orchard and garden while continuing to work at the SAFE and attend school, but he was about to add another facet to his life.

In the 1920s and 1930s, small towns invariably spawned amateur orchestras. Among several that sprang up in Salmon Arm was The Melody Four . . . or The Melody Five . . . or The Melody Six, depending on the number of available musicians. Mrs. Tweeddale was always one of them since she was the leader of the band. For years her husband Ed played the drums, but one day he laid down his drumsticks, claiming he was too old. His place was taken by Doc Ferguson until he moved to the Okanagan. That's when Ray, at age 15, was stopped by Mrs. Tweeddale on the street.

"Ray dear, how would you like to play drums in the orchestra?"

"I don't have any drums."

"Doc Ferguson is willing to sell his."

"Sure," said Ray quickly, before Mrs. Tweeddale could change her mind. The question of whether or not Ray knew how to play drums never came up, although it was well known that he had taken piano lessons until his father died and he was usually assigned the solos in the school concerts.

At that time the orchestra was the Melody Five. Mrs. Tweeddale played banjo and bass, her friend Mrs. Shirley the piano, Cec Sladen clarinet, b-flat alto sax and bass saxophone, Freddie Wood trumpet, and now Ray on drums. Most of the time they played in community halls or country schools, although they were engaged on one occasion to play in the ballroom of the CPR Hotel in Sicamous. They had no money for sheet music, but Mrs. Shirley made charts by listening to the latest popular songs wafting from that new box, the radio. This worked well until one night a man in a black fedora marched onto the platform right in the middle of a dance, picked up a sheaf of Mrs.

A START IN LIFE

Shirley's hand-written music and informed the group that they would be hearing from his client. When she protested that she didn't know she had done anything wrong, she was told that "Ignorance is not innocence but sin, madam. You can't go around playing other people's music without so much as a by-your-leave." For a time after that the Melody Five religiously used battered old sheet music, but when Mrs. Shirley became convinced that they had seen the last of the man, she began once again to score the latest songs from the radio. They never saw the man in the black fedora again nor did they discover who his client was.

After two years of playing with the Melody Five, Ray and Cec Sladen, the two youngest members, decided to strike out on their own. It was a matter of the differences in age; Cec claimed that every time they walked into a dance hall, he felt like he was escorting his grandmothers. Ray went to call on Mrs. Tweeddale, miserable but determined to tell her that they were leaving the band, but she beat him to it. "Ray dear," she said gently, "Mrs. Shirley and I think it's time you boys started off on your own. We're getting too old for this sort of thing." And so a new dance orchestra was born, Ray Williston and the Tickle Toes.

After completing junior matriculation in 1930, Ray couldn't afford the fees and books necessary for senior matric, so he took a year off school to work full time at the SAFE. When he registered for school the next fall, the principal suggested that he keep on at the SAFE until the end of September, knowing that the extra 60 dollars in wages would come in handy. A year later Ray left Salmon Arm to attend Normal School in Victoria where he found a boarding place on Fell Street with the Allen family. Realizing he would run out of money before the year was out, when he went home for Christmas in Salmon Arm, he screwed up the courage to ask for a loan of a hundred dollars at the local Canadian Bank of Commerce. The bank manager agreed. As Ray knew nothing about the customary demand for either collateral or a co-signer, he didn't question getting the loan without any encumbrance. It was not until years later, when talking to a teller from that bank, that he discovered the bank manager had co-signed the loan himself.

Ray graduated from Normal School in June 1933, a time when teaching positions were very scarce. He wrote letters of application to more than a hundred schools, but out of the half dozen students from the Salmon Arm area who went to Normal School that year, only one, Lilian Sladen, was successful in getting a school, and that was because she lived in the District—rather than the City—of Salmon Arm, and the District had an opening for one new teacher. For Ray, it was back to the SAFE where he became produce manager in the absence of Andy Collier. As well, he worked noon hours and several nights a week in the town's new drugstore, with his friend Jack Beech filling in for him on nights when the Tickle Toes played a gig.

New hope for a teaching career came for Ray in the spring of 1934, when one of the SAFE's regular customers, Mrs. Bert Butchart from the community of Hendon, approached him in the Produce Department. Looking around to make sure she would not be overheard, she said softly, "Our teacher at Hendon, Miss Reid, is going to get married this summer, so we'll have an opening for a teacher. Are you still wanting to teach?" Situated about 25 miles southwest of Salmon Arm, Hendon consisted of a one-room school and a sprinkling of farms along the Salmon River Valley, but every school in those days, no matter how small, had its own school board, and Mrs. Butchart was on the Hendon board. "If you want to apply . . . (she glanced around again) . . . you'd best hustle out there and get your application in before anyone else does."

That same afternoon Ray got time off, climbed into his recently acquired $75 Pontiac and took the narrow gravel road that followed the river to Hendon. There he met with three or four members of the school board in the Butchart kitchen. With bread baking in the oven and a fat orange cat curled up on the floor in a square of sunlight, it was the most congenial of settings for a job interview. Since everyone there knew Ray from the SAFE and realized he had no teaching experience, they asked very few questions, but when Ray got up to leave, Mrs. Butchart followed him onto the back porch. "I think you've got it," she whispered.

He was soon notified that the job was his, starting in September, and that he would be boarding at the Butcharts' home. Before summer his friend Jack Beech also got a rural teaching job, and together they worked out a transportation arrangement. Monday mornings the two would set off in the Pontiac; Ray would get out at Hendon and Jack would continue on to his school at Adelphi down the road. On Fridays Jack would pick Ray up on the trip home to Salmon Arm.

With the beginning of classes in September, Ray saw the interior of his one-room school for the first time: the pupils' desks, one behind the other, formed two rows separated by a cast-iron stove and a woodbox. On either side of the entrance were pegs for the children's coats, with boys' on one side, girls' on the other, and above the pegs and over the door stretched a shelf for books—the library. Near the door stood a bench holding a pail of drinking water and a single dipper from which pupils and teacher all drank.

He rang the bell, the children came inside to take their places, and he faced 16 wide-eyed, expectant kids ranging from Grade One to Eight. He tried to recall the Normal School lectures and the notes he'd taken so religiously, but he drew a blank. He muddled through his first week and on Friday arrived home thoroughly discouraged.

"I'm not going back," he told his mother and slumped into a chair at the kitchen table. "Maybe they'll take me on again at the SAFE."

"You'll be leaving the Hendon people in the lurch," his mother said. "Don't you think you should go back and stick it out for another week?"

"No."

However, by Monday morning his mother had convinced him to go back to Hendon. Slowly, the second week passed, and the third, then one afternoon near the end of September the school inspector turned up. A tall, gaunt man of about 50, T.R. Hall was already a well-known B.C. educator. After observing Ray teach for some 20 minutes, he quietly interjected, "I think we'll let the youngsters go home now."

This is it, thought Ray. *I don't have to quit. I'm going to be fired.* But that wasn't what the inspector had in mind. Easing himself into one of the pupil's seats and motioning Ray to another, he launched into some friendly advice. "Every young teacher starting out has problems and thinks he's the only one who ever became disillusioned and convinced the youngsters weren't going to learn anything from him. Some of the best teachers I know were ready to throw in the towel before they finished the first week." Ray perked up. As the inspector talked, the shadows of the trees seen through the windows grew longer, and yet this man seemed in no hurry to leave. He pointed out all the things Ray could be doing—and should be doing—in the classroom, and what he said in that one afternoon in the Hendon schoolhouse was a whole year's course in the art of teaching.

By the beginning of November the Christmas Concert was the favourite topic around the Butchart supper table where their two adopted children, Stanley and Shirley, were full of questions. After Mrs. Butchart explained that old Jake who lived in the little brown house across the valley was always the accompanist for the school concert, Ray went to see him to let him know the practices would begin the following week. He found a wizened-up elf who, after spitting out a blob of chewing tobacco juice, thanked Ray for letting him know about the concert. He didn't show up for practice, however, which was a pity since his violin was the only instrument in the entire community, and it then fell to Ray to borrow a piano accordion in Salmon Arm and try to learn enough to accompany the youngsters.

A START IN LIFE

Lewis's log farmhouse, a half mile from the school, was the location chosen for the concert. The family built a stage in their front room, and the day before the concert they covered the walls with building paper, then painted it with calsomine—the universal home beautifier of the Depression years. On the big night there was a shortage of seats since everyone in the community showed up. The women and children were given the chairs while the men leaned against the wall where the white calsomine rubbed off onto the backs of their Sunday suits.

Sheets hung from a wire stretched in front of the stage served as the curtain, and as the audience took their seats, the kids peeked out like jack-in-the-boxes from behind the curtain and waved. Finally, everyone stood to sing "Oh Canada," and the Christmas Concert began. The children were well into "Joy to the World," with Ray on the accordion, when from the back of the room came the sound of a violin. After that, every time the kids began to sing, Jake stood up and sawed away at his creaky fiddle. The concert was a great success.

In those days at the close of the school year, Grade Eight pupils had to write provincial exams, and the students from all the schools in the area went to a central location, in this case Silver Creek School, to write them. Until Ray's time, no Hendon student had ever passed the exam, but this time—to Ray's great pride—all four Grade Eighters graduated, one with the highest marks in the area.

Meanwhile, towards the end of the school year, Ray had received a proposition from a Surrey teacher, George Wilson, to trade schools for a year so that Wilson could try a drier climate for his chronic lung problem. Ray agreed. The salary would be the same—$780 a year—from which he could save just enough, if he managed carefully, to pay for courses at the University of B.C. for as many summers as it took to get his secondary school teaching certificate.

On the eve of his departure for summer school in 1935, the orchestra played at a first-of-July dance in Chase, about 60 miles east of Kamloops. Around midnight a deafening roll of thunder shook the hall, the overture to an all-night deluge in which the Thompson River, already high from the spring run-off, overflowed its banks, sweeping away trees, bridges and anything else in its way, including chunks of the Trans-Canada Highway. The Pontiac, which had already demonstrated many fine qualities, now proved to be almost amphibious, getting the musicians back to Salmon Arm about three in the morning. Ray had time for only a few hours' sleep before setting off in the rain for Vancouver. He picked up Jack Beech—who was also summer-school-bound—and two women who wanted a ride to the coast. To avoid the worst washouts, he decided to make the trip via the Okanagan and Washington state rather than the Fraser Canyon. Farm lands near Enderby were inundated, and in Vernon, where Ray stopped for gas, the only topic was the flooding. In Penticton the main street was flooded, store fronts sandbagged, and cars diverted to side streets, but they were told that the flooding was not as bad across the border.

Much of U.S. Highway 2 was concrete at that time. *Thwacka. . . thwacka. . . thwacka. . .* went the rhythm of the tires over the expansion seams, until one by one the passengers were lulled to sleep, leaving Ray to try to keep himself awake. Sometime after dark, when the headlights began flickering, he stopped at a Shell station where an attendant checked lights, switches and fuses, then made his diagnosis. There was nothing wrong with the lights, he said. Maybe Ray's eyes were the problem.

Back on the road Ray had not driven far when the flickering began again. He experimented, noting that when he opened his eyes wide the flickering stopped. He closed one eye, rested it, then opened it to do the same thing with the other eye. By repeating this cycle over and over, he kept himself awake until they reached the Washington coast and Highway 99. Unfortunately, Chuckanut Drive, which was at that time part of 99, was paved with smooth asphalt—so smooth that Ray also drifted off to sleep. The thud that followed jolted everyone awake. Failing to negotiate a bend in the road on its own, the car had struck a guard rail.

"Just a stick on the road," said Ray. "It flew up and hit the fender. Nothing to be alarmed about."

At the border, the Customs officer peered at the muddy array of baggage strapped to the running board, then ordered everyone out. "Have an accident?" he asked. The wooden railing which Ray had installed to hold the luggage on the running board was gouged from end to end and carried a bright strip of yellow paint.

"Some stick," observed Jack.

At UBC the Registrar, C. B. Wood, who had been one of their teachers at Normal School, had arranged accommodation for them in the nearby Dalhousie Apartments where Ray made a beeline for the nearest bed.

From the time Ray acquired it, the Pontiac's life had been one of starvation; there just never seemed to be enough gas for it. That September, while driving back to the coast after a brief holiday with his family in Salmon Arm, the car ran out of gas. Ray was still a mile from the home of the Huffs where he would be boarding while teaching at the one-room Grandview Heights School in Surrey. He set the brake, then hiked the rest of the way down the Pacific Highway. Walter Huff put some gas in a can, and while they walked back to the Pontiac together, Ray learned that Huff drove a school bus in the mornings and did accounting for the Highway Garage in Cloverdale in the afternoons. For the first week of the term the car with its empty tank sat in the Huffs' yard, but this was no great hardship for Ray because the school was less than half a mile away. Then Walter Huff put enough gas in the Pontiac to get Ray as far as the Highway Garage; there he was to ask owner Ed Hamre to give him a tank of gas "on the cuff" until he got his first paycheque. Hamre agreed, filled up the tank, then went inside to make out the bill. Ray followed him. At the cash register, Hamre took out a ten-dollar bill. "I'll put this on account too," he said. For the next

35 years, as long as Hamre was in business, Ray never passed Cloverdale without going in for mechanical repairs or a fill-up at the Highway Garage.

School began in September with 36 youngsters in Grades One to Eight. Then in January, all the children who had not been eligible to begin school in the fall but who had reached the age of six in the meantime were also enrolled, making a double Grade One class. The grades were arranged not in rows but across them, giving each row an assortment of ages and abilities. These rows competed against each other in spelling bees, arithmetic tests and reading assignments. On one Saturday of every month Ray would take that month's winning row for an outing. With six or seven kids squeezed into the Pontiac, away they'd go to Bellingham where, for an outlay of a dime for each child, he would treat them to a movie and an ice cream cone.

With the Pontiac on the road again, Ray was also able to attend his first teachers' meeting in Surrey where a gung-ho physical education teacher held forth on the need for money to stage track meets and basketball tournaments. They discussed all the usual fund-raisers—raffles, barn dances and bake sales—then someone suggested they put on a play, and the Surrey Teachers' Dramatic Club (which years later became the White Rock Players) was launched. The first production of the new club was to be *What Happened to Jones*, with Cyril Chave as director. "And you'll be Jones," he told Ray.

To advertise, one Saturday morning they erected a sign reading *What Happened to Jones* on top of Myrtle Irwin's car. Another girl in the cast, Gladys McInnes, got in the front seat with Myrtle, while actors Ray and Jack Kirk climbed into the back with megaphones. "Come one, come all!" Jack bawled out the window on one side of the slowly moving car.

"Where to?" shouted Mr. Interlocutor from the opposite window.

"To the Agricultural Hall in Cloverdale!"

"What for?"
"To see the play!"
"What play?"
"WHAT HAPPENED TO JONES!"

They shouted their way along the main streets of Surrey and Langley, then over the U.S. border into Blaine, but as they attempted to cross back into Canada, a customs man ordered all four out of the car and into the building. A sour-looking officer leaned over a thick book of regulations spread open on the counter. "Advertising and soliciting across the international border is illegal!" he boomed, pointing at the book. "Section 47, Sub-section 25, Item 14(a)." The other customs officers gathered around.

"So what have you got to say for yourselves?" the sour man shouted.

The drama club had nothing to say. They stood like thieves awaiting sentence, when from behind Officer Sourpuss came an explosion of laughter. The culprits relaxed.

"Why don't you guys join our club?" asked Jack. "You'd win all the awards."

What Happened to Jones was a huge success, and the phys ed teacher happily launched his tournaments and track meets. But, of more significance, the petite, blonde, blue-eyed Gladys McInnes and Ray Williston began a lasting romance.

In the spring of that school year, Ray received news of his appointment to the principalship of the two-room Strawberry Hill School, also in Surrey. On moving to the new posting in September, he boarded with the nearby Moss family, but before long he heard of a house on Scott Road for rent. Now it would be possible for his mother and sister Rosabelle to come to live with him. (His sister Verna was taking a secretarial course in Salmon Arm, and Norman was still with the CPR.) Shortly after the family's reunion in Surrey, Islay's cousin, "Uncle Cliff" Gibb, recently widowed in Didsbury, Alberta, moved in with the family.

When the furniture arrived from Salmon Arm, Ray spotted his drums and immediately decided to sell them. "If anyone finds out I've got drums, you can bet your life I'd have to play them, and where would I find time?" Uncle Cliff built a carrying case for them to make a sale easier, and an ad in the Vancouver *Sun* produced an offer of $75 from a man near Powell River. And that was the end of Ray's drumming career.

At Strawberry Hill School the merriest event of the year was the annual June picnic. Ray booked an interurban tram, one of the overgrown streetcars operated by the B.C. Electric on its intercity routes, then collected the transportation fee from those wanting to go. On Picnic Day they all boarded the tram at the Kennedy stop, just down the road from the school, the motorman clanged his bell, and away they went—down the hill to South Westminster, over the Fraser on the railway bridge, through New Westminster, then Burnaby, on into Vancouver and through the downtown to Stanley Park. Before the picnic lunch, Ray took some of the kids to English Bay for a swim. In the bathhouse, having decided it would be unsafe to leave all the children's return interurban fares in his pocket, Ray stuffed the money into an empty Lifebuoy soap-box and scrunched it into the toe of his shoe; he left his own money in his pants pocket. When it was time to rejoin the others at the picnic grounds, he waved the youngsters out of the water. In the bathhouse, the kids watched Ray turn his pockets inside out. His own money was gone. He grabbed for his shoe. The money was still in the soap-box. At the end of the day the Strawberry Hill gang, all picnicked out, straggled back to Lost Lagoon where the tram stood waiting for them.

In October 1937 as Ray settled into his second year at Strawberry Hill, he received a phone call from his friend Bill Lucas, principal in Princeton. "Ray, we've got an opening up here."

"For next year?"

"No. For right now."

"But I can't leave in the middle. . ."

"Don't worry. There are so many teachers on the loose your job there can be filled in 15 minutes."

"What grades would I teach?"

"Five and six—a double class. In the Elks' Hall."

"Where did you say?"

"The Elks' Hall. The school's bulging at the seams."

Princeton was at that time a thriving centre, the hub of a wheel with spokes going out to the mining settlements of Blakeburn and Copper Mountain and to the copper refinery site at Allenby. Along with Trail and Vancouver, it paid the highest teaching wages in the province. The school carried Grades One to Twelve, as well as one Grade Thirteen student, a young miner named Jake Lancaster, who sat in the hall taking courses on his own, helped out by teachers whenever they could spare time. Jake became a doctor.

"Can we go too?" asked Rosabelle when Ray told his family about the phone call.

"Certainly not!" said her mother. "I have no intention of chasing Ray around the country. Besides, we have Uncle Cliff to look after here."

Ray would have no need of a car in Princeton, and when he was offered a few dollars for the Pontiac, he sold it and caught the train to Princeton. When he enquired at his new school about accommodation, Lucas told him, "You can batch with us."

"Us?"

"Roy Thorstenson, one of our teachers. Slim Lewis—he works for B.C. Tel. And me. We rent a house." (All three teachers—Lucas, Thorstenson and Williston—eventually became B.C. school inspectors.)

They had arranged for the "girl next door" to do housework and make their meals. Lucas and Thorstenson had the double bed in the only bedroom of the tiny house, Slim Lewis a cot on the porch, and another cot was scrounged for Ray and set up in the living room. The one advantage to this arrangement was that—with friends continually milling around in the room—Ray was provided with excellent sleep-training and from that time on never had trouble falling asleep at night.

Early in the year, Ray organized a staff drama club. The first production, of course, was *What Happened to Jones,* and after launching it in Princeton, the group took it to the Nickelplate Mine at Hedley. There they played to a full house of miners who had apparently never seen a live performance although they were used to movies; they sat like stones with no reaction whatever. The actors, nonplussed by the lack of response to what they considered an immensely funny play, were fortunately saved by the fact that one of their number had brought along a bottle of whiskey and they imbibed freely every time they came offstage. However, as Jones, Ray was continuously on stage. The others began to loosen up, improvising and tossing new lines to him to see how he would react. By the time the curtain rang down, although the miners were still unmoved by the production, the cast had thoroughly enjoyed themselves.

At Blakeburn the play was put on in the cookhouse. The cast built a stage at one end of the room, with blankets for the stage curtain and for the walls of the set. When the curtains parted on the opening scene, Jones made his entrance through a window at the rear of the set. His foot caught on the window sill and he flew headlong onto the stage, which in turn collapsed into the audience. *What Happened to Jones* was a smash hit in Blakeburn.

As well as the drama club, Princeton School had the usual extracurricular activities. Responsibilities for these were dealt out to the teachers like a pack of cards: "Basketball for you . . . Stamp Club for you . . . Hiking for you . . ." Ray drew Cadet Corps, which in those pre-war years were sprouting up in every school in the country. In the official photograph taken after Ray's corps were equipped with uniforms, it is difficult to tell the instructor from the kids because many of the Grade 11 and 12 students who signed up were

A START IN LIFE

about six feet tall, while Ray—who looked like a teen-ager himself—was not quite five-foot-seven.

And then there was the school band. A travelling musical instrument salesman named Jack Martin had come to town, staying around just long enough to drum up enthusiasm among parents, sell instruments and launch the band. Ray and another teacher, Nina Jackson, were not immune to his sales pitch; both bought clarinets and took their places with the kids in the band. After Martin left town, Bert Rose, the conductor of the town band, was persuaded to lead the new school band as well, but he soon quit, his nerves frayed after two months with a band where no two kids played the same note at the same time. The principal, however, was adamant that the band could not be allowed to fold since the parents had sunk so much money into instruments, and Ray was appointed to succeed Rose. In time, the band became the main event at every school function, and in later years some of the musicians even achieved a degree of fame.

Princeton's ski hill, within walking distance of town, was the focal point for both the Amber Ski Club and the Princeton Ski Club. The former grew out of building contractor Bert "Pop" Irwin's passion for getting local kids into skiing. His motivators were his own three children—Billy, Bertie and Maisie. With time on his hands in the winter months, Irwin would move his whole family to the ski hill where he and his wife would instruct, make meals for the local youngsters, repair skis and keep the fire going. The Amber Ski Club's name came from the fact that Pop rolled his own cigarettes using Amber tobacco and flattened the empty cans to use in splicing broken skis. Later he began cutting out the little emblems from the tins to nail onto the skis.

The Princeton Ski Club, which was more into tournaments and social activities, took on the job of hosting the first Western Canada Ski Championships, scheduled for 1938. Planning for it had begun by the time Ray arrived in town, and Roy Thorstenson, the chief organizer, was quick to notice that Ray had a typewriter and appointed him secretary, although Ray protested that he knew nothing about skiing. Opening day of the events saw skiers from all over Western Canada descend on Princeton to take part in cross-country and downhill racing as well as jumping. At that time there were only a few ski-jumpers in the west, but the best of them, including Tom Mobraaten and Earl Petch, came for the event. As official starter for the downhill racing, Ray was stationed at a telephone installed at the top of the hill. The moment a competitor started down, Ray would shout the skier's number into the phone, and the man at the bottom would set his stopwatch. One or two officials patrolled the slope, but it really didn't matter where the skiers went as long as they left the starting line at the top and arrived at the finish line at the bottom. Afterwards, for his part in the championships, Ray was given a pair of Chalet skis.

Basketball was also popular in Princeton. Both Bill Lucas and Ray were on the town's senior team and Cec Ritchie, another teacher (who also became a school inspector), was the coach. They played up and down the Okanagan in the provincial "C" League, reaching the finals of the B.C. Championships in 1939.

Ray's move to Princeton had not dimmed his romance with Gladys McInnes. She came from a large Surrey family, seven girls and four boys. Her father, Neil, was a dairy farmer and her mother, Doris, kept geese and tended a huge vegetable garden to help feed her lively brood. To accommodate such a gang around the kitchen table, benches were used instead of chairs, and when friends and relatives came by—as they frequently did—everyone simply jammed up closer on the benches.

Once when Ray was invited to spend the night at the McInnes home, he was assigned a bed on the porch. As he hadn't come prepared to stay, he had no pyjamas, so he climbed into bed in the nude and promptly fell asleep. The McInnes girls, meanwhile, concocted a note for sister May who was out late: "Cousins Elsie and

Millie are here. We gave Elsie your bed and Millie is in Roberta's, so Roberta is sleeping in the bed on the porch. You can bunk with her." Then they waited.

At the sound of May returning, the whole family pretended to be sound asleep. May read the note, got into her nightie, then climbed into the bed on the porch. In the meantime, everyone inside the house had slipped out of their beds to hang over the bannister in anticipation. From the porch came May's voice, "Move over, Roberta!" Getting no response from the sleeping form, May jabbed her "sister" with her elbow. "Give me some room," she hissed. At this point Ray woke up and pulled the blankets over his head.

"Don't be a hog, Roberta," said May, lifting the blankets and pushing with her foot. There was a pregnant silence while the listeners waited. They weren't disappointed. May's scream was followed by "Oh my god, it's you, Ray!"

In 1938 when Ray achieved his third year standing at UBC, he was notified that he had been awarded a scholarship of $100, making it possible for him and Gladys to marry the following spring. The ceremony was performed on Easter Saturday in the Cloverdale United Church manse. The only witnesses were Ray's friend Jack Kirk and Gladys's sister May, while back at the McInnes home all the relatives gathered to welcome the newlyweds.

Before leaving for their honeymoon, the couple spent the night at the Grosvenor Hotel in Vancouver. Like newlyweds everywhere, they tried not to look the part, and in the morning they stood outside on the curb—along with a number of other hotel guests—waiting for a taxi to take them to the CPR boat. When drops of Easter rain began to fall, Gladys reached for her umbrella. As she opened it, a shower of confetti floated down on her. May had wreaked her vengeance.

In Princeton, Ray and Gladys moved into a rented house and settled into the rhythms of small-town life. At that time the United Church minister in Princeton was the Rev. J.C. Goodfellow, a man of many talents and enthusiasms—among them hiking and the outdoors. He sometimes led groups over the Hope-Princeton Trail. In those days the road only extended 20 miles beyond Hope with rugged trail for the remaining 60 miles to Princeton. Goodfellow's enthusiasm for the trip was infectious, and Ray decided he would hike the trail when summer school was over that year. "I figure we could do it in about three days," he told Gladys.

"We?"

"Sure! You can do it!" Gladys, though just five feet tall, was wiry and a good athlete. During her teaching days, she had been pitcher on a women's hardball team. Ray pressed his advantage. "It'll be a great experience. And besides, it's the cheapest way to get back to Princeton after summer school."

On an early September afternoon May McInnes drove them to the trail head where they spent the night. The next morning they set off in drenching rain, Ray in the white oxfords in which he had been married, Gladys in lightweight summer walking shoes. They marched over Skagit Bluffs and on past Rhododendron Flats, built a lean-to for the night at Strawberry Flats, then hiked on over Allison Pass. Late on the third afternoon, their feet painfully blistered, they limped out onto a wagon trail near a place known as Nine-Mile Coalmine. No sooner had they started down the track than a half-ton truck loaded with furniture rattled up behind them and stopped. Grateful for a ride on anything, the two hikers climbed on top of the furniture and rode grandly on to Princeton.

At the end of June 1940 Ray joined the RCAF. He was determined to fly, but at the recruiting depot in Vancouver he was told there were no current openings for pilots. The recruiting officer suggested he sign up for armaments where he would learn all about aircraft firepower, the loading of ammunition and operation of all equipment on planes. Ray was not interested, but the officer explained that if he signed up for armaments, he could switch to pilot training as soon as he arrived at the manning depot. With this assurance, Ray signed up and was given a travel warrant.

The manning depot in Toronto was in the old cow barns on the Canadian National Exhibition grounds. There, a sergeant pointed to a desk where Ray could fill in his armament course forms. Ray explained that he had been told he could switch to the pilot's course.

"It says here you're signed up for armaments, so armaments it is."

"But they said I could switch."

"Tell that to the C.O."

But as the commanding officer of the manning depot had more important matters on his mind, Ray and his complaint got sent to another office... and then another.... His civilian eyes were wide open by the time he found himself on the CN bound for Mountainview, Ontario, the armament training centre. Looking for a room to rent so that Gladys could join him, Ray was directed to Lillian Sprague's boardinghouse from which the lady also ran her family's telephone company. Business had mushroomed with the coming of the RCAF station, and several times a week Lillian collected a milk bucketful of coins from the station's pay phones. Soon after Ray and Gladys moved in, they found themselves pressed into service counting coins and wrapping them into paper tubes for the bank. Lillian then decided Ray could audit her books, and after work at the station, he laboured night after night at her kitchen table, trying to balance them. Finally he gave up when they were still out by $60.

"Sixty dollars out is good," said Lillian. As far as she was concerned, the books were balanced.

At the Mountainview station, Ray was not the only one who had gone into armaments with no intention of staying, and many of the others had decided to fight back by refusing to take notes or study, anticipating that they would be thrown out of the course and sent off on general duty. Once away from Mountainview, they figured they could remuster for aircrew. Ray's strategy was to work like hell for good marks to earn his transfer to aircrew. Neither tactic worked. Ray worked so hard he led the class and was recommended for the Senior Armament Instructors' Course. Many of the others ended up doing kitchen duty at the stations along the Alaska Highway where planes were re-routed to Russia.

After passing his SAI course, Ray was promoted to corporal and posted to No. 3 Service Flying Training School in Calgary to teach armaments to pilots and to cadet instructors. Many of them turned out to be high school teachers he had known in B.C. He soon earned his sergeant stripes, and although still not flying, he found life at No. 3 Service not unpleasant. He and Gladys had decent living quarters near Elbow Park; Gladys was pregnant with their first child, and Ray was playing on the station's basketball team in a provincial league.

On a weekend in June 1942, Ray and Gladys took the train to Drumheller to visit relatives, the Gouldings, who met them at the train in their '41 Chev. Bill Goulding insisted on showing them the countryside, especially the Badlands where archaeologists had been excavating for dinosaurs. By Sunday evening when it was time to leave for the railway station, Gladys was unwell, and it was arranged that she would stay overnight and return to Calgary by train the next day. However, the next morning, instead of getting a message that Gladys was on the train, Ray learned that she was in the Drumheller hospital where she had just delivered a healthy baby boy. Ray got permission to visit his wife and baby, but when he reached the hospital, quarantine notices were just going up. There had been an outbreak of diphtheria. A soft-hearted nurse let Ray in for fifteen minutes, but it was another two weeks before he was allowed back to collect Gladys and the baby, whom they named Hubert after Ray's father.

During 1943 aircrew ranks were decimated in the skies over Europe, and there was a sudden urgent call for more pilots. By fall

A START IN LIFE

Ray had remustered, and when he was subsequently posted to Edmonton, he saw his family off to the coast to live with Gladys's sister Rhea. In Edmonton he was posted to Initial Training School (ITS), located at the University of Alberta. The 90 or so students in the course were divided into three flights, each having its own barracks. Because of his experience, Ray was put in charge of one of them, T-flight. By this time he was used to the quirks of military life, especially the incentive system that was practised to keep the barracks tidy and clean; the flight having the most ship-shape barracks at weekly inspection would get the whole weekend off. T-flight, therefore, measured the turn-down of the blankets on their beds and dusted everything, including the light bulbs dangling from the ceiling. They even cleaned the soles of their shoes. The ultimate touch was that the last person out of the barracks on inspection day backed out of the room on his knees, polishing the floor as he went. The result of all this frenzied housekeeping was that week after week, when all the airmen were lined up on the parade square, the commanding officer would announce that T-flight had won the competition. When for the tenth week in a row the C.O. proclaimed T-flight the winner, the boos that rose up from the other flights drowned out anything else the C.O. had to say.

Ray topped his class at ITS and was allowed to state his location preference for Elementary Flying Training; in order to be close to his family, he chose Abbotsford. There, he and the other would-be flyers found themselves in training planes equipped with two cockpits, the one in front for the student, the one behind for the instructor. Ray's instructor was a Russian-American named Rasmussen, an arrogant, belligerent man, but a good instructor. The planes were fitted with speaking tubes for communication between the cockpits, but Rasmussen arranged the equipment in his plane so that he could talk to his student, but his student could not talk back.

One morning when Ray showed up at the hangar, Rasmussen was already there, his parachute on, pacing back and forth. Ray was still 30 feet away when Rasmussen shouted irritably, "What's the matter? Did you sleep in?" Ray checked his watch. He was early and there was not another soul in sight. "Come on! Get your 'chute on," said the instructor, heading out to their plane on the edge of the tarmac.

Although there was no one yet in the control tower, they took off and flew to a practice field at Sumas where they did a few "circuits and bumps," the term for taking off, flying around the field and then landing. When that exercise was finished, they landed beside the Sumas control tower which was now manned. Rasmussen got out of his cockpit, opened Ray's canopy and stuck his head in. "Don't kill yourself," he said, slammed the canopy shut and walked away.

This was Ray's first indication that he was to take his initial solo flight. However, as he was only required to take off, circle the field, then land, away he went. When he landed without a hitch, Rasmussen was smiling broadly—the first time Ray had ever seen his instructor smile. He learned later that all the instructors had put money in a pot for a sweepstake on which of them would be first to get one of his charges to solo. Rasmussen had just won the pot.

The next morning when student and instructor took off, Rasmussen sat behind the controls for a trial run, but when they landed back at the main airport, he climbed out of the plane. "Away you go," he said. "Do an hour of circuits and bumps."

Ray was nervous. His short solo the previous day had not endowed him with confidence. However, his instructor was already walking away, so he took off. Coming in for a landing, he froze. Unable to make a correction, he landed at an angle, and the plane ran off the runway and onto a field, coming to a stop perilously close to a fence. With his confidence sinking, he taxied back to the starting point and took off again; this landing was a repeat of the first. Now completely shaken, instead of going back to the take-off point, he taxied all the way around the triangle of runways, finally arriving

A START IN LIFE

back at the place where the aircraft was to be left when the flight was over. Rasmussen, catching up to him as he was walking to the hangar to check his next assignment, announced they were taking off for "more advanced stuff."

"But I need more practice in circuits and bumps," Ray protested.

Rasmussen snarled, "Listen, kid, I've no goddamn time to waste on your circuits and bumps. We're going on to something else."

Perhaps it was applied psychology on Rasmussen's part, and perhaps he knew Ray well enough at that point to be able to gauge the effect his words would have. At any rate, Ray made up his mind that if he was going to be forced to go up there and kill himself, he'd take the sonovabitch with him! He climbed into the plane with Rasmussen behind him and took off. Furious when the plane veered, he kicked the controls. Every adjustment he made was in anger, but the plane responded. Finally, over the speaker he heard Rasmussen sneer, "My, aren't we positive today?" From that moment on, Ray had no problems with nerves when he was flying.

By late spring of 1944 he was on his way back to Calgary's No. 3 Service Flying Training School and on October 27 he graduated with the top award. Ready at last for overseas postings, he and his classmates were sent home instead to await further instructions. Home for Ray was now New Westminster where Gladys and the children—two-year-old Hubert and one-year-old Dianne—lived in a tiny house that Uncle Cliff Gibb had built. It was not in Ray's nature to be inactive, so after two days of idleness there, he began looking for a temporary teaching job.

"But can you teach in uniform?" Gladys asked.

"I guess not. I'll have to buy a suit."

The tweed suit he bought was so cheap and the weave so loose that every time he bent his elbow or knee, the material would bulge out and stay bulged out, but he wore it to the New Westminster school board offices where he introduced himself to Inspector of Schools Roy Shields.

"We need a Grade 3 teacher at Herbert Spencer School," said Shields. "Are you interested?"

"Yes," Ray said, though he had to point out that the airforce might call him back on very short notice.

At Herbert Spencer Elementary, Ray quickly discovered that many of his charges had been promoted by virtue of age without knowing how to read. One boy told Ray, "I can't learn to read, you know," as if it were a fact of life, like having freckles.

"Sure you can. We'll start today after class." The boy soon decided that reading was easier than he thought, and much better than staying for extra classes after school.

Ray now was getting an inflated income: officer's pay, flying pay and teacher's pay, but such royal treatment was not to last. The war in Europe ended in May 1945, and shortly after that the RCAF discharged all but the younger unmarried airmen. Ray was required to report to Vancouver for his discharge. Although it was only a 50-minute bus ride from his home to the Vancouver manning depot, RCAF headquarters in Ottawa sent him a chit for accommodation in Vancouver and train tickets for New Westminster to Port Coquitlam, Port Coquitlam to Vancouver, Vancouver to Port Coquitlam, and Port Coquitlam to New Westminster. Ray kept the four railway tickets as a souvenir of bureaucracy gone awry.

No longer at His Majesty's beck and call, Ray headed back to his Grade 3 class at Herbert Spencer, only to be offered a job as relieving principal for all the schools in the city. It was an era when principals taught full-time, squeezing in administrative duties as best they could, and Ray's job was to teach one day for each of them in order to free them for paper work. He was just getting used to the routine when once more he was called to the inspector's office. Bill Steele, industrial arts teacher at Robson Junior High, had been forced to resign because of illness. Would Ray take over his classes?

"I've never taken an industrial arts class, let alone taught one," Ray said, demurring.

"But you were in armaments in the airforce. You must know something about machinery and all that."

"Very little."

When Shields insisted he take the job, promising that no inspector would visit his classes, Ray joined the staff of Robson Junior High School. There he discovered that Steele had not only taught industrial arts, but that anything that went wrong in the school—from electrical appliances to plumbing apparatus—had been referred to him as well. Inheriting that aspect of the job stood Ray in good stead for all the years to come.

One day between classes Ray was experimenting with the woodworking lathe when a piece of wood he had neglected to fasten down shot up and gouged him over the eye. Since it wouldn't do to let his students know of his inexperience, he hurried to an adjacent school, where he persuaded a teacher he knew there to patch him up and keep quiet about it. He still bears the scar from that experiment.

CHAPTER THREE:
A Career in Education

RAY REJOINED THE TEACHERS' FEDERATION early in 1945 and attended the annual convention in the old Hotel Vancouver at the Easter break. There he was introduced to Professor Max Cameron who had headed a recent Royal Commission on Education. His report had recommended that, in order to provide more uniform educational services, school districts encompassing many schools should be formed to replace the existing system of individual boards for every school in the province. He told Ray that while he had been travelling around the province for the Commission, he had been intrigued by a Prince George proposal that seemed to be moving in this direction. They wanted to have a supervising principal who would not only run the high school but would be responsible for all the elementary schools in the area as well, and he suggested that Ray should apply for the job when it was advertised.

Although he planned to try for any secondary school principalships that came open, Ray had already applied for admission to the University of Toronto's school administration program; his courses there would take a year, beginning at the end of June. Shortly before he was due to leave for the east, the Prince George position was advertised. Almost at the same time he learned that Penticton was also looking for a principal. He immediately applied for both jobs and was called for interviews, but he came away convinced that both had gone badly. He told Gladys that they had obviously considered him too young, and that four years away from teaching had been too long. That evening he caught the 6:30 train from the New Westminster station to connect with the CP Transcontinental at Port Coquitlam. As the train was full, he rode the day coach all the way to Toronto.

Ray's U of T classes had been underway only a week when he received telegrams from both Penticton and Prince George offering him the jobs he had applied for. He laid his problem before Dean Lewis of the College of Education, who on learning how little administration Ray had actually done, said, "If you can't administer, there's no course on God's green earth that will make an administrator out of you. But if you can—if you have the natural ability—then we can make you a better one. If you want my advice, leave all your credits here and get back there and see whether you really have what it takes. If you have, then you can come back and take your courses later."

Ray walked out of the dean's office and wired his acceptance to Prince George. He had no difficulty choosing. From his Princeton days he knew a number of Penticton teachers, most of them older than he was, and he knew he would run into their resistance to his innovations. On the other hand, taking on the first supervising principalship in the province would be a real challenge. He would not only run the Prince George Junior-Senior Secondary School but also oversee the work of the principals of the four elementary schools. He would be responsible for the budgets of all five schools and make all decisions on staffing, staff accommodation, classroom additions, double-shifting, and major parent/teacher problems.

At the Union Station in Toronto, Ray asked for a lower berth. "Only coach seats left," said the clerk, and when the train pulled out, Ray was once more ensconced in a day coach. Even after Jasper, where he changed to the Prince George line, he still had only a coach seat. Arriving at his destination early in the morning, he took a taxi to the Prince George Hotel.

"Sorry, sir," said the night clerk, "we have no rooms left."

A CAREER IN EDUCATION

"Look," said Ray, "I've just spent four long days sitting up on the train. I'm absolutely beat!"

The clerk was sympathetic and offered him an army cot in the hallway for 75 cents a night. If the proffered cot had been on the sidewalk at ten times the money, he still would have taken it. He fell asleep immediately, totally oblivious to the loggers, miners and travelling salesmen parading past him in the hallway.

The next morning, Ray walked over to the Northern Hardware Store where, he had been told, he would find Harold Moffat, chairman of the school board. The Moffat family owned, and still own, the kind of hardware store—almost extinct now—that stocked everything from nails to septic tanks. What you could not find at the Northern, you could not find anywhere. Harold Moffat was about Ray's height, a round-faced man in his early thirties. "You must be Williston," he said. "I'm Moffat." His smile was infectious.

The high school that he showed Ray was a bright, nine-room building only a year old. When the tour was over, he turned to Ray and said, "Well, there's your school. You've got no staff to speak of. Better get to it!"

When Ray accepted the Prince George job, he was unaware that the supervising principalship had been created because of endless jockeying by the local principals over who should get what for their schools, which frequently forced the board to make decisions on educational matters its members felt unqualified to make. When two of these principals heard of the new position and of the board's intention to bring in an outsider to fill it, they were so incensed they not only quit their jobs but left the teaching profession. All this caused controversy in the town, but by the time Ray learned of it he was far too busy to worry about it. His first response to his staffing problem, therefore, was to recruit another outsider, his old friend from Salmon Arm days, Jack Beech, as vice-principal. Then before looking for other teachers, he set out to find a better sleeping place than the hotel corridor.

"Try the McDonalds," someone suggested. "They take in boarders."

Ray had no sooner moved into the McDonalds' home when a man on a bike came looking for him, and that was when Ray learned that the school board had spoken to this man—whose name turned out to be Malcolm—about a house he was building on spec not far from the school. Malcolm had promised not to sell it to anyone else until Ray had a chance to see it, but he wanted a deposit on it by that night. He led the way to a small house under construction at the corner of 6th Avenue and Victoria, and Ray gave him a cheque payable in a week's time.

Now that he owned a house, the rest of the family could move up from the coast. It was arranged that they would ship their furniture via CN, then Gladys and the two children would fly up on CPAir, accompanied by Gladys's 21-year-old sister Roberta. At the airport Ray broke the news to Gladys that the house was not finished.

"I don't care," she said, as Ray led them to a car he had borrowed. "We can make do."

"I'm afraid not," he said. "There's no plumbing. But I've arranged for us all to stay at the McDonalds. There's just one other thing. . . . The McDonalds have gone on holiday."

"Who's running the boarding house?"

Ray hesitated. "Well. . . ."

"You didn't! You didn't say we'd run it?" But she could see he had. "Of all the gall!"

Suddenly from the back seat came Roberta's ripple of laughter, and Gladys realized they would likely all survive. Aside from Ray, there were only three boarders at that time, so Gladys and Roberta pitched in to make meals. Before long everyone at the boarding house had become friends. Two weeks later the Willistons moved into their new house.

That first year in Prince George, on the morning after Hallowe'en, Ray discovered that the high school bicycle racks, which had accommodated about 70 bikes, had been thoroughly demolished. It was obvious that a number of vandals had been involved. Ray was, of course, hopping mad and determined to flush out the culprits. Deciding that Grade 10 was about the right level to begin his detective work, he marched into one of the classes. Scanning a sheet of paper in his hand, he announced: "All those involved with the demolition of the bike racks stand up!"

Four boys got to their feet.

"Come with me!" he barked and marched the four down to his office. Looking at the paper again, he said, "Now go and get the others!"

The students went off and soon returned with five more students. "You're all suspended," Ray told them, "until the bike stands are rebuilt."

There was only the sound of shuffling feet until one of them timidly asked, "Could you please tell us how you got our names?"

When Ray held up the piece of paper he had been consulting, a moan went up from the group. The sheet was blank.

None of the students had money for the building materials, but Ray sent them down to Northern Hardware where Harold Moffat allowed them to charge the materials on condition the bills would be paid by a certain time. It took a week to get the racks properly reconstructed and almost three months to settle the account at Northern, but from that time on there was no vandalism at the high school.

As new families were moving into Prince George at an accelerating rate, more classrooms were needed almost immediately. The school board agreed to Ray's request for funds to buy building materials and hire a maintenance supervisor to construct the extra rooms. Ray hired the capable Harry Bailey.

Janitorial service, however, was an entirely separate matter and a prime headache, particularly in the high school. The janitor Ray had inherited was supposed to run the coal-fired heating system and keep the school clean but was doing a proper job of neither. The gym floor was in terrible shape since most gym shoes still had cheap synthetic soles (a holdover from the wartime rubber shortage) that left a dense pattern of black marks on the floor. Ray instructed the janitor to clean and varnish it during the Christmas break. When he went to the school to see how the job was progressing, the janitor proudly announced that it was finished. But instead of first cleaning the floor with solvent, the janitor had simply varnished right over the thousands of black marks. Ray fired him on the spot.

"Listen, mister, I was here long before you were," said the janitor, his voice rising. "You didn't hire me, and you can't fire me!" And he marched down to Northern Hardware. "I was hired by the school board," he shouted at Harold Moffat, "not by Williston. He can't fire me!"

"If he says you're fired," Moffat responded, "you're fired."

As no immediate replacement janitor could be found, Ray hired students to remove the varnish from the gym floor and give the school a thorough cleaning. As for the furnace, he cleaned that himself and got it operating properly.

The grounds for the high school and the adjoining Baron Byng Elementary School were totally inadequate for the growing school population. However, just across the street from them was a large semi-circular area consisting of a few crown lots and a large area designated "Duchess Park." The previous year a youngster had been struck by a car as he ran across the street from the school to the park, and as a consequence, the school board had erected barriers to close this street to vehicle traffic. Since the semi-circular road allowance that bordered the rest of the park started and ended within the barricaded block, it had been rendered inaccessible to traffic as well. Ray proposed incorporating the park into the school grounds and when he discussed his idea with Harold Moffat, the board chairman was enthusiastic. "If we're going to expropriate the park," he said, "we should get those crown lots too. That would give us the whole semi-circle."

"You're right," Ray agreed. "Let's go see George Milburn."

Government Agent Milburn pulled out a register in which the lots were recorded, found the right page, then picked up a pencil and wrote across the lot descriptions: "Reserved for schools."

The school board then agreed that if the park and the lots were to be incorporated into the school property, they might as well incorporate the crescent road itself since there were no houses on it and it was closed to traffic. Local contractor Bill Bellos was hired to clear the lots, bring in fill and level the rough ground of the entire area to provide softball and baseball diamonds, a track and a soccer field. To get fill, Bellos began moving earth from behind the elementary school. As Ray stood gazing at the backhoe in action, he noticed that it had already carved out a shallow basin as big as a hockey arena. "The perfect place for a skating rink," he decided. When he mentioned the idea to some senior students, they immediately volunteered to help prepare it.

Freeze-up came early that year and flooding for the rink began. It was slow going until Ray had one of his brain waves. That night's forecast was for very low temperatures, so he attached a hose to a nearby fire hydrant, turned it on and went home. The next morning all hell broke loose. Flooding the rink had almost drained the city reservoir, and half of Prince George was without water. The kids, however, had one heck of a fine hockey rink.

Meanwhile, no one had thought of informing city council that a couple of their roads and a city park had been taken over for the schools. Ray presumed the matter had been brought before city council since the mayor was on the school board and had approved the expropriation, but the first that council learned of it was on a routine inspection of city property. The changes came as a shock, especially to Josh Keller, the alderman in charge of public works. When he stormed into Ray's office, the mayor and the city engineer happened to be there, but Keller paid no attention to them.

"Who do you think you are," he raged at Ray, "grabbing all that city property?" By now he was shouting. "And my roads! Who gave you authority to take over my roads and barricade them?"

The outburst flummoxed Ray as he believed the project had everyone's approval. However, by then the whole undertaking had reached the point of no return, and there was nothing left but for Ray to apologize and Alderman Keller to accept the *fait accompli*.

By this time, members of the school board were getting used to their gung-ho principal and even getting used to his solutions to problems which had not yet arisen, so they were ready to listen when he came to talk to them about textbooks. High school students had to buy their own in those days, and since all the board members were parents, they all knew that textbook prices were escalating and that there was enormous wastage. If there were no siblings to use them or if the course text changed, books that had been used for barely a year languished like family heirlooms on shelves in private homes. Before the meeting was over, Ray and the board had mapped out the system taken for granted today: the school would buy the books and rent them out to the students. In the initial step, the board provided funds to buy back books owned by the students and purchase new ones to meet the shortfall. Solving this problem, however, created another because the school's office was soon knee-deep in books. There was no place to store them; even the basement was fully occupied. But space could be made, Ray decided, if the earth were dug out from under the auditorium and a room constructed there. He hired students, armed them with shovels and wheelbarrows, and had them gouge out a big cave. Harry Bailey did the rest, building a 10- X 24-foot room which he fitted with shelves, and British Columbia's first textbook rental scheme was launched. The project was so successful that a few years later the Department of Education decided to adopt it province-wide, and for starters, commandeered all the books Prince George High School had accumulated.

In the 1940s the hinterlands around Prince George were mainly populated by loggers, sawmill workers, farmers and trappers. Many were immigrants with a dream of a new life for their families; most found it hard scratching a living, but all of them were determined their children should get an education and they insisted that the Prince George school board find a solution. Sheer distance from Prince George and lack of roads made busing impossible. Between Prince George and McBride, for instance, lay a 150-mile stretch of countryside with no road and no high school.

In 1945, school inspector Harold Stafford had suggested a dormitory be built so these children could attend school in Prince George, but nothing happened until the following year when Harold Moffat and Ray mulled over Stafford's idea and came up with the idea of acquiring an unused army barrack. During the war the Sixth Canadian Division had been headquartered outside Prince George; the buildings now lay empty pending disposal by the War Assets Corporation. Harold picked up the phone and called Charlie East who, although about to be hired as city engineer for Prince George, was at that time the army captain charged with overseeing the sprawling, deserted army camp. After Moffat told him what they had in mind, East invited them out to look around.

Ray and Harold selected one of the better buildings, then gave Harry Bailey the responsibility of moving it into town. This was an enormous undertaking since the structure was actually three long buildings that had been erected parallel to one another and joined together by two connecting sections. Bailey located skids big enough to do the job in Terrace, some 350 miles away, and made preparations for skidding the building to a two-acre, city-owned lot a few blocks from the school.

Some months before moving day, well aware that scroungers

thought nothing of swiping equipment from dormant army buildings, Ray once more recruited his senior students. "See if you can round up some tools and bring them to school tomorrow." He and the students proceeded to the army camp where they disconnected all the sinks, toilets and removable fixtures in the building.

One enterprising lad, John Wasyluk, examined the walk-in refrigerator and, knowing that the dormitory-to-be would require a similar unit, decided to dismantle it. "Some of those other buildings must have walk-in refrigerators, too," he said. "Why don't I take them as spares in case of breakdowns?"

"Good thinking," said Ray.

The big refrigerators, sinks and toilets, bunks, tables and chairs were then taken to the high school and stored in the basement rifle range. But while Williston, Moffat and the board were as enthusiastic as kids with a new toy, the Department of Education in Victoria was totally uninterested and definitely unwilling to discuss a grant to cover the cost. But one day Education Minister W.T. Straith and his deputy, Dr. Frank Fairey, appeared at the Prince George High School on an inspection tour. They had finished with the classrooms and Ray was ready to bid them good-bye when Fairey said, "I understand this school has a rifle range."

"Well, yes," said Ray, hesitantly. "But it's really no longer a rifle range. We just use it for storage."

"Let's have a look at it anyway. After all, this is one of the few high schools in the province with a built-in rifle range."

When Straith and Fairey entered the long cement room and saw what it contained, they retreated speechless and returned to Victoria. Ray expected repercussions. There were none, but there was also no approval for the construction of the dorm.

The army buildings were skidded into town in five sections. The three main ones, each about 20 X 70 feet, were sited parallel to one another about 30 feet apart, then connected by the two remaining sections to form a three-legged H. The east wing provided rooms for the boys, with a teacher's apartment in the front end; the west wing, for girls, was identical. The front part of the centre section also housed teachers, while in the back were the students' dining room, the kitchen, storage rooms and the heating plant. The two main entrances were located in the connecting sections. The original plan stipulated two students to a room, but when the dorm was about to open in September 1947, twice as many as the anticipated number registered, making it necessary to have four to a room. That first year there were about 40 students, most of whom had been getting by with correspondence courses. Some were even ready for the senior matriculation program that was introduced in Prince George that year.

The first dorm staff consisted of a matron, Mrs. Evelyn Yost, and her assistant, Mrs. C. Hearn, who was also the cook. The students, who were charged only $25 a month for room and board, had to prepare vegetables, wash dishes and floors, clean their rooms and do their own laundry. Reasonable rules, regular study hours and trust in the students made for a favourable environment. Mrs. Yost, a grandmother and a nurse, ran the dorm with a firm but fair hand. She accepted the position of matron for three months—"Just to get it going," she said—but stayed for eight years. She later claimed that of the hundreds of children in her charge there was not a delinquent in the bunch.

The bookkeeping for the dorm was anything but straightforward since the school board had to have its budget approved by the Department of Education which had still not given approval for the dorm. This made it necessary for the board to hide the dorm's costs in nefarious way. A year later, when the Department finally gave consent, the school board had to disinter the expenses from their burial places and parade them as if newly born.

Over the next 30 years the Prince George dorm became a model for other dormitories in the province, and it remained in use until good roads, busing and new schools finally made it redundant. The last students left in 1978, and three years later it was demolished. In its place now stands a residence for senior citizens. In 1988 some of "the dorm kids" organized a weekend reunion to which ex-dormers came from all points of the compass, including New Zealand, eastern Canada and the United States. Ray realized just how significant it had been to those long-ago rural students when a number at the reunion told him that they never would have gone on to university or achieved their chosen vocation or indeed have received an education at all had it not been for the dorm.

After the dorm was in operation, Ray addressed the problem of additional housing for his staff and asked the city engineer what the town was going to do with the old hospital standing vacant on the edge of town.

"Tear it down, I guess."

"What? When there's not so much as an empty chicken-coop in all of Prince George?" And Ray rushed off to ask the school board to get permission from the city to take over the old hospital. "Harry Bailey could easily convert that building into apartments," he said, "and the rent from them would cover the cost of renovation."

"What about the nurses' residence? Why not commandeer that while we're at it?" These board members were getting the hang of things, and all were in favour of putting the two old buildings to work—providing Ray would look after the financing, including rent collection. The old hospital, with its pale yellow clapboard siding and the tall, spindly jackpines surrounding it, was a rather handsome two-storey wooden structure; to an outsider, it could have been mistaken for a very large private home. Ray and Harry Bailey made a rough blueprint of the layout of the apartments-to-be. No two would be alike, of course. The kitchen, for instance, was to be made into a four-room suite with a screened-in back porch, while the operating room would become another apartment, domed and skylighted. Nursery, pantry, maternity wing, men's wards and women's wards would all be transformed into living quarters no architect ever dreamt of.

By the end of summer 1948, teachers were moving into their new quarters. "But we need a classier name than 'Old Hospital'," said physics teacher Walter Thumm as he took up hammer, saw and pail of paint. And that is how PINE MANOR appeared in black lettering on a cedar slab over the front entrance before a committee could be formed to decide on a name. The five women teachers assigned to the old nurses' residence named their house "Ye Loving Arms."

In 1949 Ray learned that the Department of Education would soon be appointing some new inspectors, but he was too occupied in Prince George that year to submit an application. It was not until the following spring that he applied and was accepted as an assistant inspector—with a $1600 cut in salary. The year was half over before the Department, tripping over the anomaly that his salary was less than that of a vice-principal, adjusted his pay.

Two inspectors were responsible for northern B.C.: Earl Marriott in the Peace River country, Bill Grant in Prince George. Ray was made assistant to both men, alternating one month in the Peace, the next in Prince George. During his stints in the Peace, he was headquartered in Fort St. John and was responsible for two or three schools south of the Peace River and all the territory north of it, right up to the Yukon and Northwest Territory boundaries, and from Atlin and Telegraph Creek in the western part of the province to the Alberta border on the east.

In Prince George he was able to live at home with his family (three children by then, Sandra having been born in 1947), but accommodation in Fort St. John was another matter. He was expected to stay at the Condel Hotel, but he could not stomach the stench of the chemical toilets there. One night was enough. The next morning he packed his bag and, at the suggestion of an acquaintance, drove out to the local airport to ask the manager of the

Canadian Pacific Airlines staff house, an Englishman known only as Stan, if he could board there.

Stan, whose speech was very slow, said, "Really... this is... rather... unorthodox. I shall... have to enquire..."

"Supposing I move in while you find out?" said Ray, and before Stan could hatch another sentence, Ray had dropped his suitcase in an empty room. "Whenever the place fills up and you need my room," he promised, "I'll get out. I'll find a spot in the basement or someplace. I won't bother anybody." After that, every second month when Ray arrived in Fort St. John, he moved back into the CPA staff house. It was always a happy experience for him. The pilots became his friends and allowed him to keep his Mercury in the hangar, and as an unexpected bonus, the mechanics looked after it, dealing with the damage inflicted by trips over the primitive northern roads.

Some of the schools in the Peace were only accessible by trails across the frozen ground. Such was the one-room school at Moberly Lake, a native village about 50 miles from Dawson Creek. Following advice to "get in there before spring break-up," Ray left Dawson Creek and drove 20 miles west along the gravelled Hart Highway, then slowed to watch for tracks leading off to the right—the overland trail to Moberly Lake. On either side of the trail the flat countryside, dotted with brush and leafless poplars, was still covered with the dirty snow left when winter is over. Fortunately, although the track wasn't always dependable at that time of year, it held solid all the way to Moberly Lake.

Ray's watch read 10 o'clock when he arrived at the school. Fourteen children clustered around a pot-bellied stove. "Where's your teacher?"

"Still at home, I guess."

"Then who got the stove going?"

"I did," said one of the bigger boys.

"Good for you!" said Ray, hanging up his parka. "While we're waiting for your teacher, let's have a look at your work." He walked between the rows inspecting haphazard and untidy scribblers and quizzing the pupils. When 11 o'clock came and there was still no teacher, he gave the children assignments and left them.

At the teacherage, he knocked on the door. No response. Furious, he pounded on the door. This time he could hear stirring inside, the door opened and a rumpled man in long johns appeared. "You're fired!" said Ray.

Back at the school, he told the children to go home. "And don't come back until your parents are notified school's on again."

As Ray was leaving the village, he stopped a man walking down the road. "Good morning," he said. "I'm the school inspector and I've just fired the teacher."

"It's bloody well time," said the other.

By then the sun had warmed the surface of the trail, and instead of speeding along on top of the frozen ground, the car had to churn through the mud. The further he drove, the deeper his tires sank. As he approached the CPA hangar, a mechanic came out to see whose car was making all the noise. After peering under the car, he said, "Good thing you got home before dark." The muffler and half the car's wiring system had disappeared.

One early November afternoon, Ray parked his car near the river bank at Fort Nelson, got out and peered across at the native village a hundred yards away on the other side where he was to make his initial inspection of the Fort Nelson Indian School. A bridge spans the river now, but in the 1950s the way to get across was to pick up an iron bar and bang the bell which hung from a post, signalling to the people in the village that someone wanted to cross. If anyone in the village was interested, a canoe would be launched to fetch the visitor.

On that November day, the ground was frozen but the river was still open water. He struck the bell, but it brought no reaction. He rang again and stopped to listen, but the only sound was the echo of the bell. He didn't want to postpone the inspection, especially since he felt obliged to check out rumours about the young woman teacher, so he continued whacking the bell. When there was still no response after a half hour, he got back into his car and drove to the local airstrip. There, a pair of muklukked feet protruding from under a pickup told him he had found the Roman Catholic priest.

Ray squatted to talk to him. "Father Levesque, I banged the bell like you said, but nothing happened. The whole village seemed to be asleep."

The priest manoeuvred his husky frame from under the truck, wiped a greasy sleeve across his face, and said with a smile, "You didn't want to inspect the school today anyway, did you? Pick me up tomorrow morning and I'll get you across the river."

In the morning, the temperature had dropped to 20 below. Close to the shore where the stream ran slower, an ice island had formed overnight; further out huge chunks of ice floated by.

"That's where they'll bring in the canoe," said the priest, pointing to the far side of the ice island. "You'll need to get yourself down there." He struck the bell and the entire settlement on the opposite shore came to life. While the village people were launching the canoe, the priest noticed Ray's hesitation at going down onto the ice. Taking off into the bush, he emerged a few moments later dragging a log. "You can shinny down that," he said, sloping the log down to connect the top of the embankment with the ice island.

Needing both hands to creep backwards down the log, Ray laid his briefcase on the ground. As his foot touched the ice floe he saw that the priest had come part way down the log with the briefcase, and Ray reached for it, leaning out over the narrow gap of water that separated ice floe from embankment. The ice island, however, could not support the combined weight of the two of them, and it submerged slightly. Water sloshed over the ice, Ray's foot skidded in it, and he and his briefcase were pitched into the river.

Heavily encumbered with his wet winter clothing, Ray—still clutching his briefcase—scrambled back onto the ice, but before walking across to where the canoe with two of the villagers now waited, he hollered to Levesque, "Aren't you coming?"

"Oh God, no! You might be over there for two weeks."

"What?"

"Absolutely! If the river doesn't freeze up properly there's no telling when you'll get back." Then cheerfully he waved goodbye.

Seated amidships in the canoe, Ray shivered all the way over, and when the craft touched land he leapt out and ran to the school. "Where can I get out of these clothes?" he asked the astonished teacher.

"The teacherage is next door," she said. "You can dry your things on the clothesline above the stove. And help yourself to coffee." In the teacherage, he looked in the closet but saw nothing but skirts and dresses. However, there were blankets. He undressed and hung his clothes to dry, wrapped himself in a blanket and poured a cup of coffee from the enamel pot simmering on the back of the stove. Fishing a crumpled Edmonton *Journal* from the woodbox, he sat down with his coffee to read last week's news.

When his clothes were almost dry, he got dressed, but the teacher appeared as he was about to leave. "No rush. The kids have just gone home for lunch," she said. "I'll make some sandwiches."

Back in the school after lunch, Ray watched the dozen or so laughing, chattering kids struggle back to their seats, then settle down to listen to their teacher. The pupils' notebooks, the teacher's records and the classroom itself all seemed in order, but as the afternoon progressed, Ray began to notice a subtle change in the teacher's face. It was apparent that whiskers were beginning to show, and no amount of makeup could hide them.

The rumours were true: the teacher was a transvestite. However, there was a teacher shortage at the time and he would have to be kept on for a while. Besides, the chap was doing a good job—better, in fact, than many of the teachers in Ray's jurisdiction.

That afternoon it seemed that Father Levesque's prediction

might come true, for when Ray asked the villagers to ferry him back, their spokesman said, "Can't go." And he pointed at the canoe. "Look! She's just back from upriver." A coating of ice a couple of inches thick made the boat far too heavy to use. "We can't go until the river is better froze."

"But if it's frozen, how can you use the canoe?" Ray asked.

"Chop through the ice." They would use axes to cut their way across, then use the same channel for returning. They were waiting now until the ice cakes stopped moving downstream so they would not have to do the chopping job all over again on the return trip. While they were explaining this to Ray, the boatmen had been chipping at the thick glaze on the sides of the canoe, so Ray picked up a tool and joined them. As they chipped away, the sound of the bell reached them, but whoever was ringing it would also have to wait. The day grew darker and colder until at last the river ice was no longer moving, and when the last of the ice crust was gone from the boat, the group's spokesman proclaimed, "Okay. Now we take you."

The same two who had brought Ray over rowed him back, chopping a path through the ice as they went until they reached what had been the ice island where three people now waited to be taken back to the village. Fortunately for Ray, the river ice had become solid from island to embankment. Just as he reached shore and turned to wave goodbye, there was a tremendous screeching lurch; the ice had moved and the channel that had just been chopped open had closed again. A groan went up from the waiting passengers, but the boatmen merely shrugged and loaded the canoe for the return trip, resigned to chopping their way home again.

Ray's trips as assistant inspector to the country north of the Peace ended in September 1951 when he succeeded Bill Grant as the inspector for the Prince George area alone, and he remained in that post until he was nominated to run for the Social Credit party in

April 1953. His teaching career officially ended when Dr. Fairey fired him after his nomination was announced, but he continued his inspections without pay until the end of the school year, supervising the work of the two assistant inspectors Fairey sent to replace him.

CHAPTER FOUR:
Minister of Education

RAY WILLISTON TOOK HIS SEAT in the British Columbia legislature for the first time in the fall of 1953. W.A.C. Bennett's government had been defeated the previous spring before a budget had been passed, so the legislative session called for that fall was to be a short one—just long enough to pass a budget and deal with a few outstanding pieces of legislation. As a result, Ray had decided to leave his family in Prince George for the present and look for temporary room and board in Victoria. Another new MLA suggested the Pacific Club, a long-established men's club in the Yarrow Building where rooms and meals were available at a reasonable rate.

At the opening of the legislature, Ray was selected to second the Speech from the Throne. This is not just a matter of saying, "I so move," or "I second it"; rather, it is an opportunity for a full-blown oration. As the backbenchers were seated alphabetically, Ray sat next to Victoria MLA Percy Wright whose duty it was to move the Speech from the Throne. Ray quickly discovered that his microphone was not functioning, but since Wright's was, they arranged that as soon as Wright had made his speech, they would switch places.

As this was to be Ray's maiden speech in the legislature, he was understandably nervous. He had barely opened his mouth when CCF MLA Ernie Winch, one of the senior members, got to his feet and shouted, "Mr. Speaker, the member for Fort George is out of order!" As Ray had no idea what was happening, he kept on, but Speaker of the House Tom Irwin stopped him. Yes, Ray was out of order because he was not speaking from his proper seat. It took some tinkering with his mike before he was able to continue his speech from his own seat.

"I was somewhat mystified, Mr. Speaker," he began again, "when I was asked to second the Speech from the Throne in this debate. However, it soon became apparent that for today at least, the capitals of this province were being placed in a position of prominence. The Honourable Member from Victoria represents our legislative capital while I have the honour to represent the Western White Spruce Capital of the World." After agreeing with matters to be undertaken by the government as listed in the Throne Speech, he launched into a list of the needs of the northern communities: changes in the system of education grants; cheap sources of hydro power and the extension of electricity to rural areas; the extension of the PGE south from Squamish to Vancouver and north from Prince George to the Peace; and appropriate roads for lumber and logging trucks. He stressed the importance of recognizing that there was more than one Fraser Valley. As well as the Lower Fraser Valley funneling down from Hope, there was the Upper Fraser Valley stretching westward from the Alberta border for more than 180 miles before turning south, with dozens of sawmills, the most modern dairy farm in the province, and unlimited potential for farming and tourism. Yet there was no road in the 150 miles between McBride and Prince George, and the only telephone service was the line linking railway section houses. He emphasized that a road from Prince George to McBride had been promised for at least 40 years and that it was now the most celebrated dotted road on the map of British Columbia.

While congratulating the premier on his victory at the polls, he told the legislature that it indicated that the voters ". . . appreciate the sincerity of this government in advocating and practising economy with efficiency, in stopping the pyramiding of public debt, in abolishing patronage. . ." This was not mere lip-service to his party leader's beliefs. Ray was thoroughly in tune with Bennett's pay-as-you-go philosophy. From the outset, Bennett was determined to pay off the debt incurred by the previous administration and balance the budget. There would be no more borrowing, and no money could be spent by any department without approval of the minister of Finance, a post which had been given to Einar Gunderson when Bennett became premier in 1952. When Gunderson failed to get re-elected—both in 1953 and in a subsequent by-election—Bennett kept him on as a financial advisor to the government, appointing himself minister of Finance, a post which he held until the end of his political career. Throughout all those years he kept a tight hold on the purse strings. Expense accounts were tightly controlled; lunches—even those to discuss government business—were not paid out of the public purse, and a restrictive ceiling was placed on expense account meals for public employees or MLAs travelling on government business. All out-of-province trips on provincial business had to have W.A.C.'s approval, and if a cabinet minister or other official had to take advisors along, he or she had to give a full accounting as to why that number of aides was required.

In Ray's almost 20 years in government, he never once doubted that Bennett stuck to his original principles, and since he believed in the same kind of economy, there was no conflict on that score. In his 18 years as a cabinet minister, Ray never asked for nor was given a government car, nor was he allowed public money for social activities or office entertaining. When he travelled within Canada he never booked first-class seats—although once he was aboard, airline attendants sometimes took it upon themselves to move him forward from his seat in economy class. For overnight stays in Vancouver he booked a room in the modest but clean Burrard Motel. "All I need is a place to lay my head down," he reasoned.

Ray spent the winter of 1953-54 as a backbencher with no direct power to make changes in the area which concerned him most: education. The minister in charge of that portfolio was Tilly Rolston—who had bolted from the Conservative party along with

Bennett in 1951 and been re-elected with him as a Social Credit candidate in 1952. She took over a ministry with a great many problems, foremost among them a chaotic system of education financing. To remedy it, during the spring session in 1953, she put forward a new financing plan (generally known as the Rolston Formula), but no action could be taken on it because the ministry had not yet surveyed the school districts to determine exactly what their needs were.

Rolston was also faced with a growing battle over curriculum "frills," to which she responded by promising to "keep a wary eye open to prevent 'frills' creeping into our schools," while at the same time cautioning that "what are frills in 1952 may become necessities in 1953." The whole issue of what constituted appropriate courses for B.C.'s schools had exploded in the House on Monday, February 23, 1953, when Social Credit backbencher J. Alan Reid (Salmon Arm) rose to make his maiden speech and announced that immorality was being taught from sex textbooks in the high schools of the province. "There are sinister forces at work," he said, "who are using the lives and minds and souls of our children for political expediency." Reid then went on to quote former teacher Alfred J. Clotworthy, a 20-year veteran of one-room schoolhouses, who had been outraged by a Grade 12 course called Effective Living (often referred to as "Effective Loving") which "poisoned and corrupted the minds of young British Columbians with immoral sex teachings." Clotworthy also denounced teachers for neglecting basic training in the three Rs and for riddling the curriculum with socialist thought. Rolston and Bennett made immediate damage control statements, distancing the government from Reid's charges, but the media and the opposition had continued to explore them in detail until their attention was diverted a few months later by the defeat of the government and a new election.

When Social Credit was re-elected with a majority that summer, Tilly Rolston was re-appointed to the Ministry of Education, but she

MINISTER OF EDUCATION

was already terminally ill and in October she resigned her seat in the legislature. The education portfolio was then given to Robert Bonner who was already Attorney General. It was generally understood that Bonner was merely caretaking the ministry, and by early the following year, the newspapers were touting Ray Williston as the next minister of Education. It was common government policy, however, to select ministers who would come to their portfolios without too much detailed knowledge of the area for which they would be responsible because it was believed that, without preconceived ideas and policies, they would approach the ministry's business with broader views. By this criterion, Ray Williston had far too much expertise in the field of education to be selected for Education minister, but Premier Bennett was on the spot. He needed someone immediately in the education post who was capable of revamping education financing and dealing with curriculum problems before the situation worsened. This someone also had to be acceptable to ministry bureaucrats, educational institutions, teachers, parents—and the Opposition. His method of vetting Ray for the job was typically oblique: he appointed him chairman of a committee of the legislature charged with inquiring into a tree-cutting controversy on Salt Spring Island. The trees in question were on Mount Bruce, and residents were battling over whether the area should be part of a Forest Management Licence or dedicated for park purposes. Under Ray's guidance a compromise was struck, and the results apparently convinced Bennett that he had found the right man for the Education portfolio.

Ray's motives for being in government were almost entirely centred on his determination to improve teacher training and educational finance and to guarantee the construction of enough schools to adequately serve the student population of the province. By the spring of 1954, however, he could see that after nearly two years of Social Credit government there was little improvement in any of these areas. Without the establishment of any educational goals by either Rolston or Bonner, the ministry had been more or less rudderless. Under Deputy Education Minister Frank Fairey, the department had been working on the recommendations of the Cameron Report completed nine years earlier. But since Fairey was most interested in the technical and organizational aspects of education, he had concentrated all the department's energies on Cameron's recommendation for the creation of school districts with student populations large enough to justify the establishment of secondary schools offering the full secondary program. No attention had been paid to what was actually happening within the schools. Nor had any steps been taken to improve the organization of the department itself so that it would be capable of administering the new system that was being developed. And with the failure of the Rolston Formula, educational finance was still in chaos.

In this vacuum, on March 17, 1954, Ray put forward his own private member's education financing formula to the legislature, after taking care to state that Rolston's plan had only been intended as a temporary measure to correct the worst problems in the system. The main features of the Williston Formula were: the establishment of a basic school tax of an estimated 10 mills for the residents of all municipalities; an "equating factor" linking the number of pupils which a municipality was required to serve with the total municipal assessment; and a measure of local control through an 80/20 split between province and municipalities on all school costs above the 10 mill levy, with the province paying the lion's share.

As a private member—even though he was on the government side of the House—Ray's formula had little hope of acceptance by the government, but on April 14, the final day of the 1954 spring session of the legislature, the premier finally sent for him. "I'm appointing you minister of Education," he said. "Go to Government House and I'll meet you there."

It was the Easter weekend, the time when Education ministers were traditionally involved in teacher conferences and PTA meetings, and before Ray could leave Government House after the swearing-in, Robert Bonner handed him a sheet of paper.

"I'm happy to present this to you," he said. It was a list of speaking engagements.

"No, you can keep that," said Ray, trying to give the list back.

"No, no. These engagements are for the minister of Education, not for Bob Bonner." Ray began his speaking duties as minister of Education the following day.

Ray Williston was just 40 when he became Education minister, but he knew and was respected by ministry officials and had already illustrated to Prince George school district parents and teachers that he was on both their sides. He was also the choice of the CCF, led by Arnold Webster, formerly principal of Vancouver's Magee High School, because they believed that he would do what was necessary to improve B.C. education. In fact, after Ray was installed as education minister, one newspaper wit wrote that he was the only minister who had ever been appointed by the Opposition. In spite of all this approval, however, he showed no signs of overconfidence. In a profile written by G.E. Mortimer for the Victoria *Colonist* in March 1955, he was described as sitting "in the House as though he suspected he had no right to be there and was in danger of being asked to leave. He speaks mildly and with caution on all subjects, no matter how certain he is of his ground."

Fortunately for Ray, Dr. Fairey had just retired as deputy minister at the end of June 1953, and his place had been taken by Harold Campbell, assistant deputy minister under the Coalition regime and therefore in the natural line of succession. But Campbell almost lost the job after a note from him to former premier "Boss" Johnson turned up in W.A.C. Bennett's files. Written while Johnson was campaigning for re-election against the upstart Bennett, it assured Johnson that he didn't "have anything to worry about." There had been no point in Bennett dealing with the issue of Campbell's loyalties during Rolston's illness or Bonner's caretaking, but with a new minister ready to overhaul education, he decided to act.

Soon after Ray was sworn in, Bennett called him into his office and showed him the note. "What about this guy? Do you know him?"

"Yes," said Ray, "he taught at the normal school when I was a student teacher."

"He seems to be quite a political animal. Do we give him the gate?"

"No. I think he'll be loyal to whatever party is in power, and I'm sure he's the best person for deputy minister."

An academic, Harold Campbell had been totally frustrated by the slow rate of change in the department, and although he had formulated programs to set curriculum and teacher training reform in motion, he had been unable to interest either Rolston or Bonner. He was therefore delighted when Ray arrived on the scene, equally frustrated with education as it was and eager to take action.

With Campbell's help, within six days of being appointed minister, Ray was able to announce that a nine-member board had been struck to reorganize the entire Department of Education into six areas of responsibility. The first division was to be the chief inspector of schools with widened authority. Until this time inspectors had only supervised teachers, but with the realignment and amalgamation of school districts, the inspectors (now renamed superintendents) were in the best position to give official guidance to the newly elected school boards. Planning for the construction and siting of new schools would be the responsibility of the second division. The third division was created to supervise teacher training; the fourth was to coordinate adult education, the fifth was the Registrar's Branch which was responsible for teacher certification and school examinations, and the sixth was the Comptroller for the centralization of financial authority.

MINISTER OF EDUCATION

On the same day that Ray announced this reorganization, he also announced that in future all teacher training would be co-ordinated by the Department of Education's new teacher training division. At that time teacher training was provided by the University of B.C. and by the two provincial normal schools, one located at 12th and Cambie in Vancouver, the other on Lansdowne Drive in Victoria. Although a bachelor's degree was a prerequisite for registration in UBC's Faculty of Education, only senior matriculation was required at the normal schools. Each institution turned out teachers shaped by the strengths and biases of its own particular curriculum. Both normal schools had proud records and relished their independence; officials of one never liaised with those of the other, and neither spoke to members of the education faculty at the university. However, Ray's first announcements on the subject of teacher training left the faculties of all three institutions uneasily aware that some of their independence would soon be chipped away.

Ray's consuming interest in the reform of teacher education had been confirmed in his days as school inspector for the 30,000-square-mile Prince George area where he had supervised 155 teachers. Seventy percent of them had been underqualified. Some were first-year university graduates, some had come back into teaching after long absences, some had failed their training courses, some had come from a foreign country and had little understanding of idiomatic English, and some had no training at all. In a number of instances, persons who had not even graduated from high school had been labelled "teacher" and shoved into the classroom.

Prince George was not the only school district in the province with a shortage of qualified teachers, and B.C. was not the only province having trouble with teacher education. In other provinces, the approach to the teacher shortage problem was to reduce the length of teacher education—in some cases, to a mere ten weeks—but this only lowered the prestige of the profession in the eyes of prospective teachers. Instead of luring people into teaching, lowering the standards actually discouraged them. Ray was convinced that the solution was more rather than less training, and that the fastest way to increase the prestige of teachers in the eyes of the public was to give teacher training the benefit of university status.

At the beginning of July 1954 he announced that $100,000 had been set aside for interest-free loans to people who wanted to enter teacher training at one of the normal schools or UBC. In September, the teacher training branch organized Future Teachers clubs in all the high schools to influence students in that direction. A month later Ray let it be known that the whole teacher training system was under review. This was the cue for Dr. Norman A.M. McKenzie, president of UBC, to announce that all teacher training should henceforth be provided at his university. This was not what Ray had in mind, although he did believe that teacher training should be linked to universities. The plan he was working on was made abundantly clear in February 1955 when all teacher training was consolidated under a College of Education Board, and in order to eventually make a full degree course of study mandatory for all B.C. teachers, he ordered that Vancouver Normal School be incorporated into UBC and Victoria Normal School be amalgamated with Victoria College.

Very shortly after it began work, the new College of Education Board announced the first stage in Ray's drive to improve the quality of teachers in the classroom—the lengthening of teacher education from one year to two. This decision posed an immediate problem, however, because in the coming year there would be no new teachers entering the system. It was a situation with the potential to be what Ray later described as "the disaster of all disasters," but he resolved it successfully by two innovations. First, he appealed to all former teachers to come back to work for a year; the primary result was that married women returned to the classroom just as they had during the war years, ending forever the Education Department's earlier policy of cancelling women teachers' contracts as soon as they married. Many of these returning teachers stayed on after that first year. Ray's second move was to send personnel from the Teacher Training Division's new Teacher Recruitment Office to Britain—mainly England and Scotland—to hire teachers. It was the influx of these British teachers over the next two or three years, along with the return of former teachers, which alleviated the shortage to a manageable level.

While making Vancouver Normal School part of UBC presented few immediate problems since both campuses continued to operate as before, there were obstacles to the amalgamation of Victoria Normal School and Victoria College because the college was not a provincial institution. It was owned by the Victoria School Board which operated it in Craigdarroch Castle, the former home of coal-king Robert Dunsmuir. Now it became necessary for the government to pass legislation that would make the college a provincial institution, then affiliate the college with UBC which was the only degree-granting institution in the province. This would allow the college to expand to full four-year courses in education. (Prior to this time, undergraduates of the college had transferred to the university to achieve their degrees.) In the meantime, the college's faculty and students were moved onto the Lansdowne campus of the Victoria Normal School where the two separate institutions shared the normal school's Young Building. Rules at the normal school, however, were much stricter than they were at the college, and friction between the two staffs was immediate. After the legislation was passed late in the spring of 1955, the two schools became one under Victoria College's principal, Dr. Harold "Harry" Hickman, and though the college was subsequently affiliated with UBC, no one from the university ever interfered with the operation of the college.

Ray's strategy behind the combining of the college and the normal school was to create a single institution with sufficent enrolment to form the basis of a university. Dr. McKenzie, realizing that this was what he was up to, became equally determined that all university programmes should be centralized at UBC and that degrees granted at Victoria College should continue to be UBC degrees. With his Will Rogers appearance, McKenzie looked as if he would be perfectly at home behind a horse and plough, but a country bumpkin he was not. Intelligent, politically adept and extremely influential, he had a stubborn conviction that no monies should be spent on opening new colleges or universities in B.C. until all UBC's faculties were fully established, staffed and funded. And he could, of course, go on establishing faculties forever. He attracted a strong cadre of supporters, including—Ray discovered some 40 years later—Ray's own deputy minister of Education, Harold Campbell. McKenzie also convinced the College of Education's chairman, County Court Judge Joseph B. Clearihue (who also happened to be a member of UBC's board of governors), that Victoria College should remain under the umbrella of the university, even though Clearihue was a strong supporter of the college and sympathetic to those advocating university status for it.

Meanwhile, more accommodation for the classes of the amalgamated Victoria institution had become a priority. The pressure was partly alleviated by the construction of the Ewing Building and the installation of some army huts, but these were not long-term solutions. The question now became where to construct more permanent buildings for the college because if it was to develop into a university, more land would be needed. Expanding onto the Hudson's Bay land lying next to the college campus was the easiest course of action, but this would still not provide adequate grounds, and since the Bay's land was mostly rock, it was unsuitable for playing fields. On the other hand, the Canadian army's Pacific Command headquarters at Gordon Head in the municipality of Saanich, five miles from downtown Victoria, had just been declared surplus to Ottawa's military needs, and the question of what should be done with this prime 117-acre piece of land was already under hot debate. Ultimately, its disposal was the concern of the Hon. George Pearkes,

VC, minister of National Defence and MP for Saanich. Although he had been decorated to a degree that could have made him pompous and self-important, General Pearkes was folksy and approachable, and as he also happened to be Ray's neighbour, Ray met with him one afternoon in Victoria to explain how perfectly ideal the army camp would be for a university.

"Some people are pushing for the Hudson's Bay property," he told him, "but the army camp would make more sense."

"I'm on the spot," said the general. "I'd like to see some sort of educational facility at Gordon Head, but the municipality wants that property for housing and the City of Victoria wants it for an airport."

"The Chamber of Commerce is going to put up a fight to have the university there," Ray promised.

"See what I mean?" said the general. "I'm on the spot."

"You can't please everybody. But I think you've got a lot of constituents out there who'd like to see the college at Gordon Head." Ray knew that, although many people were afraid that a university would be too expensive for Victoria's taxpayers to support, there was a steadily growing sentiment that the college should become a fully-fledged, degree-granting institution.

On the college grounds, classroom space in the Young and Ewing Buildings was being augmented by the construction of the E.B. Paul Building, and the College of Education had begun planning for yet another major new classroom building. Fortunately, since the construction of public buildings fell under the jurisdiction of William Chant, minister of Public Works, and the design for them was the responsibility of Arnold Webb, the deputy minister, and since both Chant and Webb had also been hoping for a university at the Gordon Head site, Webb had arranged for the new building to be designed without a foundation, leaving that to be designed after it was decided whether it would be constructed on the Lansdowne or Gordon Head site. But with no decision from Ottawa on the disposition of the old army camp and no weakening in Dr. Mckenzie's opposition to a second university, both the siting of the building and the decision on whether the college would become a university were put on hold at about this time.

Although Ray concentrated on reforms to teacher training in his first year in office, by the end of April 1954, when he had been minister for a total of sixteen days, he had also organized a committee to plot a new educational finance plan and transform the Williston Formula for equitable school financing into practical applications and legislation. Under the system of open taxation which existed at that time, school districts in poor farming areas with little valuable land had limited potential tax revenue, while school districts in urban areas where there were manufacturing facilities or other large businesses could raise much more, even with a modest taxation assessment and mill rate. The wealthy urban districts could, therefore, afford to pay higher salaries to their teachers and thereby be guaranteed the cream of the teaching crop. They could also afford to hire more teachers and thus lower their teacher-pupil ratio, and they could purchase more teaching aids and build better facilities. As a result, there was a wide disparity in the quality of education provided from one school district to the next.

Before these inequities could be leveled out, however, a system had to be developed for the province-wide standardization of property assessment, and this could not happen until a provincial assessment authority was established. Fortunately, this was the responsibility of the minister of Finance, a job held by Premier W.A.C. Bennett who was eager to see these improvements take place, and the assessment authority office was in operation by the end of 1954.

Next, the Ministry of Education had to decide what constituted an appropriate level of education for B.C.'s children and how much it would cost, set a basic mill rate that all property owners across the province would have to pay in order to raise this amount, then institute a system of grants back to the school districts that would insure this level of education was uniformly achieved. When it came to working out a scale of grants, since the main costs to school districts were teachers' salaries, the Department of Education began by analysing the salaries of all teachers province-wide. When the huge spread in what teachers were being paid was discovered, Ray made what he later described as a "naive" decision to base the department's scale of grants on the median salary. The unintended but immediate result was that in order to collect the full grant to which they were entitled, all school boards paying salaries at rates lower than the median raised their teachers' salaries to the median, knowing that the basic mill rate would cover this sudden largesse to their employees. Property owners in school districts where teachers were receiving salaries above the median were penalized, however, by having to pay additional mills of school taxation to cover teacher salary costs in excess of the school grant. School construction and other capital expenditures were now shared 50-50 between the government and the school district. Such projects were first approved by local referenda, then funded through the Ministry of Finance; the school districts repaid their 50 percent through increased local taxation.

While teacher education and financial reorganization were priorities in Ray's ministry, other controversial issues were being tackled at the same time. One of these was school busing. Ray had never been in favour of short-distance busing, and when he was supervising principal in Prince George he had imposed a three-mile limit. Under the limit, pupils walked; over the limit, buses would be laid on if there were enough children to warrant the cost. This arrangement caused no repercussions in Prince George, but when he became minister, he discovered there were parents all over the province insisting that their children should be bused for short runs, sometimes for quite absurd reasons.

In the Sardis area, parents of high school students held protest meetings and signed petitions to get busing because their teenagers had to hike along the Sardis Road and cross the Trans-Canada Highway to reach their high school in Chilliwack. It was too dangerous, the parents claimed, to have their young people cross the highway to get to school. In typical Williston hands-on style, Ray decided to check out this complaint himself, and armed with his camera, one Saturday morning drove out to the intersection in question, parked his car at the side of the road and waited. Would the young people walk into town on a Saturday when there was no school? He didn't have long to wait before groups of teenagers came strolling down Sardis Road and crossed the highway with no apparent anxiety. Within half an hour, he had taken enough pictures to make his point. Back in Victoria he made up a set of photographs to which he appended a list of place, times and date to enclose with a letter to the parents who had declared the bus service absolutely essential for their children's safety. The protests ceased.

Soon after winning their first provincial election, the Social Credit government had been confronted with the "Doukhobor problem." The members of this pacifist religious sect had emigrated from Russia in 1899 to homestead on the Canadian prairies and in 1908 migrated to the Kootenays in British Columbia. They lived communally, developing orchards and wheatfields, and building sawmills, brickworks and a jam factory. However, during the Depression years the Doukhobors lost their communal land to the banks. When some 4,000 of them continued to "squat" on it, the banks gave up the idea of trying to evict them and instead sold the land to the B.C. government. In time, many of the squatters gained title to portions of it by registering their "squatter's rights." Unfortunately, a splinter group of zealots called the Sons of Freedom refused to recognize the laws requiring them to send their children to school and to register their title to the land on which they squatted. Their protests involved burning buildings, blowing up railway lines and staging nude parades.

In 1954 the government resolved to put an end to the Sons of Freedom's opposition and force obedience to the laws of British Columbia. Attorney General Robert Bonner approached the problems one at a time: the education of children, the registration of marriages, the registration of land on which Doukhobors were squatting, and the apprehension of terrorists. Because forcing the Doukhobor parents to send their children to school was a legal matter, it came under the Attorney General's Department, but the actual education of the children came under the Ministry of Education.

Far from being naive or unsophisticated when it came to dealing with the media, the leaders of the Sons of Freedom were adept at manipulating them. On May 4, 1954, less than three weeks after Ray had been installed as Education minister, John Perepelkin, one of their leaders, came to Victoria announcing his intention to interview Ray on education problems. He distributed a press release listing the questions he was going to ask and told the press that he would urge the minister to sanction the modification of the curriculum in Russian-language Doukhobor schools. The chief difficulty in getting the Sons of Freedom to accept education, he told the press, lay in such subjects as history "which deals with wars and national ambitions and results in the development of patriotism and aggressive characteristics." What the Freedomites wanted was a curriculum based on what he described as "natural and practical subjects" like reading, writing and manual and domestic skills.

Perepelkin's intended questions were duly printed in the newspapers and Ray awaited his request for an interview, but it never came. Meanwhile, Perepelkin returned home where he entertained the media and his people with an account of his reception by the minister of Education and the answers he had received to his questions. The answers he ascribed to Ray painted the government's actions and intentions in dismal colours, making the Freedomites look more and more like innocent victims of a diabolical government plot.

As minister of Education, Ray became a member of a government committee formed to meet with Doukhobor representatives and make recommendations. As a consequence, later that spring Doukhobor parents were warned that they must comply with the law and send their children to public school. By fall, the children in the Grand Forks and Slocan Valley areas were attending classes, but Sons of Freedom in the villages of Glade and Krestova refused to comply. In January 1955, when they continued to hold out, the Attorney General, citing this as an act of civil disobedience, had 40 children picked up at Krestova and made wards of Child Welfare. They were housed in a converted sanitarium in New Denver on Slocan Lake where children of jailed Doukhobors had been installed in 1953 and from which they were still attending school.

The roundup of the children was a media field day. Pictures that appeared in the press all across the country showed weeping Doukhobor parents speaking to their children through a wire fence; the photographs failed to show the nearby open gate through which people were free to come and go. Little mention was made of the fact that parents could get their children back immediately if they appeared before the court to promise they would send them to public schools near their homes.

The Sons of Freedom took advantage of other opportunities for media attention. In October 1955 when W.A.C. Bennett scheduled a cabinet meeting in Nelson, a full schedule of civic functions was arranged, including a luncheon, a ground-breaking ceremony at the site of the new bridge across Kootenay Lake, a reception and a public banquet. The Sons of Freedom began their demonstrations by staging noisy protests outside the main entrance to the Hume Hotel where the cabinet members were staying. The members solved that problem by using a rear door, but they could not avoid the Freedomites altogether because Nelson is a small town. While Ray and W.A.C. were walking back to the hotel from the civic luncheon where Ray had been guest speaker, they saw a group of Freedomites advancing toward them.

"Come on," said the premier, ducking into the barber shop they happened to be passing. As both barber chairs were unoccupied, they each took a seat. The barber draped both men, tipped back their chairs, took up his scissors and proceeded to give the premier a haircut, while the Nelson police dispersed the Freedomites who had congregated outside the barber shop.

At the New Denver dormitory, staff from the Welfare Department had difficulty keeping the children under control. On the weekends, parents would bring borscht for their offspring who didn't seem to appreciate this traditional food and took to throwing it—bowls and all—out the windows, not caring whether the windows were open or closed. Ray was appalled when, on a tour of inspection, he found 48 broken windows, dirty floors, and unsupervised children, and he immediately pulled strings to have the operation of the residence transferred from Welfare to Education. The New Denver school principal, John A. Clarkson, then became responsible for the residence as well as the school. Remembering the excellent results from hiring a capable matron for the dorm in Prince George, Ray hired a no-nonsense Scottish woman to see to the children's well-being outside school hours. On her first morning there the matron spotted a boy coming down the stairs, peeling an orange and tossing the peeling on the floor.

"Pick up those peelings," she told him.

"No, you pick them up. You're getting paid for it."

Whereupon she took the youngster over her knee and spanked him. Her action told the children where they stood and behavioural problems soon all but vanished.

During Ray's tenure as minister of Education, no parents petitioned for the release of their children from New Denver. It was 1959 before the first mothers appeared in front of Magistrate Evans in Nelson to promise that their children would be sent to school from their homes. Their requests were granted, the promise was kept by the mothers, and after August 1959 when the New Denver residence was closed, there were no major difficulties with schooling for these children.

Ray's job in the Ministry of Education led him quite naturally into another role after he commented casually during a cabinet meeting in 1955 that it might be a good time to start making plans for the B.C. centennial coming up in 1958, marking one hundred years since the establishment of the crown colony of British Columbia. The premier's response was, "That's a good idea! That's a good idea. You and Ken Kiernan will be a committee and bring a report back to cabinet."

As Kiernan was at that time minister of Agriculture, he had less access to the necessary information sources than Ray whose ministry acted as the umbrella for all the archives and museums of the province. Later that year, they brought in their report to which Bennett responded with, "That's fine. These are all good ideas. You and Mr. Kiernan will be a committee to implement them, but just remember that you have no budget."

Without funds until they could be voted for the project when the next budget was brought down the following spring, the two ministers set out to establish a core committee that would not require wages. Laurie Wallace, who later became deputy provincial secretary, was recruited as chairman of the Centennial Committee, followed by Willard Ireland, who was head of the provincial archives. Ed Espley, the comptroller in the Ministry of Education masterminded the committee's financing. They turned to UBC for the next member, Dr. Malcolm MacGregor, to the City of Vancouver for Alderman Bill Orr, and to the B.C. Electric for Ted Fox. All were paid their regular salaries by the institutions which employed them, and the City of Vancouver and the B.C. Electric covered transportation costs as well.

After the next budget was brought down, the committee added to its numbers, set up headquarters in Victoria's Weller Building and hired Larry H. McCance of Toronto as executive secretary for the festivities; unfortunately, although he had great credentials as a festival producer, he understood very little about British Columbia or its history. Six months later, the committee let him go and put Laurie Wallace in charge, and he was such a success that he was also drafted to run the centennial of 1967 marking Canada's first hundred years and the centennial of 1971 celebrating British Columbia's entry into Canada as a province. The success of the first centennial, with events all over the province, also convinced Bennett to draft Ray for all the following ones as well.

One of the interesting by-products of the first centennial was the adoption of a centennial flag—a white dogwood on a green background—which became extremely popular with the people of the province. As a result, after the festivities were over, Ray suggested that it would make a great provincial flag, and in due course the legislature passed a motion to that effect. On his next trip to Europe, the premier took the flag to the College of Heralds in London where he discovered to his shock that the province already had an official flag. What to do with the handsome white dogwood on the green background? Why, make it the emblem of the B.C. Ferry Corporation that was just coming into being in 1959.

While Ray's main ambition on entering politics had been to improve the province's educational system, he realized he had little hope of retaining that post for the long run. He had done what was necessary to save the ministry from self-destructing and placed it on solid footing for the future, but in doing so had sometimes given the premier headaches—as in the overrun on the budget caused by his teacher salary grant formula.

"As ministers," Ray recalls, "we were completely responsible for our actions, but we had to answer to the Old Man if we didn't carry them out. To keep his ministers in line—especially Phil Gaglardi who was almost impossible to control—even after our budgets were passed, he would only release the money in quarterly amounts. He monitored all the key budgetary factors in a daily report from his deputy finance minister, and then at the end of the quarter each minister had to show where he was in relation to his total budget. If you were over, before the Old Man would release the next quarter, you had to show how you intended to get it back in line." After February 1956 when Ray moved to the Lands and Forests portfolio, he became the bane of all the other ministers whenever there was a bad forest fire year. "I got into all kinds of difficulty then, spending millions and millions and millions that I didn't have in my budget. And as soon as W.A.C. took that into account, he would reduce all the other budgets so he could still balance his budget. The other ministers really used to swear at me when I had a bad fire season."

The final chapters in the story of the founding of the University of Victoria did not occur until Ray had left the Ministry of Education for the Ministry of Lands and Forests, but he was nonetheless involved. A year or so after Ray's conversation with General Pearkes, the federal government resolved the problem of what to do with the Gordon Head property by turning it over to the province where it automatically came under the jurisdiction of the Department of Lands. Ray, as minister, immediately dedicated it to the new University of Victoria and celebrated the momentous event on the Gordon Head site with a group of university advocates which included Dr. Hickman and Hugh Farquhar of Victoria College, Harry Gilliland who headed the college's education faculty, and Judge Clearihue who had now become a passionate believer in the need for an independent university in Victoria. The new minister of Education, Les Peterson, was also invited but probably on the advice of his deputy minister, Harold Campbell, managed to have another engagement at that time. The celebrants met on a dirty day in October 1957, and after tramping across the muddy fields, conducted a sod-turning ceremony, declaring it to be the start of the University of Victoria. A few pictures were taken by the city editor of the Victoria *Times*, and then with the rain still teeming down, they all headed back to town with Hugh Farquhar carrying off the sod-turning shovel in order to have it gold-plated as a souvenir. In spite of the official photographer at the event, nothing appeared in the newspaper, and Ray concluded much later that the *Times* editor's close friendship with Harold Campbell, who was still adamantly opposed to a university in Victoria, had outweighed the newsworthiness of the event.

It was 1960 before the College Council finally launched a massive fund-raising drive to make the university a reality. Premier Bennett's response was to promise matching funds up to $2.5 million, and the following year at the opening of the E.P. Paul Building on the Lansdowne campus, Bennett expressed his support for an independent university and pledged another $2.5 million for future development. The final hurdle came after Dr. McKenzie retired in 1962 to be replaced by Dr. John McDonald in the presidency of UBC. Before he took office, Dr. McDonald had been asked by the government to undertake a study of post-secondary needs in British Columbia. His report advocated the establishment of colleges throughout the province to provide the equivalent of the first two years of university education, and the addition of two new universities, one in Victoria and the other on the eastern side of Vancouver to accommodate Fraser Valley and interior students. The government adopted the entire report immediately, and in January 1963 at the official opening of the classroom block, now named the Clearihue Building, Premier Bennett announced that an act would be introduced during that legislative session to create an independent university in Victoria. The act was passed on March 14. The University of Victoria was born on July 1 of that year.

Although Ray's 1957 sod-turning ceremony at the university never made the annals of history, many years later the shovel did. It turned up again in the hands of Hugh Farquhar, by then the president of the University of Victoria, at the sod-turning for the university's McKinnon Gymnasium. "This is the second time this shovel has been used in this capacity," he announced, but as he never enlarged on his statement, only those who had stood in the rain on that dirty October day in 1957 were aware that the ground for the university had actually been broken with that shovel on that long-ago day.

From left: Ray's brother Norman, born 1910; Ray's father Hubert Williston; Ray, born in 1914 seated on the lap of grandfather Peter McCalman.

Ray and Gladys Williston on the steps of their Princeton home. March 30, 1940.

Flight Sergeant Ray Williston (second from left in front row) graduates top of his class from Initial Training School in Edmonton in the spring of 1944.

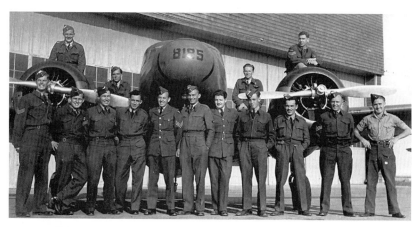

Ray Williston (standing third from the left) graduated from Service Training School in Calgary on October 27, 1944 with the top award once again.

Ray Williston and his staff at Prince George Junior-Senior High School in 1946.

Ray Williston is sworn in as Minister of Education at Government House, April 14, 1954. From left: Aide-de-camp Pennington, Lieutenant-Governor Clarence Wallace, Mrs. Wallace, and Ray holding the Bible. At the right is Premier W.A.C. Bennett and Provincial Secretary Wesley Black.

Ray Williston as the new Minister of Education at Kamloops graduation ceremonies. 1955.

The Social Credit cabinet in late February 1956, just days before the resignation of Lands and Forest Minister Robert E. Sommers. From Left: Highways Minister P.A. Gaglardi; Education Minister R.G. Williston; Trade, Industry and Fisheries Minister R. Chetwynd; Health Minister Eric Martin; Agriculture Minister Ken Kiernan; Premier W.A.C. Bennett; Attorney-General R. Bonner; Provincial Secretary W. Black; Sommers; Labor Minister L. Wicks and Public Works Minister W. Chant.

Crown Prince Akihito and Princess Michiko entertain a delegation of BC Cabinet Ministers in 1956. Ray, holding the case for his forbidden half-frame Canon camera, stands to the left of the prince, with Mines minister Ken Kiernan behind him. Health Minister Ralph Loffmark and Premier W.A.C. Bennett stand to the right of the princess, on a balcony chosen by the princess because it provided better light for the photograph.

Ray waits with Princess Margaret as Prince George 'prospector' Alex Moffat pans gold nuggets for her. On the right is Chuck Williams of Prince George. July 17, 1958.

The BC Cabinet rides the rails on the inaugural run of the Pacific Great Eastern Railway into Fort St. John, October 4, 1958. In front of the engine are Labor Minister Lyle Wicks and Highways Minister Phil Gaglardi. On the engine are the premier's assistant Bill Clancy, Health Minister Eric Martin, Premier W.A.C. Bennett, P.G.E. president Einar Gundarson, Lands and Forests Minister Ray Williston (half hidden behind his camera), Education Minister Leslie Peterson, Attorney-General Bob Bonner (face completely hidden by camera) and Agriculture Minister Newton Stacey.

Starting the revolution. 1961. Ray Williston, BC Chief Forester John Stokes and Tom Wright, chief forester for Canadian Forest Products examine small wood close to Prince George to determine the timber area required for a Pulp Harvesting Area licence for a proposed Canadian Forest Products pulpmill, the first pulpmill to be completely dependent on waste wood.

Ray Williston and John Liersch of Canadian Forest Products contemplate the small wood survey results in the forest southwest of Prince George.

The largest collection of pulp-making facilities on a single site anywhere in the world: Prince George Pulp and Paper (left foreground), Intercontinental Pulp and Paper (right foreground) and Northwood Pulp and Timber (smoke on center/right horizon).

One of the early Chip-n-Saws in action.

The development of self-dumping log barges spelled the end for many up-coast gyppo logging outfits which had previously sent their logs south in booms.

CHAPTER FIVE:
The Member for Fort George

ONE RAINY SPRING DAY IN 1954, very shortly after Ray Williston was appointed minister of Education, as he was driving up to Prince George for a weekend with his family, he found traffic had come to a halt about 22 miles south of Quesnel. Debris and gravel had collected behind a railway trestle during a flash flood, backing the water up until the pressure became too great and it burst through, taking out the trestle, the railway bed and tracks as well as the adjacent highway bridge.

By the time Ray arrived on the scene, several dozen people were milling around. Some were there to begin emergency repairs while others, including Ray's Prince George friend Ted Williams, had just come to view the damage. After greeting Ray, Ted introduced him to a local man.

The man's response told Ray that he was now truly identified with politics. "That's what's wrong with this goddamned government," the local snorted. "The bridge washes out and they send the minister of Education!"

With his new duties, Ray could not commute as often as he wanted to Prince George, and in preparation for moving his family to Victoria, he began spending his lunch hours with a realtor looking at houses. One day the agent asked him to have a look at a listing on Cedar Hill Crossroad. "The owner thinks I'm not working hard enough for her," he said. The $20,000 price tag was away over Ray's limit, but he agreed to have a quick look. In the realtor's car on the way back to Ray's office, he admitted that he liked the house but that it was too expensive.

"I know, but you'd do me a service if you made an offer—any offer—so I could show the owner that I am working for her."

Ray made an offer of $12,000 with $3,000 down and $75 a month, and hurried into the legislative buildings. Late that afternoon the realtor phoned to tell him, "You've got yourself a house."

"But you told me I wouldn't have to buy it!"

"I didn't think the offer would be accepted either, but it's a great buy. All you have to do is make a $500 deposit. Then if you find you can't raise the down payment, that's all you'll be out."

At the Canadian Bank of Commerce, manager Jimmy Thow agreed to lend Ray the necessary $3,000—providing he moved his account from the Bank of Montreal to the Commerce. However, when Ray went to the Bank of Montreal to move his account, manager Bert Twist—whom Ray had known in Prince George—wanted to know, "How come you went to the Commerce for your loan instead of coming here?"

"I knew you wouldn't give me the money because I was forever in hot water with you in Prince George about overdrafts!"

"Go and buy your godammed house! Write out your cheque and we'll cover it here!" And that was how Ray bought the house on Cedar Hill Crossroad where his children grew up and which he kept for 33 years.

The Prince George house was listed for sale, and while waiting for an offer, Ray rented it to Alan Bircher, a roads superintendent, who was looking for a larger house to purchase. The house he eventually found had tenants; could he move them into the Williston house? Ray agreed to the arrangement, and the displaced family moved in. Not long afterwards, the man of the tenant family, coming home from a night at the Legion, was struck and killed when he stepped out of a taxi into traffic. His widow subsequently took in boarders to augment her welfare payments. Meanwhile, Ray had received an offer for the house of $8000 cash, exactly the amount necessary to complete the purchase of his Victoria home. Notified that she would have to leave, the widow told her troubles to the Legion, which promptly took the matter up with lawyer Frank Perry, head of the Liberals in Prince George.

Soon a story began to circulate that the member for Fort George was putting a poor widow and her children out on the street. Ray was forced to reject the cash offer for the house. The Legion then provided the woman with money for a very low down payment so that she could buy the house herself, and Ray had no choice but to accept her offer. However, months and months went by with no regular payments from her. Nor did she pay taxes, and after a couple of years Ray received notice that the house was to be sold for outstanding taxes. However, just before the date of the sale, Slumber Lodge Inns and Motels Ltd. made the woman a cash offer for more than she had agreed to pay Ray, on top of which they would give her the house since they planned to erect a motel on the land. She paid Ray off, took the gift house and had it moved across the river onto Pulpmill Road, the winner by a mile in this whole transaction.

Another of Ray's constituents was Ben Ginter who had arrived in B.C. soon after World War II. Born in Poland, though raised in Manitoba, he was only 24 when he burst onto the Prince George scene, armed with a single bulldozer and plenty of ambition. His timing was perfect; Alcan was preparing to drive tunnels from the Nechako lake system down to Kemano, and Ginter won the contract to clear the site. He was taking a huge gamble because the contract called for him to guarantee a large number of bulldozers on a daily operating basis and to get the machinery onto the site in the fall of the year so that much of the work could be done before freeze-up and, weather permitting, throughout the winter. Ginter won the gamble, even though he bought his huge fleet of machines on credit, because under the terms of his contract he had an assured number of operating hours for each bulldozer. Thus, on the days the weather was too bad for the machines to be worked he was still paid the agreed hourly rate for them, although he paid neither the operators' wages nor fuel costs. In addition, there were no maintenance costs for the idle bulldozers. And as it turned out, that winter was so severe that the machines could be operated only a few days before the following spring.

Soon after the Social Credit government achieved a majority in 1953, they became involved in a major road construction program and Ray, who had made a campaign promise to get more and better roads for his Fort George constituents, pushed to make them a priority with the Highways Department. And the Prince George-based Ginter, a hands-on operator with a low overhead and a now fully-paid-for fleet of machines, was able to bid competitively to construct them. From his Alcan bonanza and local road-building contracts, his business soon mushroomed to become one of the biggest road construction outfits in the province.

It was at this point that Ginter was offered a brewery. During the 1950s the major brewing companies were getting rid of competition from small breweries by buying them out, then after a decent interval, closing them down. Thus, a few years after Labatt's purchased the Prince George Brewery, the company was able to show that the decline of annual production had made the business unprofitable and announced that the brewery would close in 1962. Labatt's hastened to have the government cancel the brewery's licence, and with a view to disposing of the property as quickly as possible, approached Ben Ginter and proposed that he buy it for equipment storage. Ginter refused but Labatt's did not give up easily and kept encouraging him to make a bid. At last Ginter succumbed with a very low one. Almost as soon as it was tendered it was accepted, and the Labatt's people were so anxious to unload the property that they did not even bother to take away the brewing equipment.

Convinced that the brewery could be a viable industry again, the brewmaster who had been associated with the Prince George Brewery from its earliest days to its closure arranged a meeting with Ray, as MLA, and Garvin Dezell, Prince George's mayor. He explained that when Labatt's had bought out the company, they had changed the brewing formula. "It tasted vile," said the brewmaster. "Nobody bought it, and no wonder, but if we went back to my old brew we could make a go of it."

"So what do you want us to do?"

"Convince Ben Ginter that he should apply for a licence and get the brewery going again. Everything's there, ready to go. And the staff are still here, willing to go back to work."

"Why don't you talk to Ben yourself?" Ray asked.

"Oh, he wouldn't listen to me."

"His bark is often worse than his bite," said Dezell. He turned to Ray. "What do you say? Do we beard the lion?"

"Why not?" said Ray, but when they talked to Ginter, they found him firmly negative. "I'm in road construction," he said.

"Ben, you could put all those brewery people back to work," Ray told him.

"Can they handle bulldozers?"

Dezell moved in. "This town has done very well by you, Ben. Now's your chance to do something for the town."

Ginter began to weaken because he couldn't deny that Prince George had given him all the breaks he needed to expand his businesses. "I'll tell you what I'll do," he said. "I'll put $200,000 in the bank as a credit to the brewery. The guys that used to work there can give me advice, and I'll get the thing going again."

"That's terrific, Ben!"

But he wasn't finished. "If it pays its way, that's fine. But if it doesn't, when that $200,000 is used up, it's game over. Then I close the plant and turn it into maintenance headquarters for my machinery. . . which is what I bought the damn thing for in the first place!"

"Fair enough," said Dezell.

Ray agreed to make arrangements to get the necessary licence but kept the application quiet because it was deemed unwise to let Labatt's know what was going on. Nevertheless, one day Ginter received a phone call.

"Mr. Ginter, we've had an accident in our New Westminster brewery," said the caller. "Our brew kettle got badly damaged and you can help us by selling us the one that's in the brewery up there."

Ben hedged, and at length his caller offered him more for the kettle than he had paid for the whole brewery. Up until that point he had considered his $200,000 stake merely a goodwill gesture to the community. Now suddenly he was keenly interested in the brewery business. "The kettle is not for sale," he said and hung up.

As Ginter actually looked like a typical bewhiskered German brewmaster, he decided to have his own likeness on the brewery's label and to call the product *Uncle Ben's Beer*. As soon as the Liquor Control Board issued the licence and the brewery was back in business, the local Legion and several of the hotels were persuaded to carry the new draft beer, and people began acquiring a taste for it again.

Then queer things began to happen. A stranger would turn up in Prince George, make his way to a beer parlour, take a swig of the local beer, then shout, "What's this swill you're serving here?" Next he would march over to the bar and order a big-name brand of bottled beer. "And a round for these other gentlemen," he would add, grandly waving towards the loggers and sawmill workers seated nearby. At the same time, rumours began circulating that some of the local hotels had been offered "financial assistance" for renovations, and it was not long before Ginter's Prince George Brewery was faced with cancelled contracts from most of them. The only holdout was the Canada Hotel. The proprietors, Mr. & Mrs. Bill Cutt, chose to stick with the local draft beer. Then one Sunday a young man who had been staying at the Canada for the best part of a week knocked on the door of the Cutts' living quarters in the hotel and asked if there was any chance he could buy some beer.

"No," said Mrs. Cutt, "of course not. I can't sell you beer on a Sunday."

"Gosh, I've got friends coming in this afternoon and I forgot to lay in some. I'm really stuck. Are you sure you can't let me have a dozen?"

The woeful look of the young man swayed Mrs. Cutt. "Well, I can't *sell* you any," she said, "but I guess I could *give* you a dozen, and you can replace them tomorrow. Wait here a minute." She reappeared a few moments later with a carton of beer.

"Thanks a lot," said the chap, taking the beer. "You saved my day!"

Only minutes later there was another knock on the Cutts' door. This time, two RCMP officers came in, one carrying what appeared to be the dozen beer she had just given to the young man, the other carrying a search warrant.

"You can sit down and wait till Bill gets back," said Mrs. Cutt. "He'll have something to say about this!"

"Sorry, but this won't wait," said one of the officers, and from a cluttered table nearby he picked up a five dollar bill—a marked bill planted there by the young man. "Mrs. Cutt," he said, "I'm afraid we'll have to charge you with bootlegging."

As soon as their report arrived on the desk of Colonel McGugan, commissioner of the Liquor Control Board, he promptly cancelled the Canada Hotel's beer licence. The Cutts immediately contacted Ray who, when he heard the story, was livid. From his office in the legislative buildings he phoned McGugan. "What evidence do you have that the Cutts were bootlegging? Has it been proven in court?" Ray bellowed.

"There was no doubt about the bootlegging," said McGugan loftily.

"We'll see about that!" said Ray. He was busily dialling to set the wheels in motion to save the Cutts when a friendly MLA poked his head into the office. "Hey!" he said. "You didn't have to use your phone. You could have just opened your window and the Colonel would have heard you all the way downtown!"

In due course, the Cutts' bootlegging affair came to court in Prince George. The judge, critical of all the shenanigans that had taken place, threw the case out, and McGugan had to restore the Cutts' beer licence.

In the meantime, Ben Ginter was having a hard time getting beer sales in other parts of the province because there was a tacit agreement among local breweries that they would not sell in each other's territories. Then, just when it seemed that the Prince George Brewery would have to close, Ginter came up with two solutions to his problems. First, noticing that beer in cans was becoming popular in the United States, he began to produce canned beer, a first for B.C. His second decision was to move into the Alaska market where he could undersell the American beer makers because his transportation costs were lower. Both were astute moves that finally established the Prince George Brewery as a viable and expanding business. And to top off his luck, not long after Ginter began putting his beer into cans, a province-wide brewery strike made the non-union Prince George Brewery the only one in operation in the entire province, with a ready market for everything they could produce.

He branched out into the soft drink business—again using the *Uncle Ben's* label—and then into wines, and expanded his beer production so that it could be marketed in other provinces. He dreamed of establishing his breweries right across Canada, at one point announcing that he was putting together a consortium to take over Molson's enterprises; he was forced to drop the plan when the Molson family showed not the slightest interest in selling. In the end he only succeeded in setting up Uncle Ben's breweries in Alberta and Manitoba because negotiations with other companies usually ended with Ben stomping out shouting, "I'll sue!" As he usually followed through on the threat, he spent much time and money on litigation.

In spite of this, in less than 30 years Ginter built up one of the largest B.C.-based personal industrial complexes in the province's history, at its high point employing 9,000 people. He eventually overextended himself, however, and because he was a very belligerent man at the best of times and had not endeared himself to many people, particularly his creditors, no one came forward to bail him out. His companies were placed in receivership in the mid-1970s. He fought to regain control, but in 1982, just when success seemed within his grasp, he died of a heart attack. As for the copper kettle that sparked Ben's sudden enthusiasm for the brewery business, it lasted until 1978 when it was sold as scrap for $5,000.

The roads Ginter constructed in the Fort George riding were not the only ones that demanded Ray's attention. One of the most pressing needs was for a road to connect Prince George to McBride, 150 miles away, and on from there to Jasper, Alberta. At that time, there was only a tote road through the mountains from Jasper to McBride. A dirt road ran south from McBride to Kamloops, but it was closed half the time because of a shifting sandbank, and from McBride to Prince George there was no road at all. It was as a result of this situation that on Sunday, June 2, 1957, Ray found himself a passenger in a Grumman Mallard float plane on his way to a rendezvous at Moose Lake. A car would be waiting there to take him to Mount Robson Park where he was to speak at yet one more annual rally to press for a road from Jasper to Prince George.

As the plane turned for the descent to the lake, pilot Jack McNeil shouted over the noise of the engine, "The oil pressure's dropping." And just then, like ink flicked from an outsize fountain pen, a splattering of oil hit the windscreen.

"There's your answer," said Ray, pointing to the wing. Oil was leaking from the left engine. As a pilot himself, he knew exactly what this would mean. The plane smacked onto the water, and Jack nosed it toward the sloping shore where they could climb out the forward hatch onto a tiny patch of beach, the only place where tangled brush had not encroached to the water's edge. A couple of hundred yards away, a car waited to take Ray to the rally.

"I'll work on the oil leak while you're away," said Jack, "but before you go, I'll need a hand to swing her around so the fuselage is parallel to the beach." After they had manoeuvred the plane so that the left wing was over dry land, Ray walked to the waiting car. As he climbed in, he glanced back and saw that Jack already had the engine cowling off.

On this occasion, Ray, who was as keen as anyone from that area to get the road put through, could happily reassure the 2,000 people gathered for the rally from as far away as Edmonton and Kamloops that a survey from the Alberta boundary to Prince George would be completed before winter. A half hour after he finished his speech, Ray was back at Moose Lake where he found Jack leaning against the plane.

"Get her fixed?" asked Ray.

"Nope."

"What are we going to do?"

"I dunno. I won't be able to get full power, but if we take off in a circle, I guess I can get her up. I sure as hell can't leave her here."

Ray turned his head in time to see the car that had brought him disappearing up the road. "I guess I'm going with you. But we're travelling light. We'll make it."

"Right!" Jack pointed to the left wing, its tip just touching the ground amid the underbrush. "You slide under there, and when I lift on my side, you lift on yours."

Ray crawled under the wing until he was clear of it, then hunched forward and jumped up. Unfortunately, he was right under the left engine nacelle and as he jumped, the steel propeller caught him just above his right eye.

"My God!" said Jack, scrambling for his first-aid kit. "First I have to stop the oil coming out of my engine, then I have to stop the blood coming out of my passenger."

Fifteen minutes later, with Ray's blood flow staunched with a bandage, the two of them lifted the wing from the sand, pushed the aircraft away from the shore and clambered aboard. Jack got the motors started and taxied out to the centre of the lake where he would have plenty of room for the take-off. Ray held his breath as, with half power on the ailing motor and full power on the other, they followed a semi-circular path across the lake. Then suddenly he realized they were airborne.

"I don't think we can make it to Vancouver," said Jack. "I'm going to try for Kamloops."

Because the plane was amphibious, they would be able to land on wheels at the Kamloops airport where Jack would be able to get the engine repaired. Or so they thought. But ten minutes after a safe landing there, Jack climbed back into the plane. "No go. They can't do it till tomorrow. I'm going on to Vancouver." He waited for Ray's reaction.

"Let's go," said Ray, although he hadn't missed the fact that oil was again leaking from the faulty engine. By this time evening was coming on, and lights below them identified first Merritt, then Hope, and before long dazzling city lights told them they would soon be on the ground. It takes a capable pilot to jockey a crippled plane onto any airstrip, let alone into a major airport like Vancouver with its added traffic, but Jack McNeil was as capable as they come. "My left motor is on the fritz," he told the tower. "I think I may have to come down fairly soon." The tower gave clearance for him to land immediately.

He turned to Ray. "This may be eventful. Better hang onto your hat!"

Below them, Ray could see the flashing lights of fire engines rushing across the tarmac, but Jack went about his business as if this were a normal landing. In fact, the landing was better than several Ray had experienced on commercial aircraft. Jack switched off the engines and sat back in his seat. "Nice having you aboard, Ray," he said. Ray shook his hand, then hurried to the taxi ranks.

At the Hotel Georgia he had a sandwich sent up to his room. His head was throbbing, and too exhausted to finish his sandwich, he climbed into bed and promptly went to sleep. He woke about midnight to find his pillow sticky. Switching on the light, he saw that a crimson puddle had soaked into the pillowslip. Once again he got a taxi, this one to take him to Vancouver General. There he sat in the Emergency waiting room along with half a dozen drunks, women with crying children, and a man in his pyjamas. A seedy-looking individual next to him leaned over companionably and said, "W . . . w . . . what happened to you, bud? Get in a fight?"

When the doctor removed Ray's blood-soaked bandage, he said cheerfully, "That propeller didn't cut your skin—it mashed it! And there's not a heck of a lot we can do about stitching it. We'll clean it and dress it, but you'll likely have a scar for the rest of your life." He was right. Ray carries a permanent identification mark—a souvenir of the fight for the northern highway, bud.

Some of Ray's responsibilities as MLA for Fort George were mixed blessings, and this was especially the case on the July day in 1958 when he stood on a platform at Taylor Flats overlooking the Peace River. Blue and gold ribbons fluttered overhead and flags billowed in the breeze, while round the platform were crowded press representative from all over the world. Beside Ray, the mayor of Fort St. John grinned as he looked up at the summer sky. "We're sure lucky with the weather," he said.

This was very true since the centre of attention that day was H.R.H. Princess Margaret, who was there to officially open the pumping station for the Westcoast Transmission pipeline to Vancouver. Ray's job as MLA for the region was to act as the princess's co-escort with Lieutenant Governor Frank Ross during the northern part of her royal tour. For both the lieutenant governor and Ray there was a certain degree of tension on this trip. The princess had already exhibited the willfulness for which she was noted during a ceremony in Victoria where Premier Bennett had handed her the deed to Portland Island off the Saanich Peninsula. She was then supposed to deliver a prepared speech giving the deed back to the premier, and the island would be renamed "Princess Margaret Island" and dedicated as a marine park for the people of British Columbia.

So the script went.

What really happened was that Margaret omitted the most important part of the speech, the part in which she gave the deed back to the premier. Instead she concluded her speech with "As I travel through the country, I shall feel a special pride. For, thanks to this wonderful and generous gift which you, Mr. Premier, have just presented to me, I shall be able to feel myself already a land-owner in the province. I can assure you that no other token of your affection could have given me so much pleasure." And off she went with the deed to the island tightly clutched in her hand.

Needless to say, Ray and the lieutenant governor were apprehensive as they stood on the platform at Taylor Flats with Margaret, watching the spectacular flaming pillar that was created as Pacific Fort St. John No. 4 gas well was turned on for the first time. Below them, a photographer from *Paris Match,* noting that her skirts were billowing in the breeze, dashed down the embankment for a better view. Close on his heels was a member of the Royal Canadian Mounted. "But I only weesh a photograph of zee royal leg," pleaded the Parisien. "I have not bombs, only zee camera."

"No leg," said the mountie.

On the platform, Princess Margaret made a short speech and declared the pipeline open. The ceremony over, half a dozen limousines carried the royal party to Westcoast's compressor station No. 1 where Frank McMahon, company president, was to be the guide for a tour of the plant. And that's when it happened. Although even the smallest details of the visit had been meticulously planned, when she spotted a closed door, the princess turned the knob and disappeared through the doorway. Panic ensued because not only was this definitely not on the itinerary, it was also extremely dangerous since much of the plant was still under construction. But before anyone could react, Margaret re-emerged unharmed and unconcerned. The flap was over.

With the tour complete, the official party climbed back into the waiting cars to return along the dusty gravel road to the airport. Suddenly the princess, riding in the last car, pointed to one of the other buildings in the refinery complex. "I should like to go into that one," she announced. Although no more stops had been scheduled, the chauffeur immediately complied, turning off to the right. Meanwhile, the mounties in the lead car looked straight ahead, unaware that the princess was no longer with them; the drivers of the other cars dutifully followed the mounties.

Outside the building of Margaret's choice, the chauffeur of the royal limousine stopped and smartly opened the car door for her. She alighted, and trailed by Ray and the lieutenant-governor, marched inside. As could be expected, the guys at work in the plant—most of them stripped to the waist because of the hot weather—stopped to gawk as Princess Margaret walked into their dirty, half-built, pipe-festooned plant, but she strolled among them and chatted amiably, appearing to be genuinely interested in what they were doing.

About this time it dawned on the mounties that they had lost the princess. Turning the cavalcade around, they vroomed back, spotting the royal limousine parked with its driver at the wheel. At the side of the road an onlooker, watching this drama, commented, "Talk about embarrassing! They've got a guard on every bridge and behind every telephone pole, and there's wee Margaret cavorting around on her own in a rambling, big barn that's not halfways finished."

"Yes," agreed her friend, "and all those big apes sweating away inside, including my dear husband."

A few hours later, beside the Prince George railway tracks where the royal tour would board the PGE to head south, the princess was given a gold-panning demonstration. The scenario had old Alex Moffat, who had panned for gold at Quesnel long before he opened his Northern Hardware Store in Prince George, panning sand that had been seeded with gold nuggets. Real ones. As each nugget appeared in the pan, Ray was to pick it up and put it in a velvet-lined box to be presented to the princess. However, before he could pick up the first nugget, Margaret's hand shot out and snatched it up. Moffat looked up in surprise, but he shook the pan again. Again the royal hand grabbed the nugget . . . then the next . . . and the next . . . until Margaret was jiggling all the nuggets in her little hand. The official presentation had fizzled out. Later, on the train, Ray handed her the box. "Here," he said, "you may as well put your nuggets in this."

That evening, steak was on the PGE dinner menu. Margaret ordered hers rare. When it arrived, she noticed Ray glancing at the bloody meat on her plate. She laughed and said, "If Mum were here she would say, 'Margaret, why don't you let them kill the animal before you eat it?'"

North of Williams Lake the royal train pulled into a siding for the night, and here Margaret stepped onto the rear platform of the train for a smoke. "Dammit!" she cried. "There goes my cigarette holder!" It had dropped to the tracks below. Dutifully, everyone climbed off the train to walk up and down the tracks in the dark, looking in vain for the cigarette holder. It may be there yet.

Princess Margaret had two ladies-in-waiting, plain Lady Ogilvie and attractive Mary Peak, and before each ceremony the princess saw to it that Mary Peak's outfit did not outshine her own. Lady Ogilvie she didn't have to worry about. Lady Ogilvie, however, was a charming woman and popular with the rest of the entourage, so the next day as the train moved out of the siding and she showed an interest in its operation, Ray took her up to the engine cab. Going in to Williams Lake, the engineer handed her the controls, and Ray took a photo of her running the diesel. When he told her he would send her a copy, she was delighted, but she made him promise he wouldn't tell Margaret that she had driven the locomotive. Nobody upstaged the princess.

For the stampede in Williams Lake the royal party was given a special box in the stands. Once more the Frenchman circled below, singlemindedly pursuing his goal of photographing the royal leg, but to his frustration, Princess Margaret sat down, and with her legs hidden behind the enclosure, kicked off her shoes and became absorbed in the show.

"When she eez seating down," moaned the photgrapher to the mountie who was detailed to follow him, "from here I cannot see."

When the time came for the royal tour to move on again, the lieutenant governor came to Margaret. "Your Highness, we must be going now."

The princess didn't budge.

A few minutes later he came back. "Your Highness, it's time we were leaving." Still she didn't move.

Then somebody had a brain wave, and a few minutes later a voice came over the loudspeaker: "Would everyone now stand while the band plays 'God Save the Queen'? Her Highness has to leave now." Princess Margaret, of course, had to stand. When "God Save the Queen" was over, the crowd remained standing while the princess put on her shoes and walked out.

The princess and her entourage then boarded a DC-6, the first big plane to take off from the new, still uncompleted Williams Lake airport, and headed for Penticton. Having been told about Lieutenant Governor Ross's Douglas Lake Cattle Ranch, Princess Margaret said she would like to see it from the air, so the plane circled low over the world-famous stock farm. *A lot of good, red, rare beef down there*, she must have mused.

In Penticton the royal party changed to a Grumman Goose for

the flight to Vernon, Margaret's first ride in an amphibian. As the party boarded the plane, two black specks approached in the distance: the man from *Paris Match* with the mountie in pursuit. Before long the plane descended over the shimmering turquoise and blue of Kalamalka Lake, shot along the surface with a great splash and taxied towards the beach where a crowd of local people waited to welcome the princess. After the reception the plane carried the royal party back over the lakes to Kelowna where Premier Bennett awaited the arrival of his royal guest. Ray breathed a sign of relief; his duties as an escort were over.

And Portland Island? Well, some years later, through diplomatic channels, the island was pried loose from the princess. Today the marine park bears the name of Princess Margaret, but the island is still Portland Island.

CHAPTER SIX:
British Columbia's Forestry Revolution

THE SOMMERS AFFAIR, which catapulted Ray Williston into the Ministry of Lands and Forests, began with a speech on February 15, 1955, by the Liberal MLA for Lillooet, Gordon Gibson Sr., a 25-year veteran of B.C.'s truck logging industry. In that speech, he demanded an investigation into the government's method of awarding Forest Management Licences. "I firmly believe that money talks and that money has talked in this," declared Gibson. His speech made for bold headlines in the next morning's press, particularly the Liberal-owned Vancouver *Sun* and *Province*. In time it would come out that Gibson was referring specifically to an application by B.C. Forest Products Ltd. for timber in the Clayoquot Sound area.

Forest Management Licences or FMLs (later known as Tree Farm Licences or TFLs) had been an innovation recommended by the 1945 Sloan Royal Commission as part of a new policy of sustained yield forestry that matched the rate of logging in the province's crown forests to the annual overall growth rate of the forests. Under this policy, the Forestry Service set up large "public working circles" of crown forest area to provide timber for small local logging companies, while the large logging corporations received FMLs. The holders of these FMLs were given exclusive cutting rights to certain areas of crown forest lands in return for managing the forest on a sustained yield basis and paying a stumpage fee to the government for each tree cut. They were also required to place their private timber holdings under the same type of management. The first FML was issued in 1948, and by the time Social Credit came to power in 1952, 12 FMLs had been granted and 23 applications were being studied. Since it was the job of the minister of Lands, Forests and Mines to recommend to cabinet which applicants should be awarded FMLs, the person holding that portfolio was very vulnerable to bribery pressures.

From the time he became part of Social Credit's original government in 1952, minister of Lands, Forests and Mines Robert Sommers (MLA for Rossland-Trail) had been plagued by money problems. He had been a schoolteacher before entering politics, and arriving in Victoria with his bank account overdrawn by $900, he had immediately taken out a $3,500 bank loan for a down payment on a house. For funds to renovate and furnish it, he turned to a friend, H. Wilson "Wick" Gray, the president of a small logging operation called Evergreen Lumber Sales, and within nine months of becoming a cabinet minister he owed his friend $7,000.

The period between Gibson's accusations in February 1955 and the ultimate arrest of Sommers in November 1957 was a time of rancorous charges, countercharges, accusations, denials and cloak-and-dagger assignations. These began with a March 1955 commission under Judge Arthur Lord to investigate Gibson's charges, but since Gibson had in the meantime resigned from the House, he refused to testify because as a private citizen he could be sued for slander by the forestry companies he had named. As a result, after a three-day hearing, Lord reported to the government that: "On the evidence and on statements of counsel on behalf of Mr. Gibson, I find that there has been no impropriety on the part of any person in connection with the issuance of any forest management licences." Subsequently, on May 18, 1955, FML No. 22 in the Clayoquot Sound area was awarded to B.C. Forest Products, a company very recently organized by industrialist E.P. Taylor. This FML, however, had actually been carved out of a Clayoquot Sound public working circle that had been designated for local logging operators.

The case came to a boil once again in December of that year when lawyer David Sturdy told a hearing of a new royal commission on forestry presided over by B.C.'s Chief Justice Gordon Sloan that he had evidence that the Forests minister had taken bribes. Sommers' response was a suit for libel and slander against Sturdy, but by this time the RCMP had delivered a report to Attorney General Robert Bonner to the effect that there was some truth in Gibson's and Sturdy's charges. Sommers, meanwhile, had continued in government as the minister of Lands, Forests and Mines, and when budget time rolled around in late February 1956, he rose in the legislature to report on his Forest Department estimates. The Opposition immediately launched an all-out assault on his integrity, and after 18 hours of questioning and heckling had taken place without a vote on the estimates, the premier had heard enough. When the supper break was called on Monday, February 27, he turned to Sommers and quietly told him that he would accept his resignation from the cabinet as of that minute. Shortly after ten that evening when the salary estimates for Forests came up for debate, Sommers rose again and began reading his resignation statement. At noon the next day, Bennett summoned Kenneth Kiernan and Ray Williston to his office where he ordered them to go over to Government House and wait for him. Neither of them knew what to expect since the premier gave no explanations, but while the rest of the legislature ate lunch, the two men were sworn in as cabinet ministers for Sommers' old portfolios—Kiernan as minister of Mines and Ray as minister of Lands and Forests, although he also retained his post as minister of Education.

The forest industry that Ray Williston found himself supervising was divided into two zones—one on the coast, the other in the interior—and at the time there was little recognition of the vast differences between them. The coastal zone was dominated by five companies—MacMillan Bloedel, Powell River, Rayonnier, Crown Zellerbach and B.C. Forest Products—and since these companies, along with a few mid-sized ones, turned out 80 percent of the province's timber products, all of B.C.'s forestry regulations to that time had been designed to accommodate them. Most of their products were in the form of large-sized, rough-cut timbers which were exported to be used as massive building materials or re-manufactured into lumber at their destination. None of these timbers were dried before they were exported, only stain-treated to prevent discoloration during the trip. In addition, peeler logs were utilized in a comparatively small, but well-established plywood industry, and a number of pulpmills were in production, all of them using round wood.

What little construction there was in B.C. during this period was supplied with dimension timber from the interior where a few of the bigger mills had installed dry kilns. This interior industry had been established almost exclusively along the railroad lines from Prince Rupert to Jasper, along the Canadian Pacific and Canadian National into the interior, the B.C. government-owned Pacific Great Eastern Railway, and the old Kettle Valley Line that ran through to Lethbridge. In the Prince George district alone, more than 600 small mills were turning out random-length, rough dimension timber and hand-loading most of it into railroad boxcars for markets on the prairies and to a lesser degree in eastern Canada and the United States.

But although the new minister had lived for many years in Prince George, which was surrounded by these little mills, he had only a hazy concept of the forest industry as a whole. In fact, shortly before his appointment he had been invited to Cranbrook as Education minister to officiate at the opening of a new elementary school. The building had been pre-fabricated at the coast, and in his speech before cutting the ribbon, he spoke glowingly of this new use for coastal manufactured timber. As he spoke, he could see the president of the company which had built the school standing at the back of the room waving his hands back and forth to signal him to stop. Afterwards, when he asked the man what this had been about, he was told, "Well, to tell you the truth, I had to get all my kiln-dried wood for that school from Bellingham. Coastal B.C. doesn't produce kiln-dried dressed fir lumber." A "greener" forestry minister it would have been difficult to find, but W.A.C. Bennett had chosen Ray for the Lands and Forests portfolio precisely because he came from outside the industry and could approach its problems without bias.

The media, however, saw him as the wrong man for the job, and within a few months of Ray's new appointment, they began urging the premier to lighten his load and get him back where he belonged in Education. "It is a tribute to the abilities and energy of Mr. Williston," said the Victoria *Times* on May 5, "that he has served in these two capacities for so long. But it is unreasonable to expect him to continue. Being Minister of Education is a full-time job. So is being Minister of Lands and Forests. It is unfair to Mr. Williston to keep him in the two posts. It is equally unfair to the two departments." By July columnist James K. Nesbitt of the Vancouver *Sun* had added his voice to the chorus, suggesting that Ray should be relieved of Lands and Forests, although he expressed admiration for "the technical knowledge Mr. Williston has picked up in so short a time, about so difficult, so complex a subject as the modern administration of forests. But he is a scholar, and it appears that scholars, once they put their minds to any task, are able to master it. In this way he's a walking example of the benefits of higher education."

In general the media assumed that Bennett would keep Ray in Education because Sommers was supposedly only in exile until the matter of FML 22 had been satisfactorily cleared up, after which he would presumably be welcomed back to his old portfolios, but Ray suspected that the premier was using this emergency to phase him out of the Education portfolio. "I think he'd had enough commotion in the Ministry of Education," Ray recalls. "We had completely revised teacher training and the financing system for the operation and construction of schools, all in a matter of eighteen months. I think he wanted things to go at a little slower pace there."

Ray was right. Bennett was only waiting until after the September 1956 election to move new faces into the cabinet, and then he promptly slipped lawyer Leslie Peterson into the Education slot, leaving Ray in Lands and Forests. In the course of the next sixteen years, Ray Williston was to develop a remarkably thorough knowledge of forestry as he oversaw changes both in the way that government dealt with the industry and within the industry itself. Together these changes created a forestry revolution. "It wasn't something that was planned," he recalls. "I couldn't have foreseen that this was what was coming, but as it began to happen I was able to give it some guidance and support it as it went along."

(Sommers was returned in Rossland-Trail in the 1956 election with 5,097 votes to the CCF's 2,839. Nevertheless, there came a point when Attorney General Robert Bonner could no longer ignore the charges against him, and on November 21, 1957, he was arrested as part of a conspiracy involving B.C. Forest Products, Pacific Coast Services, C.D.Schultz and Co., and Evergreen Lumber Sales. Wick Gray and Charles Schultz were charged as the agents who had perpetrated the bribery. In February 1958, Sommers was found guilty of receiving bribes and sentenced to five years in jail. Wick Gray also received five years for giving bribes. B.C. Forest Products, however, was found not guilty of being part of the bribery plot.)

On Thursday, March 1, two days after Ray had been sworn in as minister of Lands and Forests, there was a night sitting of the House—the fourth that week—and at 8:30 p.m. Ray stood up to present the estimates of Lands and Forests—estimates that he had not even had time to read over. The Opposition gave him a fairly rough ride, but it was nothing to what happened after the premier called for the vote on the minister's salary at 12:43 a.m. Then they unleashed all their pent-up frustration, hammering away at the

Sommers affair in an attempt to force the government to call a royal commission or at least a judicial inquiry. The new minister—who abhorred politics—was plunged into the thick of them. If Sommers was innocent, the Opposition members demanded to know, why did he resign? Why doesn't the Attorney General resign too? When they ran out of questions on Sommers, the Opposition began filibustering. Any topic would do. MLA Frank Howard talked about squirrels' habit of burying acorns and the effect of this habit on forest management, then questions and answers about squirrels were batted back and forth.

Ray, unfamiliar with his new department and its budgets, was only anxious to present the estimates and get the agony over with. Premier Bennett, on the other hand, was not about to put a stop to the filibustering. Let the Opposition talk and shout until they dropped, he decided, and sure enough many of them were asleep in their swivel-chairs and the sun was up before the Lands and Forests estimates finally passed. The moment Ray was finished this nearly eleven-hour marathon, he left the chamber to get a cup of coffee in the cafeteria, but before he had finished drinking it, other members began to arrive. The Department of Mines estimates, he learned, had been approved in ten minutes and the House was adjourned at 7:36 a.m.

How he was going to stay awake for the cabinet meeting scheduled for that same morning Ray did not know, but he hurried home, took a bath and returned for the meeting. No one else showed up; it had been cancelled but no one had notified him. This was the culmination of his two-day initiation as minister of Lands and Forests.

While Ray's purpose in becoming part of the government had been to improve the process and funding of education in B.C., he accepted his new role in the government with the same will to get the job done right, and while the Sommers Affair wound its way to its sorry conclusion, he began a thorough investigation to determine whether there really was corruption within the administrative structure of the Forests Branch. This was a priority because the media had intimated that the problem went deeper than Sommers, leaving the personnel of the branch all under suspicion. Ray's investigation, however, proved to his satisfaction that "there was not one single thing out of place when we opened up the books." Since all forest companies had to apply in the same way for FMLs and all went through the same processing steps, the only point at which any fixing could have been done was when the minister chose to consider or not consider an application for recommendation to the cabinet. "To this day," says Williston, "I'm sure that if Charlie Schultz acted as representative for a company applying for an FML, that company received consideration. And if certain other agents presented an application, it never got to the stage where it received consideration. I'm as sure to this day as I was then that Sommers alone juggled the books; some applications received immediate consideration, others never got looked at."

Ray Williston was proud of the fact that Forestry Branch books remained balanced throughout his 16 years as minister. At one point he challenged anyone to find fifty cents out of place and promised to resign if they did. Columnist Barry Mather of the Vancouver *Province* lamented the fact that inflation had struck even in this. "It's only a few years since we'd be asked to find a nickel out of place, but Williston is asking us to find fifty cents!"

Although the branch's personnel proved to be squeaky clean in the Sommers Affair, all was not well in Ray's new ministry. Some weeks before the scandal erupted, Sommers had arranged a six-month vacation for his secretary, the veteran Miss Noel Ferguson, and she had gone off to Scotland. Her replacement, Ellen Miller, an extremely capable woman, was acting secretary to the minister when Ray took over from Sommers, and Ray was pleased with her work. Unfortunately, as soon as Miss Ferguson learned of the Sommers affair, she hurried back to Victoria to reclaim her job. Ray first met her one morning when he buzzed for his secretary. Instead of Miss Miller, in strode Miss Ferguson in businesslike grey with white collar and cuffs and sensible shoes from Ingledews.

"I'm Noel Ferguson, Mr. Williston, and I'm your secretary."

"Where's Mrs. Miller?"

"Oh, she's gone to the typing pool."

Ray picked up the top letter from the pile. "To Dagwinder Singh etcetera. Dear Mr. Singh. . ."

"Excuse me, sir, I don't do shorthand."

Ray frowned. "You don't do shorthand?"

"No."

"You *can't* do shorthand?"

"That's right. I can't do shorthand."

"Then what's your note pad for?"

"For making notes of things you want to do."

Ray gestured towards the pile of letters. "Well, what I want to do right now is dictate some letters for you to type."

"Oh, I don't do the typing."

"You don't type! Then how do I get this mail answered?"

She pointed to a yellow lined pad on his desk. "You write your letters on that pad."

"In longhand, I presume."

"Yes," she said brightly. "Then I take them down to the typing pool."

When Sommers had assumed the Lands and Forests portfolio in 1952, he inherited Miss Ferguson, a ministerial secretary from the time of Arthur Wellesley Gray, minister of Lands and Municipal Affairs from 1933 to 1943. Miss Ferguson knew every important person in the government and outside the government. She knew which social functions should be attended and which fork to use. She could efficiently RSVP all invitations. But she could neither take shorthand nor type business letters. She was, it seemed, a "social secretary," apparently an essential element during the regime of Wells Gray.

"That will be all, Miss Ferguson," said Ray, and he left the legislative building and drove home. From his basement he recovered the tiny Hermes portable that Gladys had bought him from the first shipment of those worthy little machines to enter the country from Switzerland nearly 20 years earlier.

"Don't they have typewriters in Lands and Forests?" asked Gladys.

"Somewhere, I suppose," he said, preparing to return to his office. "I have a department of a thousand souls, but my total personal staff consists of one secretary who doesn't type."

"Why don't you fire her?"

"Not allowed. She's entrenched for life."

"For life?"

"Well, not actually life, but I'm saddled with her until she retires."

"When's that?"

"A couple of years, I think." From that time on, Ray typed most of his letters on his Hermes then sent them to the typing pool for retyping. Occasionally, he would insist that Miss Ferguson type up a letter for him, but the results were hardly worth the effort to retrain her.

It so happened that the government workers' union agreement stipulated that should a government employee wish to keep on working beyond the normal retirement date, the employee must apply for extension within a certain time period. Miss Ferguson had no intention of retiring but, unfortunately, when her time came in late 1957, she neglected to apply for an extension by the required date. She would have to leave. Devastated at the thought of retirement, she implored Ray to intervene on her behalf, but he refused. He had done his duty.

Even after her departure, however, Ray's Hermes typewriter stayed on his desk, and though it was used daily for the next 16 years, it never required repairs. It became indispensable for making sure that no one misinterpreted the decisions that came out of his office. Using triplicate forms, he typed a memo to verify each decision, with one copy going to the petitioner, one to the department head affected and one remaining in his own office files. It was a simple but very effective system, giving a permanent record of his intentions. It was so effective, in fact, that long after he was out of office, Ray received a call from a judge in the exchequer court requesting him to appear in court for 15 minutes to clarify documents tendered in a taxation case that had been in contention for several years. The documents turned out to be 15 of Ray's famous memos, all of them involving a timber concession in the Queen Charlotte Islands. He was embarrassed to discover that he had crossed out lines and written up the margins, but the memo texts were perfectly clear, and the judge questioned him for two and a half hours—thoroughly fascinated by Ray's explanations of the processes that had gone on behind the scenes. Immediately after the questioning was complete, he dismissed the case against the logging company in question.

When Ray took over the ministry, his deputy minister for Forestry and chief forester was C.D. Orchard whom Williston remembers as dogmatic and dictatorial. "He ran a pyramid type of organization. Everything had to come across his desk, and although we had a lot of good men in there, none of them could exercise any initiative. On one occasion, shortly after I took over, Gerry McKee (assistant chief forester in charge of operations) came to me to ask permission to send a telegram to Orchard who was at a forestry convention in Australia. Orchard would have to return immediately, he said, because there was a decision to be made. I said, 'You mean you can't move on this until he says so?' And he told me that was the rule around there. Nothing happened until Orchard said so. I blew sky high. 'You get out there and make that decision,' I said. 'You're not holding up everybody until Orchard gets back.'"

Orchard was by this time facing retirement, and soon after he returned from Australia, word got back to Ray that he was taking F.S. "Finn" McKinnon, assistant deputy minister and assistant chief forester, around the province and introducing him to the industry as the next deputy minister. Although McKinnon had a master's degree in forestry from Harvard, Ray regarded him as no more than Orchard's hatchet man because Orchard, instead of dealing himself with any of the dirty decisions that had to be made about the industry, always passed on that privilege to his next in command. It had come to the point that whenever Ray told people in the industry to see McKinnon about their problem, they refused because they knew the answer would be no. When Ray heard that Orchard was annointing McKinnon as his successor, he called the assistant deputy minister in. "I'm sorry, Finn," he told him, "but you're not going to be my deputy minister because you've never shown me who Finn McKinnon is. All you've shown me is the hatchet man for Orchard. I don't know where you're going and what you can do, and until I know, I'm promoting Gerry McKee over you to the deputy minister's job." McKee was an old friend and Ray knew what to expect of him; a bluff, down-to-earth man, he had been district forester in Prince George from 1945 to 1947 and had lived across the street from the Williston family. Ray's children, in fact, had made regular forays to the McKee house for cookies. When McKinnon threatened to resign rather than accept McKee's promotion over him, Ray encouraged him to tough it out. "Stay with it and show me what you've got," he told him. "Remember that Gerry is heading for retirement in a few years. You go home and think about this for thirty days, then come back and see me." McKinnon was back in thirty days to say that he had decided to stay. He worked hard to prove himself up to the job of deputy minister; it became his in 1965 when W.A.C. borrowed McKee to make order out of the chaos in the government's purchasing department. (Bennett, incensed when he learned that the previous comptroller had got one of his staff members pregnant, had struck the man in the face, then sacked him. The man sued and Bennett was forced to pay up.)

Ray Williston continued to have what he called "good luck" in choosing people. On the whole, however, it was less luck than the knack of knowing when staff members had been promoted as high as they could go, usually at the point that they became incapable of making decisions efficiently unless secure in the knowledge that someone higher up would take the final responsibility. He was never underhanded in re-arranging his staff appointments, however, and as a result never lost the men who were passed over in this way, and many of them remained his friends long after he left government.

The findings of the second Sloan Royal Commission were announced in June 1957, a year after Ray Williston became minister. Of all the recommendations, only two directly concerned the coast forest industry. First, to prevent any possibility of future bribery scandals, the report recommended that no future applications were to be considered by the ministry for what were now called Tree Farm Licences (TFLs) in the lower coastal area where cutting rights to timber stands were most hotly contested. Second, to ensure adequate timber supplies for all the major and mid-sized forest companies operating in this southern part of the coastal zone, the minister was to complete the issuance of licences to the Powell River Company, to Crown Zellerbach in the Bella Coola area, and to a few smaller companies whose applications had been held in limbo while the Sommers controversy raged. After these licences were issued, all future needs of the coast industry would be filled through public working circles in the same way that most of the timber supply was already being allocated in the interior forest zone.

The balance of the Sloan Report's recommendations concerned the regulation of the cut and the organization of sustained yield units (SYUs) within the public working circles, and it was Ray's job to translate these recommendations into action. As Education minister, he had made a practice of gathering a group of educators and ministry officials together to arrive at consensus on policy decisions, and he approached the second Sloan Report in the same way, phoning a number of people prominent in the industry to ask them to sit on a committee to analyse the report. Within a matter of days he had his first lesson concerning the way power was distributed among the five major companies in the coast forest industry. Repeatedly he was told that he had asked the wrong person from a specific company or had approached the wrong company altogether. "I couldn't name a single person to that committee without high-powered objections from some other quarter."

During this period, the coastal majors were led by MacMillan Bloedel Ltd. which had played the most important role in the formation of the Council of Forest Industries and continued to make the largest financial contribution to it. As a result, when MacBlo took a stand, none of the other companies would officially oppose it. H.R. MacMillan had retired as the company's CEO by this time and been replaced by J.V. Clyne, and MacBlo reflected the new head's authoritarian/legalistic approach to corporate management. Anyone, according to Clyne, could be an efficient manager if given the right principles to operate by and the intelligence, skills, and willingness to undertake hard work. Resource management had no place in his scheme of things.

As soon as the committee's meetings began, Ray discovered that Clyne and most of MacBlo's other top brass had adopted the general attitude that the coastal forest companies did not need the government but that quite possibly the government needed them—especially MacMillan Bloedel—and it was the industry that would call the tune. As far as wood utilization and further types of licensing were concerned, MacMillan Bloedel's officials advised Ray not to allocate any more timber on the coast at that time. When there was need for additional product, they told him dismissively, the major companies would inform the minister and he could then allocate further timber supplies. "To be honest," says Ray Williston, "I never got anywhere in my sixteen years as minister with any of those companies except Canadian Forest Products. To all intents and purposes, the rest of the coastal industry ignored me." In fact, Ray Williston never once entered MacMillan Bloedel's offices, and Clyne himself, according to Ray's perception, never acknowledged that he was alive.

One MacMillan Bloedel executive whom Ray did admire was Bert Hoffmeister. Ray had occasion to turn to him for advice shortly after he took over Forests, when W.A.C. Bennett as minister of Finance instructed Ray to increase forestry revenues for the coming year by a specific amount of money in order to balance the budget. Bennett did not care how Ray raised the money as long as he got it, but Ray's problem was how to get it without seriously affecting the industry. After some careful thought, Hoffmeister suggested that it could be done with little opposition by boosting the assessments on privately held timber. He was referring to the timber growing on the one-square-mile blocks of land which had been allocated to individuals and forestry companies in the early years of this century. They were distributed all over the province, but most covered prime timber at river mouths all along the coast. MacMillan Bloedel just happened to own more of these private holdings than any other company and would therefore pay most of the increased tax, but Hoffmeister was convinced that there would be very little outcry from the industry because the small operators would not be affected. Ray took his advice, and although his Forestry Branch staff predicted an upwelling of protest, there was none whatsoever. Unfortunately, Hoffmeister was eased out of MacMillan Bloedel in December 1957, but it remains Ray's conviction that had he stayed with the company, he would have made it much more progressive during the important years of its growth.

In the end, most of the effective members of Ray's Sloan Report committee came from the Forestry Branch, and it was largely their advice he followed in implementing the report's recommendations. This ongoing consultation resulted in the development of a close rapport between Ray and his staff, so that as soon as Orchard retired as deputy minister in September 1958, Ray abolished the pyramid-style administration Orchard had cultivated and placed the five senior department heads in control. It was mainly from these men that he learned the principles of forestry, and in the end he was so well schooled that whenever his department heads began initiating new concepts, he would complain that they were violating their own rules, and his education would begin all over again. The weekly meetings between the minister and these five were noisy affairs. "I'm sure," comments Ray, "that some days the rest of the staff thought the roof was coming off when we got into an argument, but we always came to a consensus. Nobody beaten up or anything like that."

Another part of Ray's education came from H.R. MacMillan. Soon after Ray became minister, the old man began coming to Victoria on the average of once a month to talk to him about forestry and other topics affecting the forest industry. "I am absolutely convinced that he thought that this new minister required an education," Ray recalls. Although no longer chief executive officer of the company he had founded, MacMillan still held the post of chairman of finance, but he never spoke of his own company during these visits. He dealt instead with general matters only, and Ray sincerely appreciated the opportunity to talk with him.

It happened that during the period of Ray's education by H.R., the ministry was still considering the application by MacBlo's arch rival, the Powell River Company, for its long-awaited TFL consisting of timber on northern Vancouver Island and Bute and Knight inlets. At the same time, the ministry was attempting to complete hearings begun by Sommers on an application by Canadian Forest Products (CanFor) for cutting rights in the Nimpkish Valley. When Ray reopened hearings on CanFor's application, a protest was launched by the Western Forest Management Association, made up of a group of smaller logging companies, headed by Cornelius "Blondie" Swanson of Squamish and represented by North Vancouver lawyer Ron Howard. They contended that Ray had no legal authority to conduct the hearing, based on the fact that in December 1957 Chief Justice Gordon Sloan had left the bench to become forestry advisor to the government and had been given the authority to "provide a public tribunal to examine, hear representations from interested groups and advise upon granting of timber rights, particularly forest management licences." But Sloan had died suddenly a year later, and since he did so without actually providing any advice to Ray or his ministry, the government had not hired anyone to take his place. Instead, in March the legislature had passed an amendment to the Forest Act that permitted the minister to conduct his own hearings. Therefore, in spite of Howard's protests, Ray continued the CanFor hearings and went on to hear briefs concerning the Powell River Company's application. Howard retaliated by applying to the B.C. Supreme Court for a writ of prohibition to prevent the issuance of licences to either company until the law was clarified. He succeeded in keeping the case in court for a whole year; each time the government arranged a court date, Howard managed to get a delay, although when the case was finally heard in February 1960, it was thrown out of court.

While Powell River's TFL was being held up in the courts, H.R. MacMillan came to Victoria for one of his meetings with Ray and in the course of conversation explained that there was a rumour going around in industry circles that the Western Forest Management Association's legal attack was being funded by MacMillan Bloedel in order to thwart Powell River. He wanted Ray to know that this was a lie and that it had been circulated by persons unfriendly to the company. The following day, MacMillan attended a meeting of his company's board of directors in Vancouver, and there he explained that he had told Ray about the rumour and made it plain that it had no substance in fact. There was an embarrassed pause in the meeting, and then a senior member of the board admitted that MacMillan Bloedel had in fact made a major contribution toward Ron Howard's fees.

H.R. was humiliated because his integrity was absolute and he appeared to have deliberately told Ray something that was not true. The incident also revealed to him that he no longer had close contact with the inner workings of the company he had founded. He insisted that someone else must tell Ray that he had not known of these arrangements with Western Forest Management and apologize for what he had said. There was some problem in finding someone to carry this message, but eventually a man named Shortreed did the job. The tragedy as far as Ray was concerned was that H.R. never again came calling and made no more direct contacts with him, although as the years went by, H.R.'s former vice-president and long-time friend, Ernie Shorter, did transfer some messages from him. The only time Ray saw him again was in June 1967 at the official opening of the forestry building that H.R. had donated to the University of B.C. Ray had been asked to give a speech but when he discovered that the 82-year-old MacMillan was in attendance, he departed from his text and instead eulogized the man's true belief in good forest practices and his determined attempt to carry them out. MacMillan broke down as he listened, and after the ceremony was over, the two men walked in the grounds for some time discussing general matters. It was the last time Ray saw him.

MacMillan Bloedel's part in delaying the granting of the Powell River Company's TFL did not become general knowledge until the two firms were completing negotiations for an amalgamation in July 1959. There had never been a cordial relationship between the top personnel of the two companies, and it had not improved during the negotiating period so that when this piece of information came out, Fred McNeil, director of management services at the Powell River

Company, expressed himself rather vehemently on the subject to J.V. Clyne of MacBlo. Almost immediately McNeil ceased to be a member of the amalgamated company. He followed Joe Foley, Powell River's former CEO, to the Ford Motor Company, then moved to the Bank of Montreal in 1975 to become deputy chairman and CEO. John Liersch, a former dean of forestry at UBC, had joined the Powell River Company in 1946 as executive vice-president; in the amalgamated company he was demoted to vice-president in charge of pulp and paper production. He stuck it out until February 1961 when he went over to Canadian Forest Products where he eventually became CEO. In the end MacBlo had cleared out all of Powell River's top management.

From Ray Williston's standpoint within the Forest Ministry and later as a consultant to the industry, MacMillan Bloedel/Powell River Company—reflecting the grandeur of being one of the province's largest firms—seemed to be more interested in gaining a reputation on the world stage as a leader in business rather than improving their use of wood resources in this province. Although the company's money was still coming primarily from the manufacture of timber, many of the places in which it was spent did not contribute to an improvement in their manufacturing position. Ray became convinced that had MacBlo grasped some of the opportunities which were open to it, it might have placed this province in a position on the world stage which had true significance.

In a 1989 interview he stated that "once the company had acquired a capital base and manufacturing facilities that were among the best to be found anywhere for the time, it then ceased to move forward, to renovate, to keep up to date, to continue to invest in a capital structure in a way which would have ensured greater growth and better utilization of forest resources. From my own observations, it has not been the large companies which have been innovative in the acceptance and initiation of new ventures, but the small companies with insufficient timber resources. In fact, the less the timber resource a firm has had, the greater has been the innovation introduced by the owners. MacMillan Bloedel's research was always of a sophisticated, highly technical nature, not developed towards the mass utilization of product and waste. Certainly in all my years as minister, I really never received from the firm one single imaginative proposal that generated my enthusiasm. . . . This could have been because of the size of the company, but I think it came from the fact that they felt they had already perfected the industry. . . . In a dramatic way their failure to expand forest resource-related ventures became evident when in 1981 a company which had just started in the industry in the interior [Northwood Mills Ltd.] actually became the controlling shareholder in MacMillan Bloedel."

Ray Williston remains highly critical of the other major coastal forest companies as well because, with the exception of Canadian Forest Products, they failed to appreciate the potential of the interior of the province. Instead, they saw only that the sawmills in that area were running out of timber close to the rail lines along which most of them were located. This depletion was largely the result of the slower growth of trees in the interior and failure to implement reforestation, a strategy which Chief Forester Orchard had not believed useful for interior forests. This problem had been pinpointed in the first Sloan Report, which had recommended steps to regulate the cut and organize sustained yield units (SYUs) within the public working circles. Thus, at the very time that the coastal industry had settled into a complacent status quo, the interior industry was ripe for new initiatives and ready for a revolution.

For Ray, that revolution was sparked by a chat one day in the fall of 1956 with Tom Wright, chief forester for Canadian Forest Products. The two men were friends from the days when Ray's mother had provided board for UBC students and Wright had been one of the regulars at the Williston dinner table. On the occasion of their chat, Wright had just come from the Prince George area where he had been scouting for interior pulpwood. "Have you any idea," he asked Ray, "what percentage of wood volume in that area actually reaches the boxcar?"

Ray guessed that it would be in the range of 50 to 60 percent. "Would you believe that 25 percent is sold as lumber?" said Wright. "The rest is waste."

Ray was stunned. "You can't waste 75 percent of a resource and still stay in business!"

"But that's what's happening," Wright told him. "With the trees knocked down and the waste left in the bush, the kerf sawdust and the shavings from the planing process, only 25 percent goes into the box car."

Recalling that conversation, Ray says, "You hear about people getting religion, well, that's the day I got it. I knew we had to use that waste." Having become aware of waste in the woods, he quickly learned that although some of the sawdust produced by the interior mills was being sold as fuel and some of it was being made into pressed firelogs, tons of it were being incinerated in beehive burners along with bark, log trimmings and planer shavings. Back in Prince George, he began asking what could and should be done about it. Fortunately, the local Board of Trade was headed by Ray's old friend Harold Moffat, and he persuaded the board to pay out $200 to investigate the utilization of waste in the Prince George district. That $200, according to Ray Williston, was the best money ever spent on forestry in B.C.

The job went to Industrial Forest Service Ltd., owned by Larry deGrace, a former Forestry Service employee who had operated a forestry experimental station at Aleza Lake, east of Prince George. His consulting service, headquartered in Prince George, was now involved with local sawmill operator associations, helping them to organize the division of the annual allowable cut in the sustained yield units (SYUs). Ray was aware of the man's integrity, having dealt with him on the occasions when deGrace had accompanied his sawmill operator clients to Victoria for consultations with the ministry, at which times he would even openly contradict their statements in the interests of the truth.

The report that deGrace handed to the Board of Trade in January 1960 was a thorough documentation of the state of the forest industry in the Prince George area and its potential for the future, and it became one of the most significant forestry documents ever prepared in this province. Waste within the sawmills of the Prince George area, deGrace had discovered, ranged from 36 percent to 54 percent of the total volume of logs entering the mills; more than half of this was slabwood, edgings and trimmings. In addition, a large amount of waste had already been left behind in the woods in the form of large tree tops, cull trees, cull logs and broken chunks of logs. Other timber, though mature, was too small for sawlogs so it too was left behind. The report concluded that even with the technology then available, 35 percent of the total waste (which was the equivalent of 15 percent of the total log volume in the area) could be utilized for pulp manufacture and that a kraft pulpmill with a daily capacity of 1,200 to 1,250 tons could be supplied entirely from that waste. Coming from slow-growth timber, this waste had the long fibres that would make excellent kraft pulp, useful as an additive to short-fibre pulps to make paper with high "burst-and-tear factors."

When Ray got up in the legislature on February 24, 1960, to give his semi-annual ministerial report, he had Larry deGrace's report in hand, and after expounding on the facts in the report, he predicted a great pulpmilling future for the interior. A response from the forest industry was not long in coming. In an editorial entitled "Mr. Williston's Education" which appeared in the trade magazine *Timber* (April 1960), Hugh Weatherby wrote:

> *The Honourable Ray Williston's grasp of the forestry problems of British Columbia is following a familiar pattern. He began, as most of us did, by being concerned with fire losses. He then progressed to*

reforestation, and for a time planting seemed the solution to all of our forestry problems. Then he became aware of the inadequacies of artificial regeneration and turned to the wider field of sustained yield forest management.

He's at this point now, and he's making the predictable mistakes the professional provocateurs who are prodding him expected him to make. He has discovered, with gratifying alarm, that sawmill waste in the Prince George area varies between 36% and 54% of the total volume of logs extracted. . . that 35% of this waste has a potential value for pulp. . . that the salvage of only one-half of the tree-top waste left in the woods in this area would yield 165 tons of pulp per day. . . that harvesting one-half of the stunted pine could produce 1,272 tons of pulp daily. . . .

Do I have to point out the obvious idiocy in all this? That there are approximately 800 sawmills in the Prince George district alone, perhaps five in a financial position to afford even the cheapest of barkers and chippers. . . . And tops, chunks and branches for pulpwood! Mr. Williston, to make good pulp you must have good, clean wood. . . . And sawmill waste? It's a serious problem all right, but part of it can be solved, and by the Minister who is so concerned about it. Many sawmill operators glow with satisfaction if they cut within an inch of the required dimension, which means a heavy loss in lumber values. The local scaler, naturally tolerant of his boss, goes along by keeping the scale down. Two-by-fours that measure three-by-five and must be planed down to size account for a large part of our sawmill waste.

However upsetting these utterances by a Minister of the Crown may be, they nevertheless offer encouragement, too, for they indicate that he is following the pattern, and he will soon enter the doubt period. As he gathers more knowledge of forestry, he will be able to see, understand and judge for himself. He will be able to assess properly the factual, but ambiguous and often deliberately misleading information fed to him by the ivory tower dwellers and self-interest groups. As his ability to appreciate forestry problems grows, a cold, cold wind of uncertainty will blow down his spine, and he'll wonder, as all of us did, when we reached the same point in our education, how he could have been such a fool.

For Ray, this response was not entirely unexpected. Ever since Tom Wright's revelations, he had been attempting to find a forest company to build a pulpmill in Prince George. He had begun by approaching MacMillan Bloedel, but company officials told him that Jack Prescott, one of their foresters, had already been to Prince George to look at the possiblities there and had reported that there were no opportunities whatsoever to be exploited. When Ray tried to encourage MacBlo officials to think in terms of mill waste, they pointed out that no pulpmill in the world had ever been run entirely on waste, so that was out of the question. All coastal pulpmills at that time used round wood, although a few of them also used some chips from their own sawmills. The only coast sawmill, in fact, which produced any volume of chips for sale to pulpmills was the Victoria Lumber Company, and its barkers and chippers had been installed in 1935 by Crown Zellerbach which then barged the chips across the line for use in its American pulpmills.

Now, in spite of the cold-water treatment from *Timber*, Ray went on trying to find a company willing to accept the challenge. The only one to show an interest was Canadian Forest Products, which at that time was dominated by L.L.G. "Poldi" Bentley and John G. Prentice. They had set up their new company on Canada's west coast after escaping the Nazis in Austria, but they still retained strong connections with the European pulp industry. Like their counterparts in Europe, Bentley and Prentice were interested in producing kraft pulp and only a few years earlier had sent Tom Wright to northern Alberta to look for a site for a pulpmill. Wright, however, had suggested that there were better prospects for a mill in Prince George because he knew that much of the small mature timber in that area was unsuitable for sawlogs and would thus be available for pulp. Unfortunately, by the time CanFor became interested, the SYUs in the Prince George area were already established with no provision for timber supplies for a pulpmill. It remained for Ray to convince CanFor on the strength of deGrace's report that it would be possible to operate a mill entirely on the waste from the local sawmills.

CanFor's management was willing to be convinced, but in order to persuade the financial sector to fund such a project, the company would have to demonstrate first that they had an assured fibre supply—and no one in the industry was willing to call waste wood an assured supply—and second that they had a strong marketing partner. They acquired the latter by default.

It happened that a professional engineer named Dr. Hans Klagges, a vice president of the Feldmuehle Pulp & Paper Company of Germany, had been making reconnaissance trips to the Prince George area as part of an attempt to persuade his firm to build a mill there to produce high-quality kraft pulp. When he was unsuccessful in persuading his own company to make the investment, Klagges began talks with the Reed Paper Company of England with which Feldmuehle had a close business relationship, and it was Klagges who convinced Reed, which already had interests in Canada, to join Canadian Forest Products to form Prince George Pulp and Paper Co. Ltd. In the early summer of 1960 Ray was able to announce that construction of the new company's mill would begin that September. No public mention was made of Reed's interest.

The coast industry's reaction came very swiftly. Ray received an invitation to a meeting at the Empress Hotel where he found all of the major pulpmill companies on the lower coast represented with the exception of Canadian Forest Products. Ray had been asked to their meeting, they explained, in order to save him the embarrassment that was sure to result from his continued reference to the imminent construction of a pulp mill in Prince George. Ever since the first hint had surfaced about the forthcoming mill, this powerful group had been busy contacting every North American and European designer of kraft pulpmills to discover what kind of mill CanFor was building, but there was *no* design, they told Ray, on any drawing board on either side of the Atlantic for the mill he was touting. They had even gone further in their industrial espionage by tracking the travels of John Liersch, who was now CanFor's vice-president in charge of the pulpmill project. Liersch, they claimed, had made no contact with any engineering firm with the expertise to design such a mill.

"Let's not worry about my reputation," said Ray. "Canadian Forest Products has met every commitment they've made to me so far, and I'm sure they'll proceed."

It was not until September 1, 1960, when Canadian Forest Products announced that the Reed Paper Company of England had joined them to construct a mill in Prince George, that the pulp mill officials who had met with Ray realized their error. No one had thought to check on Reed's London office, and that is where the pulpmill had been designed. Using the specifications from wood harvested in Prince George and secretly pulped in Reed's mill in Ingersoll, Ontario, they had determined how spruce should be treated to make quality kraft pulp in order to develop the specifications for the mill.

The officials of the coast majors were forced to apologize to Ray. They also told him at that time that Reed Paper, which was normally supplied with kraft pulp from MacMillan Bloedel, had some years earlier asked MacBlo to provide them with pulp made from slow-growth northern fibre, since their initial tests showed that it made kraft pulp of a quality that could compete with pulp manufactured in Scandinavia. MacMillan Bloedel, however, had assured Reed that the pulp they were sending them was already top quality. As a consequence, when Dr. Klagges approached Reed, that company's officials were still looking for a source of slow-growth fibre. MacBlo was, therefore, almost directly responsible for Reed's partnership with Canadian Forest Products.

Even with Reed on board, however, Prince George Pulp and Paper was going to have difficulty financing this new mill unless it could be demonstrated to the financial community that the mill would have a sufficient and constant wood supply in case waste wood was not available. The job of nailing down some kind of timber licence that would guarantee that supply went to company vice-president John Liersch who began working with officials of the Forestry Branch to resolve the problem. As it happened, the key to the solution was to come from an entirely different source.

Quite apart from the CanFor/Reed project, another pulp enterprise had been developing. It began when the giant mining company Noranda was forced to liquidate its worked-out Waite Amulet Mine in Quebec. With a straight liquidation, the company would have had to pay tax on the accumulated capital and operating funds; instead, with an eye to initiating a pulpmill project, the company instructed its B.C. manager, Bernard O. Brynelson, whose main function until then had been to find mining properties for development, to put the Waite Amulet profits into a half dozen sawmills in the B.C. interior. All of the mills chosen were part of the National Forest Products group of companies, including Sinclair Spruce Mills and Upper Fraser Lumber Mills on the rail line east of Prince George. In the new company, Northwood Mills Ltd., Noranda held 85 percent of the shares, the balance being retained by National Forest Products.

National then hired forestry consultant Ian Mahood who had left his position as chief forester for MacMillan Bloedel after H.R. MacMillan stepped down as CEO. It was Mahood's inspiration as he studied the proposed National/Noranda pulpmill project and its need for financing that was destined to make the whole of the interior pulp industry viable. He conceived the idea of pulp harvesting licences which could be superimposed over the traditional sawlog economy. This would be especially feasible in the interior because many of the SYUs contained a large percentage of mature timber that was too small to make sawlogs. Under the plan Mahood presented to National, their mill would apply for cutting rights to only this small timber, harvesting it by using the roads which had already been constructed into these SYUs to take out the sawlogs.

The Forestry Branch, still at work with John Liersch creating terms of reference for a document that would guarantee a fibre supply for Prince George Pulp and Paper, incorporated Mahood's concept into their plan. The other interested companies then simply sat back and waited while the team considered and discarded fifteen drafts before consensus was reached on the terms of a final Pulp Harvesting Area (PHA) licence document that would meet all the needs of the industry. The most important clause in the new licences stipulated that if not enough waste chips were produced by sawmill operators to meet the demands of the licensed pulpmill in that area, the pulpmill could send out its own crew into a specified area to harvest additional small timber—but not sawlogs—to meet its needs. This stipulation would guarantee enough wood to a pulpmill company holding a PHA licence to give financial institutions confidence that the mill would have the wood resources it required.

Subsequently, when the Forestry Branch began considering applications, Northwood Pulp & Timber Ltd., the new pulpmill company formed by Noranda with National Forest Products, applied for a PHA licence east of Prince George and strongly opposed Prince George Pulp and Paper's application for a licence. The company based its opposition on deGrace's report which had seemed to suggest that only one mill could be supplied in that area, a conclusion supported by the fact that at that time spruce wood was considered to be the only suitable fibre source and its supply was limited. However, the potential fibre supply was greatly increased when a process was developed for eliminating resins in pulped lodgepole pine.

Both Prince George Pulp and Northwood were issued PHA licences, but since both firms were somewhat skeptical that the local sawmills could supply their needs, they each spent some $3 million on the construction of an on-site "wood room" where they could convert small wood acquired under their PHA licences into chips. Ray, stepping onto the wood deck on his first visit to Prince George Pulp's new woodroom, upset proud owner Poldi Bentley when he asked, "Who in the hell designed this?" The machinery had all been designed to accommodate the large logs of the coastal industry; the company was soon forced to replace it with appropriate equipment at considerable expense. In time, changes in technology made it possible for pulpmills to get all their chip requirements from sawmills; as a result, later interior mills did not waste their money building "wood rooms." Both mills also accumulated large piles of chips before their pulp mills were operational, although no one had any experience in preserving them, and the chips heated up and some turned black. Northwood bulldozed a gigantic pile to make a base upon which future chip stocks would be stored, but Prince George Pulp tried to use the damaged chips, only to find that they produced inferior pulp. With the discovery that increasing the air supply to the piles would solve the problem, the mills began building smaller piles and moving them more frequently. It was another step in learning how to run a waste-chip-dependent pulpmill.

Prince George Pulp and Paper was the first interior pulpmill to be licensed and the first mill in the province to be entirely dependent on waste wood. The company's licence, however, reflected the government's concern for the expansion of product lines and markets. The premier insisted that the mill should be making paper as well as pulp, and Ray, not understanding the complexities of the kraft pulp industry at that time, inserted a clause requiring the 600-ton-a-day mill to turn out half its product in the form of pulp and the other half in paper. Once the mill was in production, the pulp sold at a premium around the world, but the paper—which had a burst-and-tear factor far higher than required for most manufactured products—had to compete with all lesser papers, and the company lost approximately $50 a ton by having to put the pulp through the extra manufacturing processes needed to make it into paper.

In the meantime, Noranda had placed the company's chief financial officer, Adam Zimmerman, in charge of Northwood Pulp & Timber. Although Zimmerman recalls being enthusiastic about this appointment, in his first meeting with Ray, he spoke bitterly about being assigned to this minor housekeeping job with its lack of potential. Besides, he complained, he knew nothing about forestry. He obviously knew how to run a company, however; the Northwood Pulp Mill in Prince George, completed in 1967, grew to be the largest single producer of kraft pulp in the world. In the years that followed, Northwood bought out B.C. Forest Products and the Frazer Company of eastern Canada, and in 1981 Noranda, with Zimmerman now its executive vice-president, acquired 49 percent of MacMillan Bloedel's shares. Zimmerman became MacBlo's vice-president and the dominant figure in the Canadian forest industry. (Ironically, although Ian Mahood's inspiration made the original Northwood mill possible and revolutionized the future of the entire interior pulp industry, he was never paid for his services because he had been hired by National Forest Products and that company ceased to exist when the pulpmill company was formed.)

It was 1965 before Dr. Hans Klagges finally convinced Feldmuehle Ag to jump on B.C.'s pulpmill bandwagon, and at that time they joined Canadian Forest Products and Reed Paper in building yet another mill in Prince George, this one known as Intercontinental Pulp and Paper. A $70 million investment, it had a capacity of 210,000 tons of kraft pulp a year. Together, Intercontinental, Prince George Pulp and Paper and Northwood Pulp and Timber now formed the largest single collection of pulp producing facilities in the world. Dr. Klagges was present at Intercontinental's opening ceremonies in May 1968, and afterwards, putting an arm around Ray's shoulders to walk him out to his car, he said, "Now we are using the spruce and pine, and on the next project we should be using all this wonderful aspen you've got in this country." For Ray it only brought home the fact that so often innovation and leadership for B.C.'s industries were coming from people outside the country.

Before any of these mills were in production, however, Ray and the Forestry Branch woke up to the fact that they were about to put the cat among the pigeons. Pulp harvesting licences had indeed accomplished the purpose for which they were intended—assurance to financing sources that the mills had a guaranteed timber supply—but they had also opened the door to pulpmill operators entering the lumber industry, and this was the last thing the government had intended. But in order to keep pulpmill crews out of the forests, more chips had to be produced for the pulpmills, so Ray began encouraging Prince George sawmill operators to install barkers and chippers to increase the supply. Ivor Killy was the first mill operator in the Prince George area to sign an agreement to install them, but Killy was a skeptic, and even though the first pulp mill was already under construction, he held off until other sawmill operators led the way.

Until this time the regulations for cutting timber in the interior had been the same as those for the coastal industry: all trees with a minimum ten-inch diameter at breast height (DBH) must be harvested up to an eight-inch diameter top. Although this standard had made sense in the old growth forests of the coast where trees were huge and had a gradual taper from the base, it was extremely wasteful in densely-treed, slow-growth interior forests where the trees achieved neither the height nor the diameter of coastal trees and the taper was confined to the first foot above the ground. Why waste all the wood between breast height and the ground? Ray asked. And so in 1962 he began a series of changes that would put teeth in the Forestry Department's Close Utilization (CU) regulations.

Harvesting size was changed to a minimum eight-inch diameter at a point one foot above the ground up to a four-inch diameter top. This single change revolutionized logging in the interior; because it was impractical to ask men to get down on their knees with their chainsaws in order to cut trees off a foot from the ground, companies began investing in "clippers," gigantic machines that would either clip or saw the trees off at the base. And because the trees grew so close together, it was also possible to introduce "feller-bunchers" that worked like haying machines to cut and gather the trees; they were followed by machines that could pick up entire bundles of trees, complete with their tops, and load them onto trucks. In the dense small wood stands of the interior there were few branches, so there was no need for limbs to be lopped before loading. More importantly, it meant that the tops of sawlogs, formerly left in the bush, came into the mill to be made into chips for the pulpmills.

The problem for the Forestry Branch now became how to accurately scale these small trees in order to assess stumpage. The method then in use was to calculate the board foot measure which was the number of one-inch-thick boards contained in a log; this was estimated by using the coast-generated taper scale to measure around one end of the log and up the length of the log. Using this method, interior operators were measuring from the log's small end applying the more gradual coast taper scale. The inaccuracies of this process became very obvious when interior sawmills consistently showed huge over-runs between their log scales and reported lumber sales. Some were getting as much as one and one-half times the lumber they should have been able to produce from their logs. Bert Leboe, who had a mill at Crescent Spur near McBride, had such a tremendous over-run that the Forestry Branch decided to take him to court for dishonest scaling practices. He was able to prove, however, that he was simply using the coast taper scale in the accepted manner.

In looking for a solution, Ray visited Crown Zellerbach operations in the United States where timber was scaled by weight instead of measure, and in 1963 he introduced legislation for the interior industry that would provide for measuring both the total cubic volume of wood and the relative weight to volume. To accomplish this, logs were now to be measured by length as well as by diameter at each end. To determine weight, weigh-scale stations were installed on all roads leading to sawmills so that entire truckloads could be weighed without unloading. To monitor the accuracy and establish the relationship between the water and fibre contents of the wood, regulations were also passed requiring that every tenth load be hand scaled. In this way, wood from higher elevations, which is lighter because of its lower water content, could be assessed just as accurately as that from lower elevations. Stumpage was then calculated by subtracting the cost of producing the lumber from its selling price and dividing the product in two; the sawmill retained one half, the government got the other. The new scale was also a boon to truckers who now received payment for every pound of timber that they transported.

These changes increased the chip supply but they solved only half of the problem. The small timber was still not being entirely utilized by the sawmills, mainly because their equipment could not handle it efficiently. In the "scrag mills" of some of these interior plants, each small log was held on spikes on a chain while it was passed through a bank of saws. Whatever emerged from the other end was sent through a resaw to make rough lumber which was then planed to finished size. The waste from this system was incredible, and since in most cases the log had not been barked before it was processed, the outside waste was not even suitable for pulp-making.

The introduction of cubic scale meant that, for the first time in the history of the industry, mill operators would be paying stumpage for *all* the wood in the tree. They would now have to use all that wood or lose money on it, and they suddenly developed an interest in saws with small kerfs and in sawing with accuracy instead of oversizing boards and then planing them to size. Once this part of the revolution was on its way, Ray introduced an acceptable "conversion factor" between cubic scale and the board measure in which lumber is sold. In the beginning this was set at just a little over five—in other words, from one cubic foot of log the operator was expected to get a little over five board feet of lumber—but as sawmills began upgrading their equipment, this factor was raised, forcing even more cutting accuracy and thinner and thinner sawblades. These improvements reached their height with the Macmillan brothers of Lone Butte, near 100 Mile House, who developed the first high-strain, narrow kerf saws for interior use. Their conversion rate was so high—up to eight board feet of lumber for every cubic foot of log—that Ray sent experts from UBC's Forestry Faculty to their mill to scale every log going into the mill and every board coming out. What they discovered was another step in the revolution: if the Macmillan brothers could do it, other mills could achieve the same results.

It was about this time that Ray was visited in his Victoria office by Ernie Runyon, an Oregon inventor, who wanted to show him the designs for his Chip-n-Saw, a machine which could process small timber into chips and dimension lumber. Runyon had been unable to interest any coastal forestry companies in it because they routinely chipped their small logs for pulp, but Ray was intrigued by its potential for the interior industry. The machine could be adjusted to a log's profile, and then in a single pass, it would chip off the log's sides while it was going through a set of saws which cut it into dimension timber—for example, a 2 X 6 with a 2 X 4 or 1 X 4 on either side. Unfortunately, the inventor had been unable to find a manufacturer who would produce it. Serendipitously, two weeks later a representative of Canadian Car and Foundry Ltd., the big

Ontario manufacturer of rail cars and heavy equipment, visited Ray's office. The company wanted to get into the business of manufacturing sawmilling equipment. Did the minister have any suggestions? He did, indeed, and his suggestion turned out to be a perfect fit between inventor and manufacturer. When the prototype was ready, Ray talked John Liersch into installing it at CanFor's Eburne Sawmill in Vancouver for trials to work the bugs out of the design. Ray's next project was to find a sawmill owner in the interior who would install a Chip-n-Saw permanently. By this time CanFor had constructed a sawmill in Chetwynd, but even though the company had conducted all the experiments with the prototype, its management refused to invest in one. John Ernest of Quesnel was the man who finally decided to take the chance, although he certainly did not have the financing behind him that the big companies had. The first thing he discovered was that the machine had to be stopped before each log went through so that the operator could examine it and adjust the profiler. As a result, Ernest could not get the level of production he had achieved with his old equipment. His solution was to size all logs as they came into his mill, sorting them into bins and sending whole bin-loads of same-size logs through at a time. By 1964 John Ernest was handling logs as small as five inches in diameter and reporting an average recovery of 61 percent lumber, 32 percent chips and 7 percent sawdust.

The second Chip-n-Saw went to the mill Runyon had worked for in the states, the third to a mill at Boston Bar. With each sale, the machine was improved and it was soon in demand all over the world. In due course, Canadian Car and Foundry sold out to the large Scandinavian firm Kochum, which in time produced fully computerized machines capable of faster adjustment to log profiles, eliminating the need for precise log sorting. (Unfortunately, Ernie Runyon, who had started the whole thing, had difficulty collecting proceeds on his invention, and it took years of litigation before he was properly compensated.)

The value of the Chip-n-Saw to B.C.'s interior industry was felt far beyond the milling process. Its use improved the assembly of sized dimension lumber—generally eight-foot-long 2 X 4s, with the result that random-length shipments of dimension lumber in boxcars could be abandoned in favour of paper-wrapped packages on flatcars, loaded aboard by forklift. Practically all lumber was now kiln-dried before shipment, cutting freight costs due to the reduced weight, and these improvements led to the province's expanded manufacture of pre-fabricated homes, trailers and building trusses.

The most important factor in stimulating sawmills to use small wood for lumber rather than letting it go to the pulpmills, even though it meant that the sawmills had to bark and chip it all, was that in doing so they could take advantage of a special provision of the Forestry Act. It had been on the books for more than 20 years but had been largely ignored because it did not appear to be applicable. By its terms, sawmill operators practising Close Utilization (CU) were charged stumpage of only 20 cents per thousand board feet instead of the standard sawlog stumpage which could range up to several dollars. They were also allowed to increase their harvesting quotas from the sawlog base by 30 percent. To encourage mills to invest in equipment that could process this small timber properly so that they could fit this category, Ray agreed not to change this low stumpage rate for a period of twelve years. Unfortunately, because of the cost involved, the smaller operators could not make the investment and were forced out of business, leaving them with a lot of unsaleable antiquated machines and their quotas in the sustained yield unit. Rather than have this portion of the SYUs go unharvested, Ray introduced regulations which allowed sawmill operators to sell their quotas—the only asset they had of any value.

The Ministry of Forest's encouragement of small wood utilization by interior sawmills also sparked other innovative enterprises. On the coast, trucker Herb Doman developed efficient milling equipment for small wood, then began buying up pulp booms from coastal operators, converting them into lumber and selling the chips back to the pulp commpanies. From this beginning he developed one of the major independent lumber manufacturing facilities on the whole coast, although he started with no timber supply.

The introduction of PHA licences triggered a mini-tidal wave of applications for licences in the interior pulp industry. One came from three sawmill operators in the Kamloops area, and after hearings which indicated that their plans for a 200-ton-per-day mill were feasible, Ray issued PHA licence number two to them in October 1962. The major partner in Kamloops Pulp and Paper was Ken Long, owner of Nicola Valley Sawmills, Fadear Creek Lumber and Kamloops Lumber; the others were C.J. "Phos" Bessette of B.C. Interior Forest Products and Art Holding of Holding Lumber Company. By finding a use for their chips, they could close down their beehive burners—a process Holding described as "turning smoke into money"—and provide work for their employees indefinitely. Soon after they received their licence, the trio attracted the attention of a group of Crown Zellerbach executives in B.C. who were eager to construct an interior pulpmill but had been unable to get approval from their head office in San Francisco. They encouraged the Kamloops trio and even provided a recently retired technical expert to guide them in their basic organization and detailed mill planning. This assistance was not entirely altruistic: in spite of head office opposition, they were angling for control of the Kamloops mill.

Believing that Crown Zellerbach would eventually spring for the money to finance the mill, Long, Bessette and Holding submitted their mill plans to Victoria the following summer, assuring Ray that financing was arranged, and in September 1963 he issued their licence to proceed with a mill which would use small tumble digesters to turn out 200 tons of pulp per day. The men from Crown Zellerbach were outwitted, however, because of a clause in the trio's PHA licence which stipulated that their mill had to be in production by the end of December 1965, a clause inserted because there were other companies waiting to apply for licences for the same potential chip supply. When plans for actual construction dragged on and on, Ray's ministry issued a warning; the Kamloops group's reaction was to contact the Weyerhaeuser Company of Tacoma, Washington, who, it was generally understood throughout the industry, wanted to become established in British Columbia. A new spectre then arose for Ray: the Kamloops trio could simply sell their licence to Weyerhaeuser to collect a profit, setting an example for industry speculators to follow. Therefore, on April 25, 1964, he pushed through legislation that would allow him to cancel any pulp harvesting licence if the licencee sold it for capital gain before performance.

As a result, a rather unusual agreement was reached: for the work which they had already done getting the licence, acquiring property and planning the mill, the three sawmill operators were given a 49 percent equity position in a new pulp company. Long was to remain company president. Weyerhaeuser, which would control the board, put up half of its 51 percent equity share in cash and agreed to loan the money for mill construction. To the consternation of industry competitors—and even some senior officials within Weyerhaeuser who did not understand the time-limit factor—the new company proceeded to build the small mill which had already been planned. But Weyerhaeuser officials in B.C. knew that getting the mill into production was their first priority; substantial expansion could be undertaken after it was producing. A cost-plus contract was signed with a Seattle construction company which had worked for Weyerhaeuser before, stipulating that pulp had to be manufactured by the date specified in the PHA licence or no payments would be made for their work.

The resolution of other construction problems resulted in innovations that set new standards for the industry. The millsite was five miles east of the city in the Thompson River valley, close to the local airport. Faced with the danger that smoke from its waste burners could reduce visibility for aircraft, Weyerhaeuser designed a system whereby all emissions would be discharged from a hilltop stack high above the valley floor. Because sawmill waste burners discharge both smoke and particulate emissions, the system included a waste collector and furnaces where the particles were burned to generate electricity from steam turbines. The company planned to sell the resulting energy to B.C. Hydro, but Dr. Gordon Shrum of Hydro turned their proposal down. When Ray protested, he and Shrum got into an acrimonious argument in which Shrum announced that generating power was *his* job, and since Ray's job was to promote forest industries, he should stick to that. As there was no budging him, for many years electrical generation had to be limited to the company's own requirements; only in recent years have the original plans been realized.

Kamloops Pulp and Paper went into production a month ahead of its deadline in November 1965, seven months before Prince George Pulp and Paper with PHA licence number one turned out its first pulp. When the mill was eventually enlarged, the original small digesters were put to use making pulp from sawdust—another innovation.

In December 1963 the amalgamated MacMillan Bloedel/Powell River Company applied for both a TFL and a PHA licence in order to launch a two-stage project at Kitimat: an $86 million kraft mill with a 740-ton-per-day capacity and a $64 million newsprint complex. The company already had private timber holdings in the area; unfortunately, the area of crown timber they wanted to add to it overlapped that applied for by two other pulpmill project proponents. Columbia Cellulose, which owned a sulphite mill in Prince Rupert, was planning to add a bleached kraft pulpmill there and wanted a PHA licence north of Prince Rupert and Terrace as well as the area east and south of Kitimat also claimed by MacBlo. The area applied for by Bulkley Valley Pulp and Timber Company, a consortium of sawmill operators headquartered in Houston, included the Ootsa Forest District, an area which MacBlo's management insisted was vital to their operation. The situation was further complicated by Crown Zellerbach which had traditionally bought logs in the Prince Rupert area, towing them south for use in its Ocean Falls pulpmill; the PHA licence applications of both Columbia Cellulose and MacBlo posed a very real threat to the company's future wood supply.

A MacBlo executive, hoping to eliminate the overlap with the Bulkley Valley Pulp and Timber, suggested that the consortium should be given timber rights further east, but this was not possible because B.C. Forest Products and its subsidiary Alexandra Forest Products (recently purchased from the Wenner-Gren interests) had put in a bid for timber there to supply a new pulpmill at Mackenzie, and Cattermole Timber was also contesting rights to that timber for its own pulpmill. To top off the problem, timber resources for hundreds of small independent logging operations and sawmillers had to be protected.

Before going into the hearings in April and May 1964, Ray made it clear that he believed there was enough potential pulpwood available for all the contestants because the industry was making such rapid strides in utilizing wood previously considered useless. "If it's a weed today," he said, "I'll bet it is gold-plated tomorrow." However, he stressed that he would only deal with each company's present plans, not their future expansion, and that he would protect the sawlog industry.

When MacBlo's application, which was intended to provide timber for their proposed pulp and paper mills as well as for the company's sawlog operations, came up for public hearings in April 1964, J.V. Clyne insisted on speaking on behalf of his company. He began by urging Ray to bear in mind that MacBlo was a fully Canadian company while its competitors were foreign-owned, and then went on to explain that his company was committed to the first stage of its mill plans (the kraft mill) but that the second stage (the newsprint mill) would depend on future market conditions.

When Ray asked if the company would proceed with the first stage if timber for only that stage was granted, Clyne replied, "I have to tell you, Mr. Minister, that a 740-ton plant is an economic unit but it is not an attractive economic unit. It is only marginally so and if there was no hope for future expansion, I doubt very much if my company would want to proceed." Ray's comment was "You won't guarantee expansion, but you are asking me to guarantee the wood supply for something you won't guarantee."

Clyne countered, "If we do not utilize that wood, you have the power to take it away."

"But not for 21 years," Ray told him, "and you have the chance to occupy that position for 21 years." The question the industry was left to ponder was whether he would allow MacBlo to play dog-in-the-manger for that length of time while other forest companies starved for lack of timber.

Clyne continued to respond to Ray's questions from a legalistic point of view, satisfying no one at the hearing, particularly Ray, who had to base his licensing decisions on the technical aspects of forest management. Ironically, seated just behind Clyne were some of the best technical forestry people in the province who could have answered Ray's questions in a matter of moments, expediting the hearing enormously, but they were not allowed to speak. Finally, in exasperation, Ray asked Clyne to sit down and let someone take over who could provide the answers. Clyne did so and left the hearing the next day. The incident did not help the Williston/Clyne relationship; their next meeting was two years later on the occasion of the planting of the 50 millionth tree in MacBlo's Port Alberni reforestation program. The air between them was cool.

Ray also conducted hearings for the Columbia Cellulose and Bulkley Valley applications in April 1964, then in late May went to Prince George for hearings on the applications by B.C. Forest Products and Cattermole Timber. Reporters assigned to the hearings were impressed with Ray's calm—and at times extremely blunt—

approach. A *Province* editorial proclaimed that Ray's performance at the hearings inspired "public confidence and approval. He has learned to hew quickly through the verbiage and undergrowth of public hearings and to summarize situations briefly, precisely and fairly. A government is known by its agents, not so much by what they do as the way they do it. On this basis Mr. Williston comes through with first-class honours." Added Pat Carney of the Vancouver *Sun*, "Many people felt that any politician with a regard for his own neck would refer the touchy timber issue to a royal commission, but in dealing with the applications himself, Mr. Williston is doing the job we elect him to do."

In June Ray rejected the applications of both B.C. Forest Products and Cattermole for PHA licences in the Peace, and instead divided the disputed timber areas into three crown forests or SYUs. The western area around Takla Lake and the eastern one near the Alberta border were to be managed as ordinary crown forests with the cut to be determined on a sawlog basis. The centre area was to be a pulpwood sustained yield unit, the only one in the province. Long-term cutting rights would be offered, with the two pulpmill companies being given first bids and the right to match any other bid. Said one operator in the area, "He tried to satisfy everybody, and he showed the wisdom of Solomon."

A decision on the other three applications was delayed until August of that year. None got what they asked for, but all three received a timber supply that would allow them to construct the pulpmills to which they had committed their companies. When he granted MacMillan Bloedel's PHA licence, therefore, Ray allowed only the amount of timber that would actually be required for the operation of their first stage mill. "This does not mean that in my opinion there is no room for future expansion," he said, "but rather that plans for such expansion should be based on improved wood utilization and in competition with the other wood-using plants in the area." Columbia Cellulose and the Bulkley Valley group notified

Ray of their intentions to proceed with mill construction almost immediately, although the Bulkley Valley mill which was backed by Consolidated Bathurst of New Brunswick was never built. Clyne, having told the press that "the thing was too important to make any sudden decisions," stalled on MacBlo's decision. In mid-September Ray announced an October 15 deadline for the confirmation of MacBlo's plans. Clyne then told reporters, "We are looking at all our estimates on the basis of the reduced timber now offered us. We are still considering what to do." Finally on October 10 Clyne announced that the company's mill at Kitimat would go ahead, and the Forestry Department set its licensing wheels in motion. However, on April 27, 1965, a company press release was issued to the effect that plans for the mill had been dropped. Ray learned years later from Jerry O'Brien, a pulp technologist who had been working on the design for the mill, that the company's decision to cancel the mill had actually been immediate. As soon as Ray had announced his distribution of timber resources in northwestern B.C., a MacBlo executive had stormed into the company's design department and stopped work on the spot. The staff was dismissed, with management proclaiming that the firm would show this government who was running forestry in British Columbia. In future there would be no more capital investments in this province; from now on all projects would go to Alberta.

MacMillan Bloedel's reaction, as far as the minister was concerned, was typical of the company's management style. He was convinced that had MacBlo located in Kitimat it would have had access to all the reasonably priced fibre available at that time from sawmills all the way from Smithers to the coast, "but they were obsessed with controlling all of the timber in the area. As it turned out, many mills—including Eurocan which took over that licence—are now supplied with these interior chips."

In spite of MacBlo's cancellation, Kitimat was destined to get a pulpmill. The first intimation came less than two months after

MacBlo officially bowed out, when Prince George brewer and highways contractor Ben Ginter let it be known that he was negotiating with a Finnish group to build a mill there. Eurocan Pulp & Paper Ltd., the new company formed by Ginter and the Finns, derived from a chance meeting at the Rome headquarters of the United Nations Food and Agricultural Organization (FAO) between Pentii Halle of Enso-Gutzeit Oy, a pulp manufacturer in Finland, and Geneen Deluka of Columbia Cellulose in Prince Rupert. Halle was scouting for sources of fibre because Finland's forest resources were waning; Deluka told him about MacBlo's cancellation. In the company of another Enso-Gutzeit executive, Mauri Skogster, Halle immediately flew to Kitimat to assess the possibilities, and while there, the two were introduced to Ginter by Deluka. The Finns welcomed Ginter as president and 15 percent partner in their new company, with three Finnish paper manufacturing firms taking 13½ percent each, and Halle's firm taking another 35 percent. In a competition against Crown Zellerbach, Eurocan won the PHA licence which would have been MacBlo's because Crown Zellerbach's American head office would not allow the company to guarantee a completion date for construction of the mill. The Eurocan partners selected a site for their proposed $74 million unbleached sulphate pulpmill nine miles from Kitimat at Emsley Cove on Douglas Channel.

Problems began to multiply at this point. The millsite had been newly incorporated into Kitimat municipal district, and a dispute arose over who would pay for the $2 million road to the millsite: the provincial government, the municipality or Eurocan. By late 1966 the Finns were suggesting that the dispute would make it impossible for them to meet their 1969 start-up date, and in October Ray flew to Finland to get construction back on track.

Eurocan was also having financing problems. European financial houses refused funding because there was a temporary pulp glut on the market, and the Finns had to turn to the North American financial sector. It was then they discovered that Ben Ginter was a liability; no one had told them of his stormy business dealings and his predilection for lawsuits. Finally Prudential Insurance put up the money on condition that Ginter was removed from the presidency. Although the Finns were considered the best pulpmill engineers in Europe, the insurance company also insisted that the mill designers be North Americans, and Eurocan was forced to give the contract to Symonds Engineering, the pre-eminent company in the North American field. Unfortunately, Symonds engineers were overburdened with too many projects world-wide, and the new mill had design problems from the foundation up. In addition, the designs for the sawmill which was to complement the pulp mill had not taken into account either the size or the species of logs to be handled. Finally, although Pentii Halle was not at fault for the enormous cost over-runs in construction, he accepted the blame and was forced from the company. Eurocan went on to produce some of the highest quality liner paper in the world and developed markets around the Pacific Rim. It was later sold to West Fraser Mills when the Finns improved timber utilization and reforestation standards in their own country.

Another PHA licence applicant was the U.S. Plywood Ltd. subsidiary Weldwood of Canada Ltd., operators of the major sawmill and plywood plant in the Quesnel area. On receipt of a licence in March 1965, Weldwood created a new company called Caribou Pulp & Paper Ltd. and formed a partnership with Daishowa Paper Manufacturing Ltd., Japan's largest pulp and paper producer. Before construction got underway, however, Weldwood's parent company was merged with Champion Papers Inc., a large American pulp producer, which refused involvement with a Japanese concern and immediately terminated Caribou's association with Daishowa. Champion then put the pulpmill project on hold because at that time the company was heavily committed to building a pulpmill in Alaska. When the local Weldwood management impressed on

Champion that they would have to proceed with construction of the pulpmill before the end of 1969 to meet the December 1971 production deadline or face the cancellation of the licence, Champion told Caribou's management that they would have to proceed on their own. With a pulp harvesting licence and a mill site waiting in Quesnel but no financing, Caribou's senior officer, Pitt Desjardins, sought Ray's help in finding a new partner. Ray knew that Daishowa was still interested in the B.C. pulp industry and had been negotiating for a partnership in a proposed mill at Ashcroft. He also knew that the company's officers had been highly affronted by their earlier rejection, but taking advantage of the high regard in which he was held by Daishowa's management because of his earlier dealings with them, he approached them on Caribou's behalf and was able to convince them that the economic opportunity of the Quesnel project was far superior to that at Ashcroft. Their contract, signed on December 9, 1969, meant that Daishowa's financial resources as well as its invaluable technical expertise would be put to work in Quesnel.

In the years that followed the construction of the mill, however, new problems arose for Caribou. Although the concentration of sawmills on the flat industrial area just north of Quesnel proved to be an advantage for the economic assembly of chips, the bark and wood which could not be chipped created a new problem—pollution. As a solution, Caribou agreed to build a steam generation plant in which the energy would be converted into electricity. Unfortunately, the engineer who designed the plant used heat values from coastal wood to determine the amount of waste material which could be consumed; after the plant was constructed the operators found that the resinous interior wood, grown under much drier conditions, produced heat values so much greater than anticipated that there was a large surplus of waste material which could not be used. Since Caribou had agreed not to use beehive burners to dispose of this material, the excess waste was trucked to landfills. Before long, these fills were creating seepage problems, and that method of disposal had to be abandoned. Various models of thermal electric power plants were designed to resolve the problem, but by this time power was being generated by both the Peace and Columbia River projects and extra thermal power was redundant. In the meantime, an enormous beehive burner was constructed on the flat to dispose of all the surplus waste. It was not until the 1990s that a large waste-burning thermal electric station was constructed at Williams Lake, but as this plant was also under-designed, it still has not been possible to entirely eliminate beehive burners in that area.

In the East Kootenays, Vic Brown and Al Farstad, owners of a sawmill at Cranbrook, had watched with great interest what was going on in the rest of the province, especially Caribou's partnership with Daishowa. The two men visited Japan where they made contact with various industrial leaders. Upon their return, they paid a visit to Ray's office in Victoria where Vic Brown fished in his pocket, took out a pin with a logo on it and tossed it across the desk. "Is this firm any good?" he asked.

Ray knew the logo well; the Mitsubishi Company was one of Japan's top trading companies and an associate of Honshu Pulp and Paper. The two unsophisticated enterprisers from Cranbrook had hit the jackpot and could not have secured a stronger potential partner. Their new pulp company, Canal Development Ltd., promptly applied for a PHA licence to provide them with fibre for a 750-ton capacity mill. As soon as rumours of Mitsubishi's interest in the area circulated, Ray received two more applications. Kickinghorse Timber Products, a wholly-owned subsidiary of the California corporation Cypress Mines, and Crow's Nest Coal both wanted part of the timber for which Canal had applied. Convinced that there was only timber available for one large pulpmill or two small ones, and having been informed on good authority that Kickinghorse Timber was only competing in order to keep Mitsubishi and its partner, Honshu Pulp and Paper, out of the Kootenays, Ray held hearings but decided not to award a PHA in the area at all. Instead, he divided it into two pulp harvesting areas in which the timber would be put up for auction between the three companies on a bonus-bid basis. This meant that the company offering the highest bonus over and above the normal stumpage rate of 20 cents per 100 cubic feet would get the timber. In addition, it would be able to buy chips coming from sawmills operating in the area. Farstad and Brown promptly declared their company ready to bid and the other two soon followed suit. The auction on August 2, 1965, was the first ever held for a pulp harvesting area, and it would give the winner the right to harvest up to 35 million cubic feet of wood a year. Before bidding began, Ray asked each company to deposit $700,000 as evidence that it was prepared to build a 700-ton-per-day mill if it won. After all companies did so, he then asked them to name their financial partners and explain their chip purchasing policies. The preliminaries over, Ray began the auction. With Crow's Nest mainly a spectator, Canal matched bid for bid with Kickinghorse Forest Products until the bonus offered over and above the appraised price of the timber reached $1 per 100 cubic feet—that is, a total of $1.20 with the regular stumpage rate included—at which point Crow's Nest indicated it would match the bid. Ray, however, stopped the bidding to remind the companies of their responsibilities. "This is the most difficult pulp project in the province," he told them. "You are bidding on the lowest grade of wood. It doesn't give you any rights to sawlog material. I put it to you, gentlemen, on behalf of the industry as a whole in light of the competition and appraisal that is existing, that this bidding is not realistic. I cannot see how the independent operators in this area could get a fair price for their chips if this bidding is allowed to continue." In fact, continuing could have disrupted the entire industry for no good purpose, since it was general knowledge by this time that Kickinghorse had no real intention to construct a pulpmill; they only wanted to keep the Japanese out. Ray then refused to accept any of the bids and returned all the deposits. His actions created a furor in the coast media, but everyone in the interior industry breathed a sigh of relief.

Shortly after the aborted auction, Farstad and Brown contacted Ray with a question. If we build a pulpmill, they asked, and accept chips from sawmills in the region, would this area be included in future pulp harvesting licences for other companies? Ray's answer was no, because the purpose of a PHA licence was to ensure financial backing for construction of a pulpmill as well as guarantee a fibre supply. Without some assurance that sufficient chips would be available locally, another mill could not survive in that area because, on top of the expense incurred by all interior pulpmills of shipping their manufactured pulp long distances overland to market, it would have the added expense of getting a fibre supply from long distances overland. No pulpmill company could handle both of these costs.

As Ray's answer reassured Mitsubishi and Honshu that there would be sufficient wood available from local sawmills to meet their requirements, they decided to go ahead with the mill they had agreed to finance. The new company which they formed with Canal, Crestbrook Pulp and Paper, built its mill at Skookumchuck, and it remains the only interior pulpmill built without an assured raw material supply, that is, without a PHA licence. Through performance it was able to establish a position in the East Kootenays which could not be successfully challenged, and through careful expansion the mill was able to balance the fibre supply with the mill's capacity and thus make it impossible for a competitor to become established. Crestbrook eventually bought Cranbrook's old brick high school, which had been designated a heritage building, renovating the interior to make it into a handsome head office.

British Columbia's growing involvement with Japanese pulp and paper companies was a major factor in the provincial government's decision to mount a major exhibit for Expo 70 in Osaka. Ray's own involvement with Japan had begun when W.A.C. led a trade mission to Japan shortly after Ray became Forests minister, and the contacts he made during that visit and his introduction to the Japanese way of doing business stood him in good stead during the expansion of the interior pulp industry. His contacts expanded outside industry circles when during the latter part of that first visit Bennett and his cabinet ministers were invited to the imperial palace for a reception. Their hosts were Prince Akihito and Princess Michiko.

On the appointed day, Ray was about to leave his room in the Imperial Hotel when he remembered his camera, a half-frame Canon. He planned to capture this visit to royalty on film, unaware that visitors were not permitted to bring cameras into the palace. In fact, the renowned photographer Roloff Beny had been trying for days to get permission to photograph the royal couple. However, no one seemed to notice Ray's tiny Canon as he walked into the reception.

The group from British Columbia was ill at ease in the royal presence, anxious not to give offence through ignorance of Japanese customs, but the ice was inadvertently broken when Ray, afraid the affair would be over before he got any photos, screwed up his courage and turned to the princess. "Your Highness," he said with a little bow, "may I take your picture?"

"Certainly," she said graciously, "but let us go outside to the balcony where the light is better." And the whole group trooped out to the balcony which overlooked part of the 247 acres of woods, gardens, pavilions and pools that surround the palace even though it is right in the heart of Tokyo. After Ray had taken several shots of the group, the princess called a staff member to come and take some pictures on Ray's camera so that he could be in them as well. Relaxed now, the guests talked about the splendid garden display that could be seen from the balcony, and Premier Bennett asked Prince Akihito if the gardens contained any white-blossom dogwood, the floral emblem of British Columbia.

"No," said the prince, "only the pink Japanese variety."

"Would you like to have some of ours then?" asked the premier.

"I would be honoured indeed," said the prince, whereupon W.A.C turned to Ray. "Mr. Minister, will you look after getting some of our dogwood to His Royal Highness?"

Back in Victoria, Ray asked the nursery people in his department to be on the lookout for suitable trees for the Japanese royal garden, and when early spring arrived, three dogwoods eight to ten feet tall were dug up and prepared for shipping. In spite of Bennett's tight purse strings, especially regarding unnecessary travel, he instructed Ray to accompany the trees to Japan, and the Japanese Consulate in Vancouver was duly notified when he and the trees were ready to leave.

When Ray stepped off the plane at Tokyo International Airport, he was met by two representatives of the royal family. They had come along in a small Japanese limousine with the intention of transporting Ray and some potted seedlings to the palace. When the astonished duo saw the size of the trees, they quickly sent for a truck.

Arrangements had been made for Ray to arrive at the palace at eight the next morning to help the prince plant the trees, but at the appointed time, he arrived to find that the prince and princess and the royal gardeners had been up and at it long before. They had chosen a spot, planted the dogwoods and were back in the palace. All that remained for Ray to do was to take a look at the freshly-planted trees. After that, he was invited in for tea, thanked by the prince on behalf of the Japanese people and assured the trees would be well cared for.

His return to the legislature on Monday morning astounded the media. "The stamina of Forests Minister Ray Williston is astonishing," wrote James K. Nesbitt of the Vancouver *Sun*, "and it makes one envious. He flew to Japan for the weekend, with no more effort on his part, apparently, than if he went to Seattle. He had been in a jet most of the night, he had crossed the international line twice, he had picked up hours and lost hours, he had been through the fascinating maelstrom that is the capital of Japan. Yet he stood up and made a fast-moving speech. Why he did not drop in his tracks, I'll never know."

For the next few years, the Canadian Ambassador to Japan made it a point every year to let Ray know how the trees were faring, but when that particular ambassador was moved, Ray lost contact. When the Social Credit government was defeated in 1972 and Ray was occupied as forestry consultant to the New Brunswick government, he was even more out of touch with Japan. However, on his return to British Columbia four years later, he contacted Yoshio Hayashi, the Japanese government forestry representative on the northwest coast, and asked if he could find out how the dogwoods were doing. Photographs that Mr. Hayashi arranged to have taken showed how beautifully the trees had matured, and today visitors to the Japanese royal gardens can still view the three spectacular dogwoods from British Columbia.

The announcement of B.C.'s plans to build a pavilion at Expo 70 in Japan created an avalanche of proposals, but when none of them showed any specific relevance to B.C.'s trade with Japan, the government held a design competition and chose an entry submitted by a Vancouver consortium headed by Dominion Construction Co. Ltd. The company subsequently also won overall responsibility for the building, although the actual construction was carried out by Japanese contractors.

A large part of the B.C. display was to be an outdoor area with a backdrop of upright Douglas fir logs of ascending height. The logs, 109 of them in all, were donated by B.C. Forest Products, Crown Zellerbach and MacMillan Bloedel, and were harvested from their holdings on Vancouver Island. The largest of them came from trees over 200 feet high, some of them almost six feet in diameter at the butt end. Since the design specified timber with the bark still on, great care had to be taken by the fallers in order that the bark be undamaged. In some cases, the felled trees were winched gingerly to the ground. In others, springy beds of boughs were used to cushion the fall.

Bringing these giants out of the woods and down to tidewater also took kid-glove treatment. Some were girdled with strapped-on smaller logs to protect them. To move each of the largest logs out of the forest, two logging trucks joined by a cable were required. A standard load of logs was first mounted on each truck bed, then topped with a cradle which held the special log so that it was raised high enough to clear the cabs of both trucks. The cable permitted the rear truck to act as a braking force, and the expert drivers kept in close radio contact with each other all along the tortuously winding logging roads.

At tidewater, specially-made rubber padding pampered these gigantic logs as they were lowered into the sea to be towed to Vancouver. There they were loaded onto the Japanese lumber carrier *Ho-O Maru* for delivery to Kobe, the port for Osaka. After the ship cleared Cape Flattery, she ran into a violent storm. The captain knew that if he lost any of the logs, the B.C. pavilion could not be built on time, but he could only run with the storm and hope for the best. On the third night he was awakened by a frantic banging on his door.

"It's the logs!" shouted the first mate. "They're shifting!"

Together they ran to the bridge and looked down onto the deck. Some of the logs had come loose from the special bunks designed for them. Securing them again would be an extremely dangerous undertaking, so dangerous, in fact, that the crew refused to do it, and it was left to the captain and his first mate to go out into the storm and tie them down again. The *Ho-O Maru* docked in Kobe only a few days late with all the logs intact.

In the meantime, while Ray had been on ministry business in Japan, he had gone to Osaka to sign the rental agreement for the site at Expo 70. While there he was approached by representatives of the Shimizu Construction Company, seeking a contract to transport the logs from the port to the Expo site. They had already done their homework. Extending the extra-long boom of a crane to the length of the longest logs, they had taken advantage of the after-midnight lull in traffic to take the crane for a test run from the docks to the site. Not only was Shimizu given that job but the company was also awarded the subcontract to build the pavilion. After the arrival of the *Ho-O Maru*, Shimizu transported the logs to the construction site, with each trip carried out under police escort between midnight and three in the morning. All the logs arrived safely, although on some corners clearance was just over two feet.

During construction the logs had to be sized to fit the design. The butts that were sawn off, although normally waste wood, were sold in Japan for almost $5000, and after the exposition was over, the Japanese trade purchased most of the logs themselves, providing B.C.'s government with some revenue to offset the pavilion's expenses. The tallest log, however, was presented by Ray to the president of the Honshu Company which had just finished building its pulpmill at Skookumchuck, near Cranbrook. The Honshu Company, in turn, cut the log into lumber with which it built an entire pavilion, still proudly displayed on the company's property in Japan.

CHAPTER SEVEN:
The Two Rivers Policy

IT WAS W.A.C. BENNETT'S FIRM BELIEF that if he could make British Columbia's road and rail services efficient, organize effective resource management, and provide relatively cheap energy sources, it would be possible for his government to step back and let free enterprise develop the province to its full economic potential. The Liberal/Conservative coalition that had governed B.C. from 1941 to 1952 had launched extensive road and rail projects which Social Credit was continuing, and by 1956 when Ray Williston became minister of Lands and Forests, the beginning of a framework for resource management was well in hand. It only remained for the Social Credit government to create cheap power. This would not be a simple matter, partly because of the complicated spheres of hydro power control within the province.

In 1947 the Coalition government of John Hart had partially effected the principle of public ownership of electric energy by establishing the B.C. Power Commission (BCPC) which was to see to the generation, transmission and distribution of energy in areas of the province not served by the three private hydro-electric corporations: West Kootenay Power and Light, East Kootenay Power and Light, and the B.C. Electric Company (BCE). West and East Kootenay, both subsidiaries of Cominco Mining and Smelting which was owned by the Canadian Pacific Railway, serviced the West and East Kootenays, the South Okanagan and a southern corridor stretching from Trail to Princeton. The BCE served the most profitable areas of the province—the Lower Mainland and Vancouver Island—which included the province's major manufacturing areas, giving the company the biggest say in power matters in general throughout the province. Its influence was so formidable, in fact, that when BCPC began an advertising campaign with the motto "Power at Cost," the infuriated brass at the BCE—which charged its customers all the traffic would bear—complained to the government, and BCPC was immediately told to drop the slogan.

British Columbia was not lacking in river systems with the potential to provide the increased hydro-electric power needed by the province, but the impetus to harness those rivers came first from south of the border. Even before World War II, the Americans had been developing plans to build a dam for power generation on the Kootenay River where it loops south into Montana before crossing back into B.C. There were problems with this development, however, because the only suitable site for such a dam was at the southernmost bend of the river near the town of Libby, and the backed-up waters would flood Canadian territory. The dam would also have significant downstream effects on Canada's lower Kootenay River and Kootenay Lake as well as the upper Columbia River which the Kootenay joins at Castlegar. Construction of the Libby Dam was therefore going to require approval of both countries, and as a result, in 1944 the International Joint Commission (IJC), which had been formed by the federal governments of Canada and the U.S. to resolve cross-border disputes, set up the International Columbia River Engineering Board (ICREB) to plan flood-control mechanisms and power-dam installations on the entire Columbia and Kootenay river systems just as though no boundary existed.

This commission was still deliberating ten years later when the Kaiser Aluminum Corporation of the United States sent representatives to meet with the member for Rossland-Trail, Robert Sommers, who was at that time minister of Lands, Forests and Mines, to outline a proposal for the construction of a dam on the Columbia

River north of Castlegar and just below the Arrow Lakes. Water stored in the resulting reservoir could then be used by the generating stations already in operation on the Columbia River in Washington state to provide more power for Kaiser's aluminum smelters. Sommers was enthusiastic about the project; it would mean construction jobs for his constituents, new industries, and flood control for the town of Trail which was inundated almost annually by the Columbia River. With Sommers' prompting, the provincial cabinet supported the Kaiser proposal. This dam, however, fell into the same category as the Libby Dam because of the Columbia River's international status. As soon as Victoria notified Ottawa that the province was in favour of Kaiser's plan, the federal government, concerned that a provincial government was interfering with the workings of the IJC and negotiating an international agreement, introduced Bill III reaffirming federal control over international river agreements. As a result, negotiations between the B.C. government and Kaiser Aluminum ground to a halt.

It was March 25, 1956, before the first real step was taken to establish the political framework needed to allow hydro development to proceed on the Columbia River system. On that day President Eisenhower and Prime Minister St. Laurent met at White Sulphur Springs, New York, and there agreed that Canada-U.S. talks on the Columbia should begin at the state department level and that the IJC was to be given a deadline of 1958 to bring in its report.

The necessity for closer liaison between the federal and provincial governments now became apparent to both Ottawa and Victoria, and Jean Lesage, federal minister of Northern Affairs and Natural Resources, came to Victoria on July 4, 1956, to meet with Premier Bennett. Ray Williston was also a party to their meetings because four months earlier he had become minister of Lands which included the Water Rights Branch. He also found himself abruptly plunged into the world of international politics when it was decided that he,

Arthur F. Paget who was comptroller of Water Rights and Gordon Kidd who was chief engineer in the Water Rights Branch would join the Canadian delegation that was to meet with their American counterparts to set up the political framework for development of the Columbia River. Paget suffered from a deteriorating back condition and was in constant pain, but he knew more about B.C.'s water resources than anyone else in the country, and although he did not suffer fools gladly and was abrasive in his dealings with people he considered incompetent, Ray appreciated the man's first-rate engineering abilities and accepted the task of soothing the egos Paget wounded. It was Paget who subsequently argued most strongly to Ray that the IJC studies could result in a series of Columbia River dams which would not be in the best interests of British Columbia. He insisted the province should devise its own plan of development, but he recommended that in order to avoid built-in, homegrown biases the government should give the assignment to Glen Crippen, an American engineer whose work on the Alcan Kitimat project had impressed him. Crippen by then had decided to remain in Canada and had become half of Crippen-Wright Engineering of Vancouver. Within two weeks of the Lesage/Bennett/Williston meetings, Crippen-Wright was commissioned by the provincial government to prepare a report on the practical development of the Columbia, and Ray secured a government grant of $250,000 to pay for it.

The Liberal government in Ottawa had also been looking at alternative plans to those being developed by the IJC. In the early 1950s the Department of Northern Affairs and Natural Resources had hired B.C. Engineering Ltd. to prepare a plan for diverting Columbia River water from behind a proposed Revelstoke Dam to the Fraser River by way of the Latchford River drainage system and Shuswap Lake. The plan was also to include power-generating dams on both the Columbia and the Fraser. The company's report was delivered in early 1956, but it was quickly apparent that the project would cause huge human population displacements and that it held the potential for serious side effects to the Fraser River salmon fishery. In spite of these disadvantages, General A.G.L. McNaughton, chairman of Canada's IJC team, told the Commons external affairs committee that Canada should proceed with the project before this country lost its power resources to the U.S. for all time. "People are realizing in Vancouver that the thing standing in the road of cheap power is Fraser development. We must ask the salmon industry to sit back and look at this problem from the point of view of the real interests of the people because a great hardship is being worked on the people of that region—out of all proportion to the value of the fishing interests." The report—and McNaughton's stand—caused immediate divisions within the Liberal party. When it failed to win government approval, McNaughton urged that another survey be undertaken, and in July 1956 the Department of Northern Affairs and Natural Resources commissioned a study to be carried out by Montreal Engineering Ltd. on the best plan for developing the entire Columbia River system.

Meanwhile, what was intended to be the first of a series of state department level meetings for preliminary discussions on downstream benefits took place in Washington, D.C., in May 1957. Because this was federal politics, however, Ray, Kidd and Paget were not permitted to participate directly in the sessions taking place in the White House. Instead, they were accommodated in Blair House, the vice-president's residence, and adjournments were called in the meetings from time to time to allow the Canadian team to consult with them. Ray, joked Lesage, was the team's "back room boy."

The meeting made substantial progress toward formulating policy, but there were no follow-up meetings because less than a month later the Liberal government in Ottawa was defeated, and the new minority Conservative government found it expedient to ignore power issues for a time. The Columbia, however, was far too important to both countries as a source of energy for the Conservatives to sit on the fence indefinitely, and after they achieved a majority in the elections of March 1958, the Conservative government began actively liaising with British Columbia on this issue.

A brand new factor was added to the Columbia River deliberations after 1956 when the B.C. government announced plans to push the Pacific Great Eastern Railway northward from Prince George into British Columbia's Peace River country. The news attracted the attention of Percy Gray, a British planner and architect who specialized in the design of large-scale resource-centred industrial developments in remote areas of the world. To find out more about the Peace, Gray visited B.C. House in London where he discovered documents that had been compiled during World War II by Gerry Andrews, who later became B.C.'s Surveyor General. In 1942, Andrews had begun surveying a route for a Canada-Alaska Railway up the Rocky Mountain Trench. He had completed a good portion of the exploration and feasibility studies when the threat of Japanese invasion decreased and rail plans were abandoned in favour of the highway to Alaska. It was Andrews' studies for this rail route up the Parsnip and Finlay rivers that Gray found at B.C. House. Gray's next move was to fly to Prince George where he hired a plane to take him over the Trench. Thoroughly impressed with its potential, on his return to England he brought up the subject over cocktails with a neighbour, Bernard Gore, the British representative for the Swedish industrialist Axel Wenner-Gren, whose company had just developed a revolutionary type of monorail. Although a Disneyland-style prototype had been built in Germany, the company still needed a place to demonstrate that it could efficiently move both freight and passengers, and a monorail line up the Rocky Mountain Trench from the extended PGE to the Yukon and into Alaska held exactly that potential.

Gore took the concept to his immediate superior in Sweden, Berger Strid, but Strid's first question was "Where will the freight come from to keep the monorail in business?" Since there was no industry in the area, if the company built such a rail line, it would also have to develop industries alongside it. With Gray's help, Strid prepared a proposal which would include large resource developments along with monorail transportation; then he and Gore came to B.C. to see for themselves. Strid was stunned to find such a vast area so sparsely populated; there were only three native Indian villages and perhaps another fifty people in a more than 200-mile long wilderness.

"I didn't know such a place existed," he marvelled.

In Victoria, he presented his proposal to the government. Then, to prevent speculators from purchasing strategic land and staking resources on the eventual monorail route, he requested that a reserve be placed over the entire area while his company carried out its explorations and determined a route for the rail line. The government's announcement of the proposed development and the establishment of the reserve on February 12, 1957, immediately sparked strong political and media controversy. It was pointed out that Wenner-Gren had not carried through on his huge "Capricorn" development plans for southern Rhodesia, and although he had a close association with Israel and had donated considerable funds to projects in that country, his wartime connection with Nazi Germany was still in dispute. Now it appeared that this man with a questionable past was being given thousands of acres of B.C. land for exploitation. In fact, the land had been reserved to the government, not the company, and the government had no plans to consider land grants to Wenner-Gren until his company had made a substantial investment in the monorail project.

Meanwhile, because Wenner-Gren's proposed industrial development in the Trench would also provide freight for the PGE, the government encouraged him to proceed with surveys of possible rail routes and available resources as quickly as possible. Wenner-Gren contracted the engineering firm British Thompson Houston Ltd. to find an energy source to run the monorail, and since the German prototype had been so efficiently powered by electricity, they focussed first on finding a source of hydro-electric power. Ralph Chantrill, the engineer assigned to the project, did a survey of the whole Peace River system, beginning by designating Portage Mountain as the central point of the study and giving names to the possible damsites above that point and letters of the alphabet to those below it. Above Portage Mountain, he saw the possibilities for a dam on the Peace at its junction with the Wicked River, a second one at Carbon River, followed by a third at Portage Mountain; below it, there would be dams at Hudson's Hope (Site A) and Fort St. John (Site C). These dams and their generating facilities would be constructed one by one as the demand for electricity warranted. When his engineering survey was complete, Chantrill—who had designed hydro projects in Egypt, the Belgian Congo, India and eastern Canada—came to the conclusion that the Peace River system had the potential to be one of the world's major hydro-electric sites.

This news shifted attention from the monorail and resource development to the feasibility of harnessing hydro power on the Peace, a concept never seriously considered before because provincial engineers had estimated that only some 300 megawatts of capacity would be available from that source. In any case, power generated there would have been too distant from the main industrial areas of the lower mainland to be worth developing. Now, however, the Social Credit government was specifically looking for a source of energy to encourage new industries in the north, and Chantrill's findings had suddenly opened a door. As a result, Ray as minister of Lands and Forests became very, very supportive of Wenner-Gren's projects.

By the fall of 1957, engineering studies were proceeding at the Wicked River site under the supervision of the provincial Water Rights Branch. This was to be a relatively small dam, a starter project to get the first power on line, but it would back up sufficient water behind it in the Parsnip and Finlay valleys that each of the dams to be built later downriver could also generate power. To test the suitability of the site, drill holes were made from each side of the canyon and angled toward the centre of the river bed, revealing solid rock all the way down. However, after the engineers had been on the job for about a year, but before the final decision on the dam's construction was made, Water Rights Comptroller Paget ordered that the centre of the river also had to be drilled to establish the bottom. A barge was brought upriver in sections, assembled and anchored in the middle of the river, the essential equipment ferried aboard, and drilling began again. The engineers were understandably shocked when the drills went straight down 400 feet without contacting firm rock. Instead of a solid rock foundation extending across the river bottom, the river at this point flowed between two extraordinarily deep bedrock folds. The Wicked River site had to be abandoned and with it the site at Carbon River because a dam there could not be made high enough to create the water storage necessary for power generation.

Attention was then focussed on Portage Mountain, just west of Hudson's Hope. From that site, a T-shaped reservoir could be formed. Water would be backed up 70 miles to the junction of the Parsnip and Finlay rivers and from there north-south to establish a storage lake some 200 miles long and about 20 miles across at its widest point, with an estimated 58,000,000 acre-feet of usable water storage capacity. (An acre-foot of water equals an acre of water one foot deep.) To accomplish this, the dam at Portage Mountain would have to be a major one with a head of about 600 feet. (Head is the distance water falls before striking the generating turbines.) The end result of this revised plan was that far more power would be generated by the first stage of dam construction than had been anticipated from a dam at the Wicked River site, so there would be more power than Wenner-Gren needed for his monorail and other initial industries. On the other hand, since the cost of building at Portage Mountain would be far greater than anticipated for Wicked River, the company would have to pre-sell all of its excess electricity in order to finance its construction. Nothing daunted, Wenner-Gren launched a subsidiary, the Peace River Power Development Company (Peace Power), to raise the necessary capital. The company attracted high-profile British and Canadian senior executives to its board of directors and management, including William C. Mainwaring, former BCE vice-president, who became president of the new company.

For W.A.C. Bennett, the magnitude of the revised project meant that here at last was the source of power necessary to industrialize the entire north, while power from the Columbia River could fuel the southern half of the province, and he soon began making references to his government's "Two Rivers Policy." Among both the federal Conservatives and the general public, however, there was a perception that the Social Credit government now favoured the Peace over the Columbia. In fact, Bennett favoured the Peace project *before* the Columbia. He was convinced that nothing could stop an eventual agreement for power generation on the Columbia, but he worried that if that agreement was reached before the Peace project was underway, industrial development in the north would never happen. As a result, his orders to Ray Williston as the minister in charge of water resources were simple. "Whatever you do, you've got to get the Peace project started—irrevocably started—before a deal is finalized on the Columbia River. Unless you get it started, there will never be a Peace project."

Meanwhile, Ralph Chantrill and Seattle engineer Jack Stevens approached Peace Power with a proposal to make Portage Mountain power the "peaking provider" for the entire west coast of Canada and the United States. With back-up generation of this magnitude always available to them at peak usage times, the utility companies of that area could make better use of their own generating capacity since they would not have to keep so much water stored in reserve to meet emergent situations. Peace Power would gain both from the sale of the power and from fees paid by the utility companies for the guarantee of its constant availability. In this system the electricity would be considered interruptible or "dump" power and would thus handily circumvent a Canadian law which prevented the export of continuous or "firm" power on long-term contracts to the U.S. This law, still in effect in the 1950s, had been passed prior to World War I after Canada had failed in a bid to get Niagara Falls power back from the U.S. after it had been bound up in a long-term contract.

While the Chantrill/Stevens plan would provide eventual markets for Peace Power, the company's immediate concern was financing dam construction; to attract investors, it had to secure major long-term contracts for the sale of firm power. Because of the law preventing export, there were only two possible purchasers—the BCPC and the BCE. In 1957, however, the BCPC serviced too few customers to enter into a contract of sufficient size to attract capital to Peace Power. The BCE's management, on the other hand, refused to even consider a contract, claiming that they did not wish to be tied to a Peace Power contract that would leave them unable to accept Columbia River power when it became available. In reality, their stand on the issue was motivated less by strategic management considerations than by political ones: the BCE was one of the old hidebound Tory companies of the province and its management still bitterly resented Bennett's defection from the party. They were tied very closely to the federal Conservative party, which although still dragging its heels on Columbia River Treaty negotiations, did not want to see the Peace project proceed, in the belief that the people of B.C. would not support the Columbia River project once power from the Peace became available.

The intensity of the BCE's opposition to the Peace project was made very apparent to Ray in November 1957. He was invited to a ceremony at the Hotel Vancouver where he was to pull a remote control switch that would officially open the company's Cheakamus, Clowhom and Lajoie power houses. Afterwards, BCE's chief engineer, Tom Ingledow, speaking to the audience about the company's future power projects, ridiculed the B.C. government for supporting the Peace River project, citing the impossibility of transmitting power such a long distance economically. His criticm was levelled directly at Ray as the minister responsible. However, before Ingledow could finish his remarks, Dal Grauer, the president of the BCE, grabbed him firmly by the shoulders and pulled him back to his seat; Grauer then took over the podium himself and continued in a more conciliatory manner.

Ingledow's criticisms were based on the fact that at that time the BCE had the highest power transmission capability in North America—approximately 365,000 kilovolt amps (KVA). The company's engineers contended that this was the upward limit because, even at this voltage, the line loss in transmission was about 15 percent, high enough to put it on the borderline of economic feasibility. In any event, they said, power surges resulting from sudden interruptions in the flow of electricity could not be controlled when transmitting electricity at this voltage all the way from the Peace to markets in the lower mainland. Chantrill, however, had researched recent Russian experiments in new electrical transmission technology and discovered that they had been able to transmit voltages of up to 1 million KVA with greatly reduced line losses. The Russians' problem with power surges remained, however, as the surge arrestors they used were inefficient and too large and cumbersome to be practicable, but Canadian engineers were already developing smaller, more efficient units which resolved this problem not only for Peace Power but internationally.

In the meantime, progress on the Portage Mountain Dam was gradually slowing as financing failed to materialize. The BCPC could not sign a large enough contract to attract the necessary capital, the BCE *would* not sign, and the federal government would not allow Peace Power to sign export contracts for firm power. Without contracts, the company could neither build nor operate the dam and its generating plant, and without being able to guarantee that the power would be forthcoming, it could not even begin to negotiate peaking power contracts with the American utility companies.

Meanwhile, the B.C. Power Commission had brought in a new general manager from Manitoba, H. Lee Briggs, who had begun an aggressive campaign to expand BCPC's services, and since prospects for power from the Peace River appeared to be fading, he made plans for an alternate electricity source. To improve the power supply for Vancouver Island, he proposed the construction of a dam on the Homathco River which drains into the head of Bute Inlet. A transmission line would then have to be built to the mouth of the inlet over extremely rugged terrain and across the islands in Georgia Strait to carry the power to Vancouver Island and down its entire length. Briggs proposed financing this expensive project by selling some of the power to the BCE, but since that company was laying plans to build a thermal plant on Burrard Inlet, its management turned down the offer. His next plan for raising the necessary funds involved increasing utility rates for all the commission's customers, but when early in 1958 he approached the premier for permission for the increase, Bennett refused; he had enough power projects to deal with already. Briggs interpreted this act as a deliberate attempt to undermine the BCPC's ability to grow competitively against private power, especially since he had just discovered that although the BCE had refused to accept power from Peace Power, it had cannily bought shares in the company in an effort to gain control of it.

All this was taking place while Bennett was shuffling the province's direct debt in order to be able to declare the province debt-free. The BCPC was carrying $32 million in bonded debt held at 3.1 percent interest, and Bennett now ordered Briggs to pay off this debt and refinance it so that it would become the government's indirect debt. Briggs protested because the current re-financing rate was 5.1 percent which would add $260,000 to the BCPC's annual costs. Bennett remained adamant.

For Briggs this was the last straw and on November 12, 1958, he retaliated by calling a press conference to air his views. The premier denied his allegations. Briggs called another press conference the next day, and another the day after that. Six hours after the third one, the BCPC's board of directors, although agreeing with his point of view, fired him, then all three members promptly resigned themselves.

With power controversies raging on every side, Bennett realized that he would have to select someone from outside the province as the new BCPC head, preferably someone with international standing, and it was at this point that he learned that the respected diplomat Dr. Hugh Keenleyside was interested in leaving his post at the United Nations and returning to private life in Canada. Keenleyside accepted the chair after being assured that the other members of the commission would be men of integrity. Bennett responded by appointing F. Arthur Lee, the retired superintendent of West Kootenay Power, to head the technical department, F.A. Smith, former senior financial officer of International Utilities of Edmonton, to manage finance, and Ray Williston to act as liaison with the government.

Ray's new post came with no additional pay but it did offer a few perks, one of them being a membership in the Union Club where most of the Commission's meetings were held. But it was not long before he was called into W.A.C.'s office where, in answer to the premier's question, he admitted he was a member of the club.

"Who paid for your membership?"

"The Power Commission."

"You've got 24 hours to get over there and get it off the books," said Bennett. "If you want a membership, you pay for it yourself."

Bennett's new appointments to the BCPC did not resolve all of his power problems. Briggs' continuing accusations about debt-juggling, hostility to Wenner-Gren's plans in the north and general apprehension about the cost of Columbia River development had been siezed upon by the Opposition and the media until they became such highly charged public issues that there was even some danger of the government toppling. In an effort to clear the air, Bennett announced an investigative commission chaired by Dr. Gordon Shrum, the noted physicist and University of B.C. professor. Shrum—advised by his friend Lester B. Pearson to aim for an outcome "where both sides think they have won"—issued his report in August 1959 and had the pleasure of hearing both sides claim the report exonerated them. Briggs' charges were not substantiated, but Bennett accepted all Shrum's recommendations for improvements in the way the province handled power matters, including one which called for the establishment of a B.C. Energy Board to oversee power production and generation, especially that from the Columbia and the Peace. Shrum was appointed the new board's chairman. (Briggs ended up on the National Energy Board which opposed development of the Peace River, although ironically it supported the BCE which Briggs had opposed.)

Meanwhile, both the Canadian and American governments had been urging the IJC to complete its report on the Columbia River development options as the 1958 deadline had already passed. Much of the hold-up was the result of the Americans' belief that if they procrastinated long enough, they would eventually gain the extra power they needed free of cost when Canada—in its own interest—decided to build dams on the Columbia. The American negotiators were influenced in this by the U.S. Corps of Army Engineers which had its own agenda: the corps did not want a treaty because it would limit the number of dams its engineers could construct on the U.S. side of the border. When General McNaughton got wind of this, it brought out his propensity for drama, and amongst other threats, he announced that the governments of Canada and British Columbia were once more considering the diversion of the Columbia's waters into the Fraser River. Even though the Fraser diversion had long since been rejected as impractical and politically suicidal, the threat apparently had the right effect because the American IJC team ceased procrastinating.

With the prospect of the imminent renewal of Columbia River Treaty talks, on March 2, 1959, Ray met with Alvin Hamilton, federal minister of Northern Affairs and Natural Resources, to organize a federal/provincial policy liaison committee so that there would be a united Canadian front when the two countries sat down for the final negotiations. Hamilton chaired the meetings of this committee on behalf of the federal government, backed up by External Affairs Minister Howard Green, Minister of Justice E. Davie Fulton, who was to be Canada's chief negotiator with the U.S., and federal Assistant Deputy Minister of Finance A.F.W. Plumtree. British Columbia was represented by Ray as chairman, Attorney General Robert Bonner, Deputy Minister of Lands E.W. Bassett, Dr. J.V. Fisher (who was an economic advisor to Premier Bennett), Water Rights Comptroller Art Paget, and Hugh Keenleyside of BCPC. Their job was to hammer out Canada's policy with the assistance of General McNaughton's Canadian IJC team and a technical liaison committee.

A few weeks after the committee was formed, the International Columbia River Engineering Board (ICREB), which had been set up in 1944 by the IJC to study the possibilities for power development on the Columbia, presented its detailed six-volume report, *Water Resources of the Columbia River Basin*. This became the focal point for all subsequent planning. The report presented three alternative plans. All three included dams at Murphy Creek and on the Lower Arrow Lake near Castlegar, at Duncan Lake just north of Kootenay Lake, and at three sites north of Revelstoke—Mica Creek, Downie Creek and Revelstoke Canyon. The main differences in the plans had to do with the extent to which waters of the Kootenay River would be diverted into the Columbia. Two of the plans, the Non-Diversion Plan and the Copper Creek Diversion, would permit the United States to build the Libby Dam, backing the Kootenay's waters up into Canada. The Non-Diversion Plan would allow no diversion of the Kootenay into the Columbia, while the Copper Creek Diversion would allow partial diversion of the river, including a high-storage area contained between two dams at Copper Creek and Luxor, but it would cause the flooding of a major portion of the East Kootenay Valley.

The third plan was officially named the Dorr Diversion, although it was commonly known as the McNaughton Plan because the general had a large hand in developing it. As he was obsessed with storing as much water in Canada as possible at as high an altitude as possible and then taking out maximum energy on the Canadian side as the water worked its way down to the sea, he advocated that the main storage areas should be in the East Kootenays and the stored water be directed through Canada as far as possible. To accomplish this, three dams would be built on the East Kootenay River near the border to raise the river's level high enough to reverse its flow into the headwaters of the Columbia just past Canal Flats. It would then be futile to build the Libby Dam and its generating stations because the Kootenay's major flow would go through Mica Creek and down the Columbia through Revelstoke. Problems with this plan included the fact that West Kootenay Power's existing dams would be starved for water and the East Kootenay River would become a lake up to 20 miles wide from the border to Invermere. The result would be immense transportation and communication problems for southeastern B.C. and the displacement of thousands of people.

British Columbia's Crippen-Wright Plan, which was closest in design to the Copper Creek Plan, had been more thoroughly researched than any of the ICREB plans, with test holes drilled at all of the damsites and basic feasibility studies prepared for each dam. Of most importance was its recommendation that no final decision should be made on flooding the East Kootenay Valley until negotiations with the Americans resulted in some indication of probable benefits. Of all the plans, this one would cause the least dislocation of people in B.C. Interestingly enough, it was remarkably similar to the report completed by Montreal Engineering in November 1957 for the federal Department of Northern Affairs, although the B.C. government was not aware of it at that time. Such was General McNaughton's influence with the federal Conservative government that it had been generally ignored in Ottawa and never released.

Canada's federal/provincial liaison committee now had before it all the major reports on the river's development except for that of Montreal Engineering. Therefore, at the end of March, Ray formally raised his doubts about the soundness of the McNaughton plan with its resultant flooding of the East Kootenay Valley. His stand was supported by the federal government's technical advisors; the federal ministers continued to support McNaughton. Fulton, in fact, stated that because of the general's enormous prestige, it would be politically difficult to come up with a treaty plan that did not have his approval. And there the matter rested until the following month when B.C.'s technical advisors told the government that if the McNaughton plan went through and B.C. had to compensate the Americans for the lost power of the Libby Dam, the cost of B.C.'s own power would rise to unacceptable heights. With that, Ray informed the liaison committee that B.C. flatly refused to allow the flooding of the East Kootenay Valley, effectively quashing the McNaughton Plan although not silencing its proponents.

The committee now turned to closer scrutiny of the other plans, all of them involving the construction of dams at Mica Creek, the south end of Lower Arrow Lake and Duncan Lake. No detailed engineering studies had been undertaken for any of them, however, and since further negotiations required the B.C. government to know exactly what each of these projects was going to cost, Ray authorized the BCPC—which had eventual responsibility for all public power projects in the province—to undertake detailed designs and specifications for the three dam projects. Keenleyside organized a consortium of high-profile engineering companies, including Montreal Engineering, Crippen-Wright Engineering, and H.G. Acres and Company, and they began work in the summer of 1960.

In the meantime, Premier Bennett had been wrangling with Ottawa over financing for dam construction. For a time Davie Fulton led him to believe that a federal grant would be forthcoming, but in May 1960 when the federal government finally presented its proposal for financial support, the offer was only a loan covering 50 percent of the project's water storage costs at the current market interest rate plus 1/8 percent, with repayment tied into earnings from the sale of power. When generation and transmission costs were added into the total sum required for development, this loan would represent only a small fraction of the actual costs. The B.C. government could recoup little of these costs from the sale of power because the federal government insisted that all downstream energy due to Canada from American generating plants must be used in Canada—a stand encouraged by the BCE because it would provide the company with cheap power. To sell this power back to the United States—that is, leave the power in the U.S. where it was generated in order to avoid building transmission lines to bring it into Canada—the province would require export permits, and legally those permits could be for interruptible or dump power only. The B.C. government was boxed, and Bennett became convinced that these federal policies were simply a prelude to Ottawa's takeover of the whole project in the national interest just as soon as a treaty with the Americans was signed. As far as Bennett was concerned, such a takeover would be just fine as long as Ottawa guaranteed delivery of power into Vancouver from the Columbia at around four mills per kilowatt and B.C. was given all the flood control benefits in a lump sum to use on projects to compensate the East Kootenays.

About this time, Davie Fulton announced that downstream benefit energy could be delivered in Vancouver for 3.77 mills per kilowatt. Since neither final construction costs nor transmission costs had been determined, Ray got on the phone to Fulton to demand where he had got this figure. When Fulton stuck firmly to his 3.77 mills figure, Premier Bennett rose to the occasion. "Well then," he said, "if the federal government will guarantee the 3.77 mills, British Columbia will start dam construction immediately." Ottawa would give no such guarantee, which was just as well because Montreal Engineering, the firm appointed by the federal government to verify Fulton's figure, soon found that a more realistic figure would be somewhat more than 5 mills per kilowatt for construction and transmission.

Convinced more than ever now that Ottawa had plans to take over the Columbia River project, Bennett called Ray into his office in August 1960 and ordered him not to spend any more money on it. Ray was flummoxed. The consortium of engineering firms that the BCPC had contracted to do detailed surveys on the damsites—the largest consortium of its kind ever assembled in Canada—was already at work, billing him month by month. Unless it continued work, no firm commitments or estimates were possible on the practicality of the sites or on costs. In telling the story in later years, Ray Williston said, "Only once in my political life have I done something entirely opposite to what I was told to do." He decided not to stop the engineering work, but in order to avoid a confrontation with Bennett in his capacity as minister of Finance, when bills arrived from the engineering companies in September, he didn't pay them. Nor did he pay October's bills. When the end of November came, Bennett still had not changed his stand, and by now the bills amounted to more than $565,000. Toward Christmas, Ray approached Attorney General Robert Bonner, and after admitting that he had authorized expenditures against Bennett's specific orders, he suggested to Bonner that perhaps he should resign. But Bonner took no action and Ray went back to his office to contemplate what he would do after politics.

THE TWO RIVERS POLICY

In the wider political arena the controversy continued to grow over the relative costs of Peace and Columbia River power, fuelled at least in part by the federal government's National Energy Board (NEB) which was determined to kill the Peace River project. With no detailed figures on the cost of Columbia River power available to prove otherwise, the NEB could claim that Peace power would cost far more and be totally uneconomic. The media took up the cry. On December 27, 1960, Bennett finally responded by ordering a royal commission to compare the merits and costs of the two projects. He gave the job to the B.C. Energy Board which he had created the previous year with Gordon Shrum at its head. In making the comparison, the board was to ignore any flood control benefits which would be derived from the Columbia project and any possible enhancement of electrical output generated at existing West Kootenay Power plants after the Americans installed a dam at Libby. In addition, they were to compute Peace Power's costs as if that company was under public ownership. Shrum would have no difficulty establishing figures for the Peace project because all the engineering and costing out had been done by Peace Power, but he would have to organize the detailed engineering of the Columbia to establish its costs. It was at this point that Ray went to Shrum with an offer.

"It's going to take you a year to get those figures yourself," he told Shrum, "but I can give you the whole shebang for $565,000 tomorrow morning."

Shrum, according to Ray, didn't bat an eye. "Done," he said.

Bennett must have been aware of the transaction because as minister of Finance he received daily reports from all sections of his department and scrutinized them thoroughly. He had to have noticed that Shrum spent $565,000 for engineering studies within days of accepting the job, yet he made absolutely no comment to anyone on the subject, either at the time or later. And Ray stopped planning for his life after politics.

While all this was going on, the policy and technical groups had continued meeting in Ottawa with the Canadian section of the IJC to discuss the principles formulated by the IJC for the co-operative development of the river and decide on those which would be acceptable and beneficial to Canada. The IJC's code stated that individual projects should be undertaken in the sequence that would provide, so far as possible, the most favourable benefit/cost ratio; that co-operative development of the river should result in advantages in power supply, flood control, or other benefits or savings in costs to both countries, as compared with any alternatives available to one country alone; that "downstream power benefits" and flood control savings should be evenly divided; and that each country should assume all costs of building its own structures.

In terms of the best cost/benefit ratio, the liaison committee decided that dams at the foot of Duncan Lake and Lower Arrow Lake should have priority because although they were strictly storage dams and would not generate any power for B.C., their construction was comparatively simple and they could provide the greatest generating power for U.S. plants already in existence, half of the power from which would then belong to Canada. Initially there would be no need to generate power from dams on the Canadian side because B.C.'s share of the power coming from the American dams would actually be surplus to what the province required at that time for its industrial capacity. On the other hand, the even division of flood control benefits was questioned by British Columbia's representatives on the liaison committee because practically all of the relief from flooding would take place in the United States, and although this 50/50 split was eventually accepted by Canada, Ray remained opposed.

Decisions on the other projects were harder to come by since the B.C. government refused to allow the flooding of the East Kootenay Valley and McNaughton continued to hold out for his diversion plan, mainly, it was believed, because he harboured an implacable hatred of the Americans and his plan would prevent them building the Libby Dam. In spite of his lobbying, an agreement was finally reached on a plan the federal-provincial negotiators would recommend to their respective governments, a combination of the Copper Creek Plan and B.C.'s Crippen-Wright Plan. Before submitting it to the federal cabinet, Fulton, who was now chairing the meetings, wanted to be sure of unanimity and called together all the members of the committee as well as those of his cabinet colleagues who were directly concerned. Twice in the course of that day-long meeting, Fulton gave each person the opportunity to present his views. General McNaughton, who everyone knew opposed the final plan that they had agreed on, spoke more often and longer than anyone else, although he had earlier intimated to Fulton that he would not oppose the plan if there was unanimity otherwise. Finally Fulton asked the question: "Is there anyone here who wishes to vote against the recommendation for acceptance of this plan by the government?" His question was mainly for the benefit of McNaughton, and everyone looked in his direction, but the general did not raise his hand. He later claimed that he did, but neither Fulton nor anyone else in the room saw him do it. Certainly Ray did not see him raise it, nor did Hugh Keenleyside, who was sitting immediately across the table from McNaughton.

With all the principles and units of development decided, it only remained for Canada's negotiating team to meet with the Americans. With Fulton as chair, the team consisted of federal Deputy Minister of Northern Affairs and Natural Resources R. Gordon Robertson, Assistant Under-Secretary of State for External Affairs A.E. Ritchie, and B.C.'s Deputy Minister of Lands E.W. Bassett. (In Premier Bennett's usual parsimonious style, Bassett was allowed just three advisors: Gordon Kidd, Arthur Paget and BCPC engineer A.W. Lash.) In the negotiations which followed, it was agreed that the initial treaty would have a life of 60 years and would continue in force thereafter unless either party gave ten years' notice of termination. The final document included controls to assure that both countries would complete their undertakings. Canada agreed to build both the Arrow and Duncan dams within five years of ratification by both federal governments. For each month late there would be a penalty of $192,100 and $40,800 respectively. The Mica Dam was to be completed in nine years with a penalty of $4,500 for every month late. These penalties would be withheld from flood control payments by the Americans. On the other hand, calculation of the downstream power benefits due to Canada were to be made as if the American utilities were making "best use" of the water provided by Canada: if the U.S. did not add the necessary generators in time, it would still have to give Canada as much power as if they had been added.

The treaty negotiators' job was completed in early January 1961, but at this point a new problem arose. Eisenhower and the Republicans had been defeated in the November 1960 election, and because it is the American practice that most senior staff change when the party in power is defeated, those who had negotiated the treaty document would be leaving when President Eisenhower handed over power at the end of January. There would be no one left to recommend the signing of the treaty, and negotiations would have to begin all over again. President-elect Kennedy, however, indicated he would have no objection to the treaty being signed before he was inaugurated; after all, the only costs to his country would be those for the installation of more generators. And if the treaty proved to be a bad one, he could blame Eisenhower; if it turned out to be good for the U.S., he could take the credit.

With this problem resolved, another arose. Fulton had become alarmed over Bennett's decision to have Shrum's Energy Board study the relative merits and costs of the Peace and Columbia projects, and on January 4 he sent Ray the draft of a note of reassurance which he intended to present to the U.S. government. It read in part: "The B.C. government is prepared to proceed with Columbia River development in accordance with the treaty, and the studies [of the Energy Board] are for the sole purpose of speeding up the preliminaries to ratification." Ray could find no fault with the wording, but when Bennett learned of it, he sent Diefenbaker a letter informing him that he was alarmed about the financial implications of the treaty. In fact, Bennett was not at all averse to the signing of the treaty just as long as Canada made no move to ratify it until all the projects had been engineered and licensed and the financing agreed on.

The signing took place in Washington on January 17, 1961, the same day that Ray turned 47, with Prime Minister Diefenbaker signing for Canada and President Eisenhower for the U.S. Afterwards, Bob Bonner and Ray returned to Victoria, elated to have a copy of the document in their hands at last. In a meeting with the premier and their cabinet colleagues, they reported that B.C. was now firmly committed to building three storage dams—Mica, Duncan and High Arrow—and operating them in cooperation with the Americans. Since these dams would regulate the Columbia's flow, the province would receive a cash payment from the State of Washington for flood control. In addition, because water would be released on a pre-arranged schedule, B.C. would be entitled to half the electricity it generated at American dams on the Columbia.

After listening carefully, the premier took off his glasses and waved them at Ray. "How will this power be converted into dollars to build the dams?"

"We'll sell whatever we don't use."

"How will you sell it and for how much?"

Ray knew that what Bennett meant was *how much can you sell it for in the U.S.* because the BCE had already announced that it would only purchase this downstream power at the same price that the Americans would pay for it—although the company was still cannily insisting that it all had to be transmitted into Canada. Ray could not answer the premier's question because contracts and selling prices had not been part of the Columbia River negotiations up to that point. Within days he was off to Washington state to bargain with utility companies there. Bonneville Power, the largest of them, was a federal agency which generated electrical energy and sold it to distributors but was not permitted to purchase power, so Ray opened negotiations with some of the 39 small private utility companies in the state. Some of these companies generated electricity from their own dams on the Columbia, others contracted for power generated by Bonneville, but all of them were dependent on Bonneville because it was the agency which controlled water storage. Eager to do an end-run around the agency by buying B.C. power, they were nevertheless adamant that if it could only be sold to them for short periods, it would still be classed as "dump" power rather than "firm" power, and the established price of dump power in the U.S. was still only 2 mills per kilowatt-hour. On the other hand, they told him, they would be willing to pay 5 or 6 mills per kilowatt hour if Ray could give them contracts for long term purchasing of firm power.

"And how much *should* we be selling this power for?" the premier asked when Ray returned to tell him the bad news.

Both of them knew that the selling price would have to be based on the construction costs of the storage dams, and according to Ray's experts, preliminary engineering estimates had set that at 4 mills for each kilowatt available to B.C. from the American generating stations.

"So," said Bennett, "for every kilowatt we sell to the United States for 2 mills, one kilowatt would have to be sold in British Columbia for 6 mills." Ray had to admit that the premier's arithmetic was correct. Bennett stood up to dismiss him. "You're in the political business, Ray. You'll have to think of something smarter than that!"

Ray now had two options: he could persuade the BCE to buy firm power at 6 mills or he could persuade the federal government to change its policy on long-term, firm power export contracts. He knew that neither solution was available in the short term, but one or both had to happen before B.C. could move forward on implementing the terms of the treaty.

It was while Ray was pondering this stalemate that Bill Mainwaring of Peace Power came to his office. "The only solution," Mainwaring said, "is for the government to take over the B.C. Electric." Mainwaring's main reason for suggesting this, of course, was because the BCE had refused to contract for Peace power, thereby hamstringing his company. Expropriation of the BCE had long been part of the CCF's platform, but as far as Ray was concerned, it was not a viable solution for Social Credit because free enterprise governments do not take over private companies. In addition, he knew that if the government did take over the BCE, it would logically be forced to take over East and West Kootenay Power and Mainwaring's own Peace Power as well.

Bennett was not as willing to dismiss the idea of expropriation. If the BCE stuck to its decision to pay no more than the Americans would pay for dump power and if it continued to refuse to contract for power from the Peace River, neither the Peace nor the Columbia projects could proceed on an economic basis; in effect, this private company could hold up the government's plans for provincial development indefinitely.

The B.C. government's hand was strengthened in mid-spring when Shrum gave Bennett his preliminary report: if Peace Power were publicly owned, his figures showed that costs for the Columbia and Peace would be "practically indistinguishable." But either river, the report continued, could supply all the province's needs until 1975, so there was no point in beginning work on a second river before the first was fully developed if the government's aim was merely to provide power for B.C. The loophole Bennett needed, however, was contained in the next paragraph in which it was explained that if the two projects were to be built at the same time, export of Columbia River power to the U.S. would be essential, and this would be very practicable since the downstream power benefits were already in the U.S. Leaving them there would save the construction of almost $100 million's worth of transmission lines.

Bennett now had sufficient justification to proceed with the takeover of both the B.C. Electric and Peace Power for the good of the province. He had no plans to take over East and West Kootenay Power, partly because those companies served only a restricted area in the southeastern part of the province. But the main thing that stopped him was the fact that the city of Kelowna received its power from West Kootenay—and Bennett was the member for Kelowna. Because of the impending treaty on Columbia River power, neither company could build more dams or invest in further capital expansion and was therefore not permitted by the Utilities Commission to raise its rates. Kelowna and the other southern interior city governments which they provided with electricity resold this low-cost power at a slightly higher rate to householders, with the profit being used by these city governments to reduce local tax rates. Making the two companies part of the public utility system would not only increase utility rates for these householders but also force an increase in local taxes, and both would have serious repercussions for the premier at election time. Therefore, in spite of Ray Williston's arguments that East and West Kootenay Power should be included if the other power suppliers were to be taken over, they were never part of Bennett's takeover plans.

Meanwhile, Bennett had been developing a stratagem by which he could shift some of the blame for his planned expropriation of the private utility companies onto the federal government. Public power utilities in Canada, including Ontario Hydro and Manitoba Hydro, did not pay federal taxes. The BCE, however, as a private company, did pay federal taxes, and its customers paid more for their electricity as a result. The premier had already made a speech in the legislature in February 1961 in which he announced that, in order to establish fairness across the country, the taxes paid by the BCE to the federal government should be returned to British Columbia's provincial government, and he threatened that unless the next federal budget provided this relief, there could be serious consequences. The implications of this speech were generally ignored, but Ray Williston—along with the other long-time members of the Social Credit caucus—knew that "the old man never, never bluffed. When he said something very serious was going to happen, it happened. He wasn't a bluffer."

In June 1961 while the B.C. cabinet was in Juneau, Alaska, attending the second joint conference of representatives of the governments of B.C., the Yukon Territory and Alaska, a new federal budget was brought down; it made no mention of changes in the payment of taxes by privately owned power utilities in Canada. Bennett had his excuse for expropriation, and that same day he announced that there would be a special session of the B.C. legislature on August 1; he gave no reasons or explanations.

On August 1 a few minutes after the Throne Speech, the premier detonated his land mine—the Power Development Act—which provided for the takeover of the B.C. Electric and Peace Power and their amalgamation into a new crown corporation to be called the B.C. Hydro and Power Authority. He named Shrum as its chairman. Only five people had been brought into Bennett's confidence ahead of his announcement—Attorney General Bonner and the four bureaucrats who had drafted the legislation. Ray was as stunned as everyone else, especially to learn that he was now a director of the new company and had been relieved of his directorship of BCPC.

The introduction of the bill was greeted with outrage on the part of the CCF because expropriation of the BCE had been one of its major platform planks in the previous year's election campaign. On the government benches there was considerable embarrassment because many of the Socred members—including Ray Williston—had roundly denounced the CCF's takeover plans. But when the CCF's

Randolph Harding criticized Robert Bonner for his turnaround, Bonner replied, "If the Honourable Member wishes to make a speech based on my discarded opinions, he is welcome."

As part of his plan to improve service by the new B.C. Hydro and Power Authority, Premier Bennett announced a $50 million B.C. Hydro parity bond issue at five percent. Although half a percentage point lower than the interest on the parity bonds the government had been issuing since 1957, it was still considered an excellent buy for this type of security on the current market. While banks and brokerage houses had never been particularly enamoured of parity bonds because they tended to shift the market away from other investments, and the Vancouver *Province*'s business columnists had regularly panned them, the public liked them because they paid a respectable rate of interest and could be cashed any time for face value. As a result, even before these new bonds were in the hands of the public, they were trading at a quarter-point premium on the open market.

However, to the government's surprise, a short time later a rumour began circulating that the government was in financial trouble and would not be able to live up to its promise of the bonds' cashability. This was the work of John de Wolf, a former leader of the B.C. Conservative party, who was orchestrating the campaign from the Toronto offices of the stock brokers Burns Fry Ltd. He reasoned that if enough people could be encouraged to cash in their bonds at the same time, a crisis could be achieved. Through the *Province*, the story spread like measles, bond-owners began selling as fast as they could, and what had been a rumour of financial difficulty became reality. The bond institutions and the banks felt no responsibility to discourage this sell-off and were certainly not inclined to lend the government money to cover the outflow.

As the crisis built to government-toppling proportions, one evening the premier received a phone call from a man who identified himself as William F. Nicks, president and CEO of the Bank of Nova

Scotia. "I have $50 million which will be freed up tomorrow in New York," said Nicks. "If you want it, you can have it."

For once, the premier was speechless. His government did not even have an account with the Bank of Nova Scotia. What strings were attached?

"The only stipulation," Nicks continued, "besides repaying the loan, of course, is that you remain silent about where the money came from. Those sons-of-bitches make me mad! Promoting panic selling is a hell of a sleazy way to try to bring down a government."

The transaction was completed on the spot, and the next day when it became apparent that the government had received a financial shot in the arm, the thousands of people who had cashed in their bonds turned around and began buying them back. "Where did the money come from?" the Opposition and the newspapers asked. There were endless rumours, the most pervasive being that it had come from Harry Stonehill, a wealthy man with a shady reputation who had been deported from the Philippines—and who would later be deported from Canada. No proof could be found, however, and eventually the story died.

Bennett's method of repaying Nicks for the favour was characteristically indirect: when the B.C. Ferry Corporation was formed in late 1961, the premier insisted that its banker be the Bank of Nova Scotia. Some years later, Ray was approached by a puzzled Stuart Hodson, B.C. Ferry head, who complained that Bennett had refused to allow him to change banks even after he had received an offer of better terms from another bank. Neither he not anyone else in his Corporation could understand the Old Man's stubborn insistence, but then none of them knew about that late-night call from Toronto.

In March 1962 the B.C. Power Commission was also incorporated into the new B.C. Hydro and Power Authority, with Keenleyside kept on as co-chair with Shrum, the latter responsible for the Peace project, the former for the Columbia. Ray and Ken Kiernan also became directors of the new authority.

Although the U.S. government had ratified the Columbia River Treaty two months after the signing, actual construction work was stalled while awaiting Canada's ratification. Most of the delay was political. One of the causes was General McNaughton from whom very little had been heard between the time the treaty was signed in January 1961 and April 1962 when he reached retirement age and was relieved of the chairmanship of the Canadian section of the IJC. Then, claiming he had been fired "by the arbitrary decision of a dictator [Diefenbaker]," he embarked on a vitriolic attack on the government and the treaty, using as the basis for his arguments an economic analysis that had been prepared for him in 1959 by Larratt Higgins, an economist who had been employed at various times by Ontario Hydro and Imperial Tobacco and had served for a year on McNaughton's IJC team. According to the general, the report, in which Higgins denounced the treaty for its "grave legal, economic and political defects," proved beyond any doubt that Canada had lost control of its water resources and had been "stolen blind" by the Americans. Because of his prestige and the high respect in which he was held by many Canadians, his denunciation of the treaty was fodder for the press, and after a summary of Higgins' report was published in the *Engineering Record*, Southam Press decided to serialize it right across the country. Instead, Paddy Sherman, at that time legislative reporter for the Vancouver *Province*, persuaded Southam to allow him to research the entire issue and write the story. When Ray learned Sherman had been assigned to the job, he offered him access to all the documents in his files which related to the Columbia River negotiations. It was this source, plus interviews with the main players in the drama—including McNaughton—that became the basis of the balanced analysis that Sherman handed to Ray at the annual Christmas party of the legislative press gallery, and although it was critical of the provincial government's actions in some aspects of the negotiations, Ray accepted it as fair and to the point. The *Province*'s management, however, was very critical of Sherman's article because it ran completely counter to the newspaper's editorial slant, and they delayed publishing it by demanding numerous re-writes. Finally, Ray forced them to publish it by threatening to reveal to the House—and assembled media—that he had provided all the original documentation for the article and the newspaper had refused to publish it because they did not like the truth. Four pages long, with maps, diagrams and photos, it appeared in the *Province* on January 24, 1963, just days before Ray was to open the legislative debate on the Columbia.

Although McNaughton's views were entirely discredited in this highly acclaimed and widely read article, when Diefenbaker's government fell in April 1963, the new Liberal government—which had taken up McNaughton's cause while in opposition—insisted on certain modifications to the treaty before they would ratify it. In fact, this was merely an exercise in political face-saving because the new consultants hired by the Liberals agreed substantially with the old ones, rejecting McNaughton's complaints and strongly supporting the treaty as it stood. In the end, the changes that the Liberals demanded were so superficial that neither the United States nor British Columbia objected.

During this delay, IJC negotiations on downstream benefits had continued. Although External Affairs Minister Paul Martin was the ostensible chairman for Canada, Ray chaired the meetings on his behalf, while Charlie Luce, the new administrator of Bonneville Power, co-chaired on behalf of General Webber who represented the federal government of the United States. Advising them were teams of experts, never less than 35 for the Canadian and American federal governments and for Bonneville Power, but never more than eight or nine for Ray. "That's all you need," Bennett told him. "These guys know what they're doing. That's all you're going to get."

From the very outset of treaty negotiating sessions, the premier's advice to Ray and his team had been simply "Do what's best for British Columbia," but when it came to the monetary aspects, as minister of Finance he became much more involved. It had not taken him long to be on first name terms with Donald Fleming, his Conservative counterpart in Ottawa, and after April 1963 on even better terms with Paul Martin, the new federal Finance minister. For Ray and his advisors, however, the change of government meant they had to struggle to establish working arrangements with a whole new slate of Ottawa appointees. And for Canada's prime minister, the assassination of President Kennedy in November of that same year brought the additional problem of dealing with a new American president with a very different attitude to Canada. In fact, throughout the eight years of negotiations on Columbia power, the only constants on the whole political scene were Bennett's Social Credit government in British Columbia and Ray Williston and his advisors.

Neither Conservative nor Liberal governments in Ottawa were ever in any doubt where Bennett stood on the subject of downstream benefits. By May 1961 he had made it clear that he wanted to export all the power from the American generating plants that was due to British Columbia under the treaty terms. At the end of August 1961 when his takeovers of the BCE and Peace Power were complete, he made his position even clearer by assigning to his new Power Authority the entire energy output of the Peace project for use in the Lower Mainland market. By this manoeuvre, he could classify all of the downstream benefits from the Columbia as surplus power which by the terms of the treaty he was allowed to sell off. The United States, insisted Bennett, would have to buy all of this power at 5 mills per kilowatt because this would yield the $450 million (US) required to build the three dams to which B.C. was committed—High Arrow, Mica and Duncan. The Columbia project could then go ahead at virtually no cost to B.C. or Canada. But his entire plan was currently a non-starter because Ottawa still had not budged from its opposition to the long-term export of firm power.

On the American side of the border the obstacles to an agreement were export conditions, price and the duration of the contract.

From the beginning of negotiations in 1956 the Corps of Army Engineers had been against a treaty. Without one they could have continued building dams on the Columbia indefinitely to supply peaking load for the northwestern states while the existing dams were supplying the base load. Charlie Luce of Bonneville Power also objected to a treaty because he feared losing control over the private utility companies in the state; even after it became a reality, he continued to fight to ensure that any power due to Canada did not wind up in the hands of private utilities on his side of the border.

The managers of a half dozen of these private companies, however, were equally determined to escape Luce's control by buying Canada's share of the power. To ensure that an agreement favouring their interests would come out of the talks, they began secretly feeding information to Ray's office, telling him exactly what points the Corps of Army Engineers and Bonneville would be making in their efforts to abort the treaty. As a result, when Ray's group came to the table, they were well prepared to counter American arguments. In addition, although Canada's federal negotiators were not well organized and often failed to listen to their technical advisors, this became unimportant as time went on because their top engineers developed the habit of feeding information to B.C.'s engineers who then fed it into the discussions.

By the beginning of 1963, in spite of the machinations of the Army Engineers and Bonneville Power, the U.S. section of the IJC had agreed that Canada could, if it wished, sell its share of the downstream benefits to the United States. Now it only needed the Canadian federal government's consent to long term export of power. When the premier wanted to know what Ray's team was doing to put pressure on the federal government, Ray prescribed patience. "The Americans need that power," he said, "and their government will pressure Ottawa to change its stand on the sale of the downstream benefits." And on June 3, 1963—less than two months after the Liberals were returned to power in Ottawa—the

Canadian government agreed to the sale of B.C.'s downstream benefits on long term contracts to the United States. This agreement was signed on July 8 by Prime Minister Pearson and Paul Martin for Canada and by the premier and Ray for British Columbia.

This hurdle was no more than cleared when on July 29, 1963, Chief Justice Sherwood Lett of B.C.'s Supreme Court ruled that the legislation enacted for the takeover of the B.C. Electric was illegal because that company had been incorporated under federal statutes, and that compensation had been inadequate. B.C. Power Corporation, the BCE's parent company, returned to court two days later to demand the company's assets back; the B.C. government countered by asking for a stay of proceedings until it could launch an appeal. Hearings on both were adjourned while lawyers went to work devising a richer financial settlement. This move was agreeable to the corporation because in launching the suit it had not been as keen to reclaim the company as to make the government pay more for it. In the meantime, the Royal Bank had instructed its branches to suspend trading in the $50 million B.C. Hydro parity issue just announced by the government. According to a Royal spokesperson, the bank was awaiting a court decision on whether the takeover of the BCE was legal, but there was more politics than financial acumen behind the move because the Royal had lost the power account when the BCE was taken over. The result of the Royal's move was another rash of B.C. bond selling and another financial crisis for the government which they rode out without the help of Mr. Nicks.

This was the state of the government's affairs when Bennett called a provincial election for September 30. In reality he was looking for a vote of confidence from the people for his takeover of the BCE, but when questioned by the press for the reason an election had been called at that time, Ray told them that if B.C.'s citizens gave a strong mandate to the present government, it would help convince the Americans to meet B.C.'s price of 5 mills for downstream Columbia benefits. During the election campaign, both the

NDP under Robert Strachan and the Conservatives, now led by Davie Fulton, worked hard to convince British Columbians to pull out of the Columbia River Treaty, but they were foiled by an announcement on September 7 by the Americans that a consortium to be called the Columbia Storage Power Exchange had been formed to buy the downstream power. Spearheaded by the utility companies in the Wenatchee area, and composed of 39 of the small private corporations, county cooperatives and other distributing units in Washington state, the consortium made it plain that it was open to further negotiations on price. Financial settlement of the BCE takeover deal was announced on September 25, and five days later the Bennett government swept to victory with an even greater majority than before. Ray returned to the bargaining table with the Americans, and although the negotiations had been stuck at 4 mills before the election, B.C.'s price of 5 mills was now acceptable. Since an advance cash payment for this power would be required, the new consortium also accepted the responsibility of floating the bonds to buy the power.

Agreement between the Canadian and American negotiators on the total price, however, was not as easy to come by because the exact number of kilowatt hours available from the downstream benefits could not be precisely measured until they were actually generated. A price based simply on kilowatt units was therefore not practical, so a depreciated lump sum method of evaluation was accepted. It had already been agreed that the contract would have a 60-year lifespan, although at the insistence of the Americans only the price for the first 30 years was to be negotiated at this time because they believed that within this period they would have enough nuclear power stations in production to supply all of the northwestern states' requirements for future base load energy. After that, they could use their dams on the Columbia to store enough water for peaking needs only, and it would become immaterial to them whether Canada stored water or released it.

This was the situation when Ray Williston and Charlie Luce faced one another for the next round of negotiations in Ottawa on December 9, 1963. Offers and counter offers on the total lump sum payment were exchanged with both sides compromising, but they came to an impasse $28 million(US) apart. Another eighteen hours of negotiations later, they were still $28 million apart, but by that time tempers had flared and it seemed the negotiations were going to blow up.

What Ray and his team of B.C. negotiators did not know was that W.A.C. Bennett and Paul Martin had already agreed on the lowest payment they would accept from the Americans. Ray had already exceeded this secret figure, but unaware that he had done it, he was prepared to continue his tough bargaining stance, even though Luce was becoming more and more angry and agitated. Watching him, Paul Martin became convinced that he would walk away from the table and that would be the end of the whole agreement, but political etiquette did not allow Martin to simply command Ray to accept Luce's last offer. Instead, Martin went to Hugh Keenleyside and suggested that he "cool Ray off" and get him to reduce his demands.

An adjournment was called at this point by the Canadian team. In a private room nearby, Keenleyside, looking at the figures chalked up on a portable blackboard, suggested the $28 million difference should be split down the middle. After a brief discussion, Ray and the others agreed. When the meeting reconvened, Ray stood up and proposed that they split the difference. General Webber, pressured by Washington state's senators Warren Magnuson and "Scoop" Jackson who desperately wanted this power for the state's small utility companies, immediately jumped up and shouted, "We'll take it!" Charlie Luce, momentarily stunned by this betrayal, was on his feet moments later yelling "No!" but he was drowned out by the applause as everyone else—Canadians and Americans—happily accepted the compromise. As the meeting adjourned in joyous confusion, Arthur Laing, Canada's minister of Northern Affairs and Natural Resources, seized the blackboard on which the fateful figures had been worked out and carried it off to be framed as a historic artifact. Where it ended up is anybody's guess. On December 12 Ray returned triumphant to Victoria.

This remarkable compromise did not mark *finis* to the negotiations: a new roadblock was thrown up almost immediately. On December 19 Laing leaked word to the press that Washington wanted the Canadian government to act as trustee for the lump sum payment to ensure that British Columbia would actually use the funds for the purpose stipulated under the treaty—the construction of the three dams on the Canadian side. Laing concurred, telling reporters that it would be only proper for the federal government to retain the American payment and release it in small amounts as it was actually spent on treaty projects. Bennett was furious. There had been never been any love lost between Laing and Bennett—dating from Laing's aborted leadership of the B.C. Liberals during the mid-1950s—and the premier now regarded Laing's announcement as both a political and personal insult.

The outraged Bennett absolutely refused to accept the American proposal and just days before Christmas he sent Ray and his delegation back to Ottawa with instructions that if the money transfer problems could not be resolved to B.C.'s satisfaction, any further treaty negotiations were to be cancelled. Then he took himself off to Hawaii, saying that he would be unavailable for further consultation.

The meeting in Ottawa lasted all day, but Paul Martin could not secure the consent of his federal colleagues to release the money to B.C. without an ironclad agreement that the federal government would be safeguarded from any liabilities incurred if B.C. failed to carry out its treaty obligations. The B.C. team had not been given authority to provide such assurance, and as day wore into evening, the negotiations came to an impasse. Having tried unsuccessfully throughout the day to contact Bennett to tell him about the crisis that had developed, Ray was stymied. Hugh Keenleyside, already resigned to failure, had settled in a corner of the room to draft a press release announcing the breakdown of the entire Columbia River Treaty negotiations.

It was in the midst of this highly charged scene that Bennett chose to phone, curious about the results of the meeting. Paul Martin, Robert Bonner and Ray joined him in a four-way hook-up. When he had absorbed the details, the premier put forth a compromise suggestion: the funds should be paid directly to B.C., but if at any time the Exchequer Court of Canada deemed that the province was not carrying out the terms of the treaty, that court would give the province 90 days in which to remedy its default. If the province was still delinquent at the end of the 90 days, the federal government could withhold any other funds due to B.C. on any account. As Finance minister, Bennett was supremely confident that his province would not default on the treaty.

Bennett's compromise was instantly accepted by the federal bargaining team and the meeting ended. Unfortunately, as it was now well into the evening, the negotiators from the west had all missed their planes home and, with Christmas so close, every domestic flight had been solidly booked. Martin arranged a military plane for them, however, and they set off for Rockcliffe air station where—so they were told—they could also get some dinner. But when they arrived at the RCAF Officers' Mess, the dining tables had been cleared and a Christmas party was in progress. There was no kitchen staff on duty who could supply them with dinner. "But don't worry," a young officer told them, "you'll be fed on the plane."

At the flight counter there was no sign of the duty flight crew who were supposed to be standing by. Finally an airforce pilot who had been called away from the party breezed into the waiting room to ask where they wished to be taken.

"Vancouver, Victoria and Portland."

"All the way to the west coast?" he asked, pausing in the act of donning his flight gear.

"That's right."

"Well then, you'll have to wait a bit while we get a crate ready. There's a turbo-prop we can use, an Elizabethan."

"Sounds ancient," said one of the Americans.

While they waited for their plane, the passengers hustled back to the mess to purchase liquor for their Christmas celebrations at home. The aircraft turned out to be a troop carrier with bare-bones amenities. The seats, crowded together, were made of canvas with metal legs bolted to the floor. Just before take-off, Jack Davis, Liberal MP for North Vancouver and assistant to the prime minister, rushed up to hitch a ride home for Christmas. Once in the air, the ravenously hungry negotiators sat back to await dinner.

Only there was no food aboard. "But don't worry," the captain sent word back from the cockpit. "We have a refueling stop in Winnipeg. We'll take your supper aboard there." However, when the turbo-prop lumbered down the runway of the Winnipeg airforce station, another Christmas party was in full swing, and no one was expecting the plane. The pilot eventually rounded up a crew to service the plane, but food services were all closed.

Then a helpful corporal spoke up. "There's a snack bar down the road. I'll see what I can find for you there." He returned with a stack of paper plates; on each rested one slice of bread with a circular hole carved from the centre, and in each hole rested a poached egg. "I'm sorry," he apologized, "but that will be two dollars a plate."

In the air once again, the hospitable Americans offered drinks all round, and the Winnipeg-to-Vancouver leg passed pleasantly, with the only sad face in the lot that of Jack Davis who sat glumly in the back of the plane, doing his best to ignore his fellow passengers. Davis had gone on record as opposing B.C. getting the money in advance. Following refueling in Vancouver, the plane continued to Victoria where Ray and his team arrived just in time for Christmas Eve breakfast. The flight crew, unfortunately, had to continue on to Portland, book rest and then return the plane to Ottawa.

In the White House on January 22, 1964, while President Lyndon Johnson and Prime Minister Lester Pearson acted as witnesses, Dean Rusk and Paul Martin signed the protocol and power sale agreements. Ray was there as provincial representative, and afterwards he managed to secure permission to bring the actual Parker pen set used for the signing back to Victoria.

Two final matters had to be resolved before negotiations were complete: the Canadian parliament had to ratify the treaty, and a sole contract had to be negotiated and money exchanged for the 30 years of downstream benefits that the Americans had agreed to purchase. On September 16, 1964, Bennett, Pearson and Johnson met at the Peace Arch on the B.C./Washington state border to celebrate the Columbia River deal with the handover to Bennett of a cheque for $273,291,661.25 for downstream benefits and flood control. It was only a facsimile cheque, however, because Premier Bennett had already put the money to work earning interest by loaning it to the province of Quebec some hours before the meeting. And although it appeared that the money was being transferred from government to government, it had come, not from the U.S. government, but from the Columbia Storage Power Exchange, the consortium of small utility companies which would be receiving the additional power. In addition, in the years ahead, B.C. would receive another $69,600,000 in flood control benefits, paid in three installments as the dams were completed.

In 1961, as soon as Peace Power had become part of the new B.C. Hydro and Power Authority, Ray had cancelled the reserve that had been placed on the Rocky Mountain Trench area for the benefit of the Wenner-Gren interests. The Forest Service was then given the responsibility for clearing the T-shaped reservoir which would be formed behind the Portage Mountain Dam. The trees here were spruce and balsam with a scattering of aspen and other deciduous varieties, none of them of any great size or dimension, but still valuable for lumber and pulp chips. The service's first priority was to clear the trees in a band on either side of the Peace, Parsnip and Finlay rivers in order to form a channel in which boats could operate, salvaging timber as the waters rose. This was not as important on the Peace as it was on the Parsnip and Finlay because the Peace's waters would be impounded at a much greater depth and would cover any trees left behind.

It was in the summer of 1964 while preparations were underway to clear these working channels that Ray was visited by J.M.E. Fortin, the president of Tractau Lectric Company. He owned just the machine to do the job: the R.G. LeTourneau Tree Crusher, a 200-ton behemoth which stood as high as a two-storey house and measured 56 feet long. At its front end, extended on four reaching arms, was a horizontal battering ram for knocking down trees which would then be pulverized by the machine's two 8-foot by 30-foot blade-studded rollers.

Ray was skeptical of the Tree Crusher's usefulness in the river bottom terrain, but his project managers felt it was worth the experiment. On September 17, 1964, he signed an agreement to rent the machine for 400 working hours at $300 per hour, provided that Fortin transport his machine to the chosen site near Finlay Forks from its home base of Thurso, Quebec, demonstrate its feasibility, and have it in operation within six weeks of signing the agreement. The Forest Service would pick up the transportation costs. Fortin then contracted Cattermole Timber to operate the machine, and that company assigned employee John Dahl to the job.

Almost immediately things began to go wrong. It was November 9 before the dismembered Tree Crusher arrived at Kennedy Siding, its sections accommodated on six flatcars. A caravan of logging trucks, cranes, cats and graders waited to transport the parts to the assembly area 32 miles away, but because of problems loading the equipment and accidents due to icy roads, it was November 18 before the machine was ready for a demonstration run with Fortin and approximately 50 dignitaries and media people in attendance. The results were far from impressive, but Fortin was not disheartened. A five-day snowstorm intervened before the machine began moving toward the actual worksite, and 23 minutes into the trip the Tree Crusher bogged down in two feet of black muck. Attempts to free it by digging or dragging it out with a cat succeeded in moving it a mere 30 feet. Finally heavier cats were brought in to remove the muck down to solid gravel, and the Crusher was pulled out on a bed of logs. By now the temperature had dropped to zero and the wind was blowing at 50 miles per hour. By December 2 the machine had been stuck in the mud three more times and still had not arrived on site, much to the embarrassment of the engineer assigned to the project, H. Miles-Pickup, who had to find answers to the questions posed by the press and local citizens. His only consolation was that, except for the cost of transporting the machine to B.C., the government had spent nothing on the experiment. When the Tree Crusher was finally in place, it bogged down so completely that it was absolutely impossible to move it. Tractau Lectric salvaged the generators and abandoned the rest to the elements.

The Forest Service then worked out a system for clearing the working channels by sending in pairs of huge caterpillar tractors with cables stretched between them which would topple the trees as the cats moved forward in tandem along the river banks. At the same time, timber licences were issued to Cattermole Logging and Alexandra Forest Industries in the reservoir area, especially along the Parsnip River south of Finlay Forks where that river joins the Finlay and Peace rivers. The trees were felled and left on the ground, to be harvested by tugs after the waters rose. Tests had demonstrated that the wood would retain its value in the icy waters for several years.

To provide a site for timber and pulp operations on the Parsnip near the southern end of the Trench, Ray designated a new townsite to be called Mackenzie after Alexander Mackenzie who had first seen the Peace in 1793. To provide a symbol for the town, the remains of the Tree Crusher were dismantled, dragged up to a small parksite outside the town and reassembled there, and in 1967 Mackenzie's new mayor, John Dahl, invited Ray back for its dedication. It was calculated that this new town would be situated on the edge of deep water after the dam at Portage Mountain was completed and the reservoir filled, but that it would be high enough to be out of danger from flooding during spring freshets. No provision was made for the possibility of too little water in that end of the reservoir because it was anticipated that the generators at Portage Mountain were only to provide peaking power to the Pacific Northwest, and the water level would always remain high. The Americans did not complete their nuclear reactor construction program, however, and the dam became a firm energy provider. As a consequence, in recent years low water in the reservoir has become a serious problem for the industries in Mackenzie.

Mackenzie attracted a host of resource companies. Bob Cattermole, whose company was one of the largest harvesting timber from the reservoir, was so anxious to establish a milling facility that as soon as the townsite was designated he moved in to clear a site for his mill. Unfortunately for him, the government's agreement with the Wenner-Gren interests at the time of the takeover of Peace Power gave them first site choice, and the land Cattermole had cleared had been chosen by Wenner-Gren for the company's Alexandra Forest Industries mill. Although Wenner-Gren had since sold out to B.C. Forest Products, the deal still held. Ironically, the site further up the reservoir which became Cattermole's second choice turned out to be far superior to Alexandra's location. As for Wenner-Gren's monorail, having recognized in 1960 that their proposed Portage Mountain dam would flood the trench, the company's engineers had surveyed a new rail route from Prince George through the Yukon to Alaska and had started construction on a line from Summit Lake just north of Prince George toward Fort St. James. This short line was later taken over by B.C. Rail.

Ever since the 1961 takeover of Peace Power, while Ray had been shuttling to negotiating sessions on the Columbia River Treaty, work on the dam at Portage Mountain had been underway in earnest. A coffer-dam had been built to isolate the damsite while three diversion tunnels were constructed to channel the water of the Peace around it, then the site was cleared down to base rock, drainage tunnels were installed and the base concreted. It was at this point that Ray accompanied Art Paget on one of his regular inspection tours of the worksite, and he was there when Paget decided that the coffer dam would be inadequate to hold back that year's run-off. Data on the Peace had been collected for less than 20 years, but Paget was convinced that the snowpack that winter indicated a record run-off, and he announced that the height of the coffer-dam would have to be increased by 20 feet to be prepared for it. The reaction of the project engineers was predictable: no so-and-so civil servant could just walk in and make such a ridiculous demand, but Ray put his money on Paget and ordered the work be carried out. And Paget was right. The run-off that summer came within 10 feet of the top of the newly heightened coffer-dam. Failure to have increased its height would have meant the flooding of the damsite and a possible year's delay while it was cleared and prepared again.

As the dam was to be an earth-filled, rock-faced structure spanning the whole of the wide river valley, a search to find materials for fill began very early in the dam-building process. These investigations had been focussed for more than two years on aggregate located about ten miles away when a three-man international team of soil specialists concluded that much better fill was located close to the damsite but at a slightly higher elevation. As a result, the consortium which won the contract for the actual dam construction was able to bid millions of dollars lower than its nearest competitor by opting to move the fill by belt rather than truck. Sufficient power to operate equipment that sorted the fill materials by size before they were sent to the damsite was provided by installing generators at intervals along the conveyor line. The consortium began placing the fill in July 1964 and finished construction in 1967, almost a year ahead of schedule, realizing a substantial profit.

As work on the dam progressed, the project engineers began to see the need for changes in the design of both dam and generating plant. The first blueprints for the power house located the generating facilities above ground on the south side of the river, in spite of the fact that an exposed power house was a big worry in the cold war years. Then suddenly, even though much of the initial work had been done on the outside facility, the engineers decided that the quality of the rock discovered while the diversion tunnels were being carved out would permit an underground power house which would reduce the friction that tends to accumulate in long overland penstocks. This change, however, was to place the designers and engineers at a disadvantage throughout the remaining construction period for they never had a sufficient lead-time over the contractors. The construction company eventually sued B.C. Hydro over the extra costs caused them by the changes. Shrum refused to settle out of court, and the case dragged on for years and cost so much money that both sides took out millions of dollars of insurance on the life of the judge hearing the case so that they would at least have some compensation if he should die before it was resolved and they were forced to start all over again.

As the dam headed toward completion, Shrum and his engineers decided that only one of the tunnels that had been built to divert water around the coffer-dam would be needed—along with the ten penstocks carrying water to the generators—to control the water level in the reservoir. Since at this point it was still thought that the Portage Mountain dam would only be used to provide peaking power for short periods, it was anticipated that the reservoir would never be drawn down very far. Consequently, Water Comptroller

Paget decided that there was not enough leeway between the normal run-off level of the reservoir and the tunnel's diversion capacity. Should there be excessive run-off in the future and the single tunnel fail to handle it, the extra water would pour over the top of the dam, eroding its earth-filled centre, and a 58-million-acre-foot wall of water would sweep all the way down the Peace to the Arctic Ocean. For safety's sake, Paget ordered that an additional diversion channel must be built. Shrum's engineers disagreed, but with Ray upholding his order, Paget was able to force them to design the addition. When it was put out to tender, however, the lowest bid was $56 million, and Shrum decided it was not going to happen. Ray and Paget were adamant that it was.

This impasse brought them all before Premier Bennett. "Gentlemen," he said, "there seems to be a problem." Ray explained the situation, Shrum then told his side of it, and finally Paget detailed his reasons for demanding that it be done. The premier settled back in his chair. "Well, gentlemen, that seems to settle the matter, doesn't it? Doctor Shrum, you will attend to this, will you? Good afternoon, gentlemen." And in fifteen minutes a dispute which had raged for months was resolved.

The diversion channel was duly constructed, and the following year, just as if Paget had ordained it to justify his order, the Peace run-off was the highest on record. To accommodate all this water—an amount roughly equivalent to that flowing over Niagara Falls—the new channel ran to its full capacity. Since the lower portion of this channel had been shaped somewhat like a ski-jump to prevent damage to the river below, the water on this occasion shot right across the valley, smashing some temporary construction buildings on that side to kindling. Out there with his movie camera taking pictures of the rainbow effects as the sun shone through the flying spray was Dr. Shrum whose reputation would have suffered considerably if he had not obliged the premier.

While construction was underway at Portage Mountain, Ray

created a right-of-way for the transmission lines from the Peace River to the Lower Mainland, making it wide enough for intermediate lines to follow the same corridor. Most of it was routed over crown land, so as minister of Lands, he was able to establish it in a single piece of legislation. As Minister of Forests, he sold the timber on the right-of-way, then turned the land into a multi-purpose recreational and cattle-grazing area. The transmission towers, ordered from Italy because they were lighter and less expensive, were different from any previously used in B.C. V-shaped and set up on standard bases by helicopters, they were tethered to the earth by four cables and stabilized by the transmission cables.

As the dam neared completion, in early May 1967 Ray and his 25-year-old son Hubert, freshly graduated as a medical doctor from UBC, drove to a point 90 miles north of Prince George and launched their 14-foot wooden canoe into the waters of the Parsnip River. The ice had only been out of the river for ten days and the spring run-off was making the white water considerably whiter, but the flies and mosquitos had not yet emerged. Together father and son paddled the 80 miles down the Parsnip to Finlay Forks, then the 70 miles down the Peace to the damsite, stopping along the way to talk with forestry crews clearing the river valleys. It was a trip that no one would be able to duplicate once the reservoir began to fill, and they made it with only three cracked canoe ribs and a slight dent in the keel.

On September 12, 1967, when the last load of gravel was added to the dam at Portage Mountain, a naming ceremony was held at the damsite. Shrum had lobbied the members of the Power Authority board to have the dam named after the premier and had secured everyone's approval, so that when the Honourable George Pearkes, B.C.'s lieutenant governor, rose to dedicate the dam, no one was surprised when he announced that the dam was "a tribute to Premier William Andrew Cecil Bennett whose vision and confidence in the future of British Columbia inspired the success of this great project from its initial conception to its ultimate completion. Every man's works shall be made manifest." The dam at Portage Mountain now became known as the W.A.C. Bennett Dam.

In spite of the prediction by Ian Barclay of B.C. Forest Products that it would be ten years before tugs could operate safely on the reservoir behind the new dam, they began working there within the first year after the dam was closed and the water began to rise. Other problems did develop, however. It had not been anticipated that the rising water would saturate the silty soil along the banks of the Peace, causing such large landslides that they produced tidal waves right across the reservoir. As a result, the tugs already at work rounding up floating timber had to be kept out of that portion of the reservoir until the banks stabilized.

A much larger problem was the unexpectedly huge quantity of timber debris that floated to the surface of the reservoir to be carried by the prevailing winds down the Peace, accumulating just above the dam. Faced with the threat that the penstocks would plug up, preventing water from reaching the generators, the engineers decided that a barrier had to be constructed above the damsite. Church Brothers, who were local contractors, were given the job of putting a heavy cable across the reservoir, anchoring it on either bank. That cable was no match, however, for the force of the wind driving the debris down the waterway, and after it had been replaced and ripped out several times, that solution was abandoned. Instead, a clean-up operation using tugs was established just above the dam, and to the present day, floating debris is collected there for salvage or burning.

By the time the reservoir reached the necessary level, the first three turbines in the power house were ready to begin operation. This was the occasion for a second naming ceremony at the W.A.C. Bennett Dam. On September 29, 1968, the power house was named for Dr. Shrum, and to Ray's astonishment, the reservoir was named

THE TWO RIVERS POLICY

Williston Lake. This was the premier's decision, and he had remained absolutely mum about it so that neither Ray or any of his colleagues had an inkling before it was announced at the ceremony. It was somehow very fitting that Ray and his son had paddled down that waterway only a year and a half earlier.

It was believed at the time that these three generators, the largest of their kind yet constructed, would provide sufficient power to meet the load growth in the province for the next ten years, but within that time the increase in demand was so dramatic that the remaining seven turbines and generators were either already operating or being installed. In 1980, long after Ray had left government, a 70-foot-high concrete dam to generate even more power was completed in the Peace Canyon, nearer to Hudson's Hope.

In 1967, the Duncan Dam became the first of the Columbia River dams to be completed. Situated on the Duncan River north of Kootenay Lake, it is a 130-foot-high earth-filled dam holding back a 28-mile-long reservoir. The High Arrow Dam, later re-christened the Keenleyside Dam, became fully operational on October 10, 1968, one week after the Bennett Dam's generators were turned on. Used as the major control mechanism for the whole Columbia power system, it is a concrete dam, 170 feet high, holding back the 145-mile-long Arrow Lakes reservoir. Its completion was marked by the presentation of a cheque from the U.S. government for the first $52 million in flood control benefits. Although all early plans included a dam at Downie Creek 40 miles north of Revelstoke, that site had to be abandoned when drilling revealed that the rock there was largely composed of schist, a crystalline metamorphic rock that splits and slides easily because of its high mica content. The loss of this site meant that the dam at Revelstoke would have to do the work of two dams and therefore have to be that much higher. Completed in 1984, it is also earth-filled and stands 575 feet high. No generating plants were built into any of these dams when they were constructed, but the Revelstoke Dam and the earth-filled, 800-foot-high dam at Mica Creek at the northernmost bend of the Columbia were designed so that they could be used for the generation of power later.

The controversy over the Columbia River Treaty and the construction of dams on that river and on the Peace did not end when construction was underway nor after Social Credit was defeated in 1972. By the time the Mica Dam was completed in 1973, the New Democratic Party was in power in B.C., and the virtues of the McNaughton Plan were once again trotted out when his grandson was given the go-ahead by that government to investigate the files in Hugh Keenleyside's office to ferret out the "skulduggery" that was believed to have scotched the old general's plan. When nothing incriminating was discovered, McNaughton's spirit was assuaged by giving his name to the 130-mile-long lake behind the Mica Dam, a lake that had formerly been known as Kinbasket.

After the NDP hired former Saskatchewan Power & Light head, David Cass-Beggs, as the new head of the B.C. Hydro and Power Authority, he tried to breathe life into a proposal he had made in 1963 that the water in McNaughton Lake should be pumped over the Rocky Mountains to provide power and irrigation water for the Saskatchewan River basin. The plan never got beyond the proposal stage as it was not practical from either an economic or engineering standpoint.

In 1973 a seminar was organized at Simon Fraser University by a group of pro-NDP professors critical of the Columbia River Treaty's terms. Ray, then acting as a forestry consultant in New Brunswick, received a letter asking him to speak at the seminar but warning him that there were no travel funds or fees available for the speakers. Ray was determined to pay his own way there, believing if he did not attend, the former government's side of the story would never be told. Although he had no documents pertaining to the negotiations and agreements with him in New Brunswick, he prepared a speech, making extra copies to be available as handouts. When he arrived for the seminar, however, there was no advertising for the session he was to give—although the seminar itself was highly publicized—and he even had difficulty finding out where he was to speak. His audience, therefore, was extremely small, but anticipating that those who did attend would be highly critical of what he had to say, he was happy to recognize a few friendly faces including his former deputy minister, Walter Rauvsep who had taken over from Paget.

Ray spoke directly from his written text, and when he was finished, he invited questions. Not a single question was volunteered. Afterwards he gave a copy of his speech to the meeting's chairman who expressed surprise that he had gone to the trouble of preparing copies. The next day he returned to New Brunswick. It was only years later that he learned from a researcher that tapes of all the seminar speeches had been submitted to the provincial archives, but his speech had not been included. "Why weren't you there to tell your side of the story?" he was asked. When Ray explained that he had spoken at the seminar, the researcher contacted the university and was told that the tape recorder had broken down the night that Ray spoke. When it was pointed out that Ray had given a copy of his speech to the chairman, the university spokesman expressed ignorance of that fact. Ray then sent a copy of his text to the archives for inclusion, although it was somewhat late to set the record straight.

Ray's one consolation continues to be the fact that the international community applauded the work of his negotiating team. Dr. John Krutilla of Resources for the Future Inc., a private U.S. research agency, who had told a UBC audience in 1963 that the treaty had been drafted without proper economic study and was instead a political compromise unjustified on economic grounds, nevertheless expressed his admiration for the Canadian team's bargaining skills in his 1971 book *The Columbia River Treaty: The Economics of an International River Basin Development*. In it, he says in part:

> In reviewing the results of the international understanding for the development of the Columbia, we should be aware that a great disparity existed in the size, wealth and economic resources of the two riparian countries. To the United States the Columbia development in relation to total United States productive capacity or even power generating capacity was comparatively small. Accordingly, a sizable misjudgement about the economics of the undertaking could be accommodated without serious consequences for the country's economy, its credit status or capability for undertaking effective public works activities in the future.
>
> This may not have been the case with Canada and most certainly was not so for British Columbia. If we consider the problems faced in general by small political units or by emerging developing nations, the care exercised by British Columbia to function within its capital constraints and to secure a sufficient margin to cover any contingent miscalculation in return for committing its resources is an example that warrants emulation. There is no doubt that Canada and British Columbia in particular figured with a very sharp pencil. Analysis was used to illuminate policy choices and to evaluate the magnitudes in the trade-offs when economic and political long run and short run and similar conflicting objectives were being weighed in the balance.

CHAPTER EIGHT:
Minister of Lands

WHEN RAY BECAME MINISTER OF LANDS IN 1956, he took on a very complex bureaucracy which not only dealt with crown lands and water resources, but also governed unincorporated residential and agricultural lands as well as parklands. Many of the problems which these branches faced had their roots in regulations and practices which had been in place almost unchanged since the first settlers arrived in the province. As a result, one of Ray's first priorities was the updating of antiquated procedures which often involved revising or designing new legislation.

As a teacher and a pilot, he had developed an intense interest in maps which gave him extra enthusiasm for assisting with changes in the Surveys and Mapping Branch of Lands. In too many cases, that branch was dealing with the results of a hundred years of errors in private property surveys, errors which had been compounded with every survey carried out beyond them. Since the survey system almost universally in use at that time relied on a series of designated topographic points networking the province—and relating right back to Greenwich, England—that required surveyors to align their survey pins to the nearest point, it had been inevitable that an area of properties aligned to one point would meet up with the properties aligned to the next one—frequently with results that did not match the government's topographic maps.

Shortly after Ray took office, he met the unhappy victim of a whole series of these errors. Having bought a small homesite south of Penticton, this man had hired a surveyor to complete the mandatory survey that had to be filed in Victoria, only to discover that his plot of land lay at the juncture of two survey areas that failed to agree on the government maps. Therefore, all the properties in every direction had to be re-surveyed in order to correct the mistakes, and the law held the individual liable for the entire survey bill. In another case just north of Victoria in View Royal, a sizable piece of property shown on the map did not actually exist; errors on earlier surveys had absorbed it into the adjoining properties.

To correct the problem and remove responsibility for mistakes from the shoulders of the person unfortunate enough to choose the piece of property that joined two survey areas, Ray's Surveys and Mapping Branch introduced "integrated surveys." In this system, known points were established in every community and all new property surveys were aligned to these points. After that, whenever a new survey failed to correspond to the map, the branch would send out one of its own crews to make the necessary corrections. This procedure was aided by aerial photographs of specific points in the community and the use of the newly invented telerometer to accurately measure distances electronically.

Being the boss of Surveys and Mapping also allowed Ray to resolve one of his pet peeves: in all his years in education he had never been able to obtain a good teaching map of British Columbia, one which showed the true nature of the terrain. All he had been able to buy were colourful—and sometimes faulty—maps made in the United States. Now, determined that the branch would publish the kind of map needed by schools, he found himself facing a bureaucratic brick wall. They could not see the need for it, therefore it was not needed. Finally he "put both feet down" and issued an order, and the resulting map became the best seller ever put out by the branch—just as Ray was convinced it would be.

His second mapping success was one that showed all B.C.'s air facilities, especially the little community airfields that private pilots

The Peace River swirls past the site of the "plug" at the entry to the diversion tunnel area as engineers prepare to blast it out of the way.

Blowing out the plug to allow the waters of the Peace to enter the diversion tunnels. The tunnel entrances are in the rock at the lower/center of the picture.

Signing of the protocol and power sale agreements in the White House on January 22, 1964. Seated: Ex-Minister Paul Martin, Prime Minister Lester Pearson, President Lyndon Johnson. Behind Pearson stands Minister of Northern Affairs and Natural Resources Arthur Laing, next to him Postmaster General Jack Nicolson (white hair), Washington State Senator "Scoop" Jackson, Washington State Senator Warren Magnuson, and Ray Williston at the edge of the picture.

Carving the Bennett Dam's $56 million spillway that Gordon Shrum initially refused to build after it was ordered by the Water Resources Deputy Minister Arthur Paget. 1965.

Ben Ginter signs the arrangements for Eurocan's pulp mill licence while Ray looks on in October 1965. Behind them stand Hamish C. Cameron of Bull Housser & Tupper, Barristers and Solicitors, representing the Finnish consortium which partnered Ginter; Mauri Skogster, representing Enso-Gutzeit Oy, the majority partner in the consortium; and Clarence Cooper, lawyer for the BC Forest Service.

Ray Williston (in the bow) and his son, Dr. Hubert Williston (in the stern), canoeing the Parsnip/Peace River system in May 1967 before the closure of the W.A.C. Bennett Dam flooded the area. They are shown at the confluence of the Wicked and Peace Rivers.

Ray's personal 1967 centennial project was to run the equivalent of the distance from Victoria to Prince George—500 miles. Here he completes the 500th mile on the Victoria YMCA track.

Ray Williston and Prince Takamatsu in the Japanese Imperial Palace on May 26, 1970.

Ray Williston in Fredericton, New Brunswick, in February 1974. City Hall is on the right, the Press Building on the left.

Ray rode the open rear loading ramp of this Russian military helicopter to survey timber on the border between Burma and Bangladesh in 1973. Communication with his Bengali assistants and the Russian aircrew was accomplished in sign language.

Ray Williston in the offices of BC Cellulose with the Hermes portable typewriter he purchased in 1938. It was on this machine that he typed his famous forestry memos. May 18, 1976.

Ray and Gladys Williston celebrate their 40th wedding anniversary in April 1979 in West Burnaby United Church hall surrounded by grandchildren.

Ray receives an honorary doctorate from the University of BC in May 1982. Presenting the award is UBC President Dr. Kenney.

The pleasures of retirement. Summer 1987, Ray reads the paper while wife Eileen hams it up, swinging a pick at the rock pile that was to become the spectacular rock garden at their home in Gibsons.

Ray Williston receives an honorary doctorate at the University of Northern British Columbia from Chancellor Iona Campagnola in May 1997. Seated to her left in photo is Lieutenant-Governor Garde Gardom and seated to Ray's right is Education Minister Paul Ramsay.

rely on. Working with the association for the province's small plane owners, he organized the assembly of all available data on municipal and private airstrips. From this information, the Surveys and Mapping Branch produced a map that was then sold by the association throughout the province, becoming a source of great pride to Ray as it was updated and refined every few years.

In the 1950s much of British Columbia's population was located in rural communities where few of the amenities that urban dwellers got for their tax dollars were normally provided. However, some of these rural residents had taken advantage of a clause in the Water Resources Act to organize "improvement districts" in order to install local water systems. Under this Act, they were responsible for constructing the system, hiring people to operate it and signing up the subscribers; the Water Resources Branch provided administration and arranged taxation of the subscribers to pay for the installation and operation. Local organizers also saw improvement districts as the logical way to develop sytems for garbage collection, ambulance services, mosquito control, sewage disposal and electric power, as well as to construct hospitals and community halls and lay out parks and cemeteries. As a result, when Ray took over the Lands ministry, more than 300 improvement districts of all kinds were being administered by a three-man section of Water Resources and a single lawyer. When he began looking for a solution, he discovered more rural confusion—one tiny department in the Ministry of Municipal Affairs was responsible for the administration and policing of the provincial building code in all the unincorporated portions of the province, with the result that construction fiascos were a regular occurrence.

The hinterlands of B.C. had obviously outgrown direct administration from Victoria, and by 1965 the government had developed the concept of regional districts. Legislation was passed and an administration established under Municipal Affairs, but the arduous task of surveying the province into administratable areas and establishing legal boundaries took many more years. Some districts were fairly easily designated as they could be delineated by natural geographic boundaries (the Sunshine Coast Regional District, for example), but others waited several years before boundary disputes could be resolved. In the meantime, these areas remained under the jurisdiction of the Ministry of Lands.

In the Okanagan, several dramatic incidents complicated the procedure and brought in all the forces of the Water Resources Branch and Municipal Affairs as well as Health and Welfare. The first came about when an enterprising dredge operator began contracting himself and his equipment out to land owners along Okanagan Lake and the South Thompson River, offering to carve keyhole-shaped canals into their property to give them private mooring basins. This little operation was, of course, illegal because property in this province may be owned only above the highest water level, and the channels that were cut through the publicly owned foreshore to create these basins prevented legal unimpeded access along the beach. By the time Water Resources heard about this enterprise, a large number of basins had already been dug, and it became Ray's job to order the basins refilled and the foreshore restored—and to listen to the enraged outcry from the offenders.

This episode was not even settled before it was brought to Water Resources' attention that a man named Eddie Haymor had constructed a concrete ferry dock on the foreshore of Okanagan Lake near Summerland. Haymor, a barber from Edmonton, had bought Rattlesnake Island in the lake just south of Kelowna, and on it he planned to build an exotic, middle-eastern-style amusement park. Needing a dock on the lakeside from which to ferry building supplies and later his customers to his island, he had attempted to buy Canadian Pacific's old ferry wharf at Summerland. When that deal fell through, he had built his own dock. Since regional district regulations were not yet in effect for the Okanagan, when Haymor refused to remove the dock, it fell to Ray to order the bulldozers in to demolish it.

Meanwhile, construction on the island itself had been halted by Department of Health officials in Kelowna because Haymor planned to discharge sewage effluent directly into the lake. At the same time, Municipal Affairs building inspectors also saw to it that Haymor's construction plans were turned down.

The legislation to create the North Okanagan Regional District was not passed until after the Social Credit government had been defeated in 1972, and under normal circumstances Haymor and his problems would no longer have been any of Ray's business, except for the fact that Haymor, frustrated with bureaucrats and the destruction of his plans for paradise, became irrational. Declared mentally incompetent, he was placed in Essondale, the provincial mental institution, and while he was there, the new NDP government negotiated a deal to buy the island from him for $40,000 in order to make it part of the adjacent provincial park. After his release, Haymor flew to Lebanon where he rounded up some friends and weapons and occupied the Canadian Embassy in Beirut, demanding that the Canadian government help him get his island back. In return for vacating the premises and returning to British Columbia on a ticket provided by the embassy, the officials there promised that the Canadian government would help him, and that he and his friends would not be charged for the invasion.

Ten years later Haymor was still without his island, but eventually, with the help of lawyer Jack Cram, he sued the provincial government for its return or, failing that, proper compensation. Although Ray privately supported Haymor's claim that he had been short-changed in the sale of his island, when the case came to trial in 1987, Social Credit was back in power, and he was directed to testify on the government's behalf. Cram was as volatile as Haymor, however, and in the course of the trial, after he had bombarded Ray with a stream of insulting questions, Ray blew his stack and shouted back at him. The judge called a recess so that Ray could cool down, and when they returned after the recess, in spite of his annoyance with Cram, Ray questioned how Haymor could possibly have received justice when the sale of the land was negotiated while the man was in a mental institution at the behest of the other party to the sale—a point which Cram had completely failed to make at the hearing. Perhaps because of Ray's observation, Haymor won and was awarded some $240,000.

During his tenure as minister of Lands, Ray was intimately involved with the creation of a number of provincial parks, partly because Parks was a branch of the Forest Service and the Lands Branch was responsible for providing most of the crown land required for parks, but also because, as an outdoor enthusiast, designating more provincial parkland was almost as important to him as improving provincial education standards. And although in time Parks became a separate department, the acquisition of new parkland continued to be carried out by the Ministry of Forests.

Soon after taking over the portfolio Ray became aware that there was no public recreational land on the shores of the Shuswap where he had grown up or on Okanagan Lake, and that on neither lakeshore was there any land suitable for a park that had not already been alienated to private ownership. As a result, he persuaded the government to purchase parkland at Celista on Shuswap Lake across from Sorrento and near Summerland on Okanagan Lake. The Summerland site was an expensive strip of steep, treeless sidehill, but after extensive landscaping and tree planting, it became very popular with the camping public, as did the park at Celista.

These two purchases led to an examination of some of the other interior lakes for possible recreation areas, and it was discovered that they were already popular with Americans who were flying in to buy up all the lake frontage property and, contrary to British Columbia law, were running their property lines right down to the water as is customary in their country. Ray put an immediate moratorium on the sale of all lakefront property, then set up a system whereby a government survey team was sent in to map the properties around lakes where purchasers were showing an interest; the surveyors' job was to place the prime recreational area in reserve for a public park and divide the secondary recreational areas into lots. Since it was impossible to know whether the reserved park area would prove large enough in the future, the other lots were only leased to private individuals for 21 years with an option to renew at the end of that time if their land was not needed for public purposes. This system remained in effect until very recently when leaseholders were allowed to buy their lots.

Ray Williston had an even closer association with the establishment of another of British Columbia's provincial parks: Rathtrevor near Parksville on Vancouver Island. During the 1950s when this property with its 7,000 feet of waterfront was owned by George Rath and his two sisters, it was possible to pitch a tent under the Douglas firs, use the pit toilets, pump water from the well and, best of all, swim from the clean sandy beach where the tide seemed to go out for miles—all for 50 cents a day. And summer after summer during those years, Ray Williston and his family were among the people who camped there.

Rumour had it, however, that the Raths might sell out, and Ray's old friend, Parksville school principal Roy Thorstenson, and his friend Parker Bonney, a forester with Crown Zellerbach, began pushing to have the property bought for a public park. Gossip had it that it had been valued at $110,000. "That's just chicken feed to that gang of yours down in Victoria," Thorstenson told Ray in an effort to get him to take up the cause. Prodded by the two men, Ray finally opened negotiations with the Raths, but it was impossible to get George and his sisters to agree with one another on a price or even on whether the property should be sold at all. Frustrated, Ray let the matter drop, and campers went on paying their fifty cent fees to the Raths.

In August 1960, with a week to go before Ray embarked on the campaign trail for his third provincial election, the Willistons were back at their favourite campground, this time accompanied by their old friends, the Moffats of Prince George. When Ray suggested they erect a volleyball net on the beach so that the families could get a game going, Harold pointed out an old cedar log. "We could cut a couple of posts from that." And he handed his newly sharpened axe to Ray. "Here, you're the forestry man in this outfit." Ray positioned the log and began chopping, but in one of his mighty swings he missed the log and the axe sliced through his moccasined right foot and across the flexor tendon. He fell to the beach, writhing in the sand.

Harold took one look at the gushing blood, wrapped the wound, got Ray into his car and sped to Nanaimo Hospital's Emergency Department. As it was a Saturday evening, they had to wait while the emergency room nurse phoned the physician on call. "The next time you do this," he told Ray as he began to stitch the severed tendon, "would you please aim a bit further down? This is so damn close to the bone, it doesn't give me much room for sewing."

In spite of the seriousness of the wound, the doctor said he would be sending Ray home after he had patched him up. "We've no spare beds. It's that cheapskate Social Credit government!" Nanaimo had been making plans for a new hospital, but they were not having much luck prying money from the provincial government, and the resultant squabble was the main topic of conversation in local medical circles. "That bunch are so goddamned tight-fisted they'll never get re-elected," he said.

Ray suppressed a smile. "You don't think so?" he said.

"I'm certainly not voting for them," said the nurse.

Ray interjected a few words in support of the government, trying to explain why hospital funds had been temporarily held back. The nurse looked sharply at him, picked up his chart, glanced at it, then held it for a moment under the doctor's face. The doctor rolled his eyes but stuck to his task of closing the wound. As he tied the final stitch and cut the thread, he said suddenly, "After we get the cast on, I think we'll find a bed for you and keep you overnight."

"No thanks," said Ray, wondering what broom closet the bed would be in. "I'm leaving after the cast is on."

But when it was applied, it stretched from heel to knee with the foot flexed upwards. "How am I going to walk?" Ray asked.

"With crutches. Here's the name of a doctor in Victoria," he said, scribbling on a prescription pad. "You should see him in two weeks."

A week later the election campaign was in full swing, but with the cast on, Ray could not manage the foot controls of his car, and Gladys had to drive him to all his meetings as well as manhandle the luggage at overnight stops—a sight that was grist for the media mill. The press also took glee in pointing out the significance of the minister of Forests chopping his foot instead of the log he was supposed to be working on, and the Vancouver *Sun* carried a Norris cartoon of him with axe in hand and both feet in buckets.

In the meantime, Ray's right leg became excrutiatingly itchy, and finally he went to the Victoria doctor he had been referred to and begged him to saw off the cast. The doctor did as requested, but immediately put on a new one. When Ray complained, he was told, "You have to live with this foot the rest of your life, you know, and if this tendon doesn't heal properly you'll end up with a 'dropped toe'." As this did not sound like something to be wished for, Ray did as he was told and was still wearing the cast when he was re-elected on September 12.

The following year the death of one of the Rath sisters brought the other two siblings back to the bargaining table with Ray, but by then the value of the property had skyrocketed to $365,000. Ray still believed the land should become a park, but no amount of rhetoric helped when he approached cabinet, and prying loose that much money from Bennett for a park in 1961—when he had just expropriated the BCE and Peace River Power—was out of the question. Nevertheless, Ray refused to give up on the park idea, and he began talking to business people, to service clubs, to lumbermen, to anyone who would listen. His bullheadedness was rewarded when Jack Christianson, head of the Tahsis Company, came to him with a proposition.

Christianson's company logged not only at Tahsis but also west of Strathcona, the oldest and one of the largest of the provincial parks. In 1911, when the land had been set aside for Strathcona, some deskbound civil servant with no thought for the topography of Vancouver Island had drawn a ruler line on the map to establish the park's western boundary. By the 1960s it was still not much more than a line on a map because no one, except perhaps the odd hermit, lived in that remote area. It was just beyond this western boundary that Jack Christianson's logging shows ended.

"Ray," said Christianson, "I can get that Rath property for you."

"You can? How?"

"I'll buy it for you," he said, "but from now on, instead of stopping at the boundary of Strathcona Park, I'll just keep right on logging up those river valleys. You debit me for the stumpage and when it reaches the worth of Rath's property, $365,000 or whatever it turns out to be, I'll hand you the deed for it, pull out of Strathcona, and nobody needs be any the wiser."

"You've got to be out of your mind!"

"No, I'm dead serious."

"But if it ever came out that you were logging in the park, it'd be 'game over' for me. I can see the headlines now: FORTY THOUSAND ANGRY ENVIRONMENTALISTS MARCH ON LEGISLATURE. The government would really be in for it!" But although Ray was horrified, this was the first solid proposal to get Rathtrevor that he had received, and he ended the meeting by saying, "Let me mull this over, Jack."

What he hated most to think about was what the Opposition members would do if they got wind of such an arrangement. He knew he would hear Bob Williams' cries of outrage all the way from

Vancouver! On the other hand, it was thoughts of the Opposition's reaction that finally prompted Ray to meet with Jack Squire, NDP member for Alberni, because the Squire family had often camped next to the Willistons on the Raths' beach, and Jack had always been an advocate of getting it for a park.

He related Christianson's proposal, then added, "But if it ever got out, all hell would break loose."

Squire clapped his hands together. "Go get it," he said, "and I give you my word of honour that you'll never ever hear about it from the NDP."

Ray decided it was worth the gamble. He gave the okay to Jack Christianson, who in turn bought the Rath property. Christianson could have made a lot of money by "flipping" it to another buyer, but he kept his word. He logged in Strathcona Park, and when in October 1963 the stumpage reached the value of the Rath property, he handed Ray the deed to it and withdrew his equipment from the park. In 1964 Liberal MLA Alan Macfarlane brought the park acquisition up in the House, suggesting it had something to do with a current timber sale in Wells Gray Park, but the matter was soon dropped for lack of evidence of hanky-panky. No one ever mentioned the cutting in Strathcona Park. Decades have now passed, the lush second growth has provided new forests, and there is very little sign that timber was ever logged. Meanwhile, Rathtrevor Provincial Park has provided camping and swimming pleasure for thousands of families for more than thirty years.

Another provincial park was acquired by default. In the mid-1960s E.E. "Ted" Osborne, a logging operator and owner of Tyee Airlines of Sechelt, formed Alpine Outdoor Recreation Resources Ltd. to log the Cypress Bowl area above West Vancouver, with the stated intention of developing a multi-million-dollar ski resort. Since the bowl was crown land, partly within the boundaries of the municipality of West Vancouver, permission to log had to come from the Department of Lands and Forests with the agreement of West

Vancouver. Fortunately for Osborne, his application was received in Victoria about the same time the Forest Service discovered that Cypress Bowl had an infestation of balsam woolly aphids which was resistant to all then-known sprays. It was decided that logging by Alpine would not only clear the way for a ski resort but also get rid of the aphids, and in 1967 Osborne received permission to log and develop ski facilities within specific geographical boundaries. Permanent occupational rights, however, would only apply to the small area on which Alpine's amenities were to be constructed; the rest of the logged land was to remain with the Crown.

Once logging was under way, a barrage of criticism erupted: the company was taking out more timber than necessary; the areas cleared were too steep for skiing; clearing would affect water run-off; the skiing facilities would never be built. By 1969 questions had arisen concerning the viability of Alpine Recreation Resources itself, and it became apparent that even the construction of an access road and parking areas for the planned ski resort were beyond the financial capability of the company. Osborne began searching for financial aid and his search took him to a Manila-based firm, Benguet Consolidated, which had interests in Philippine mines, California real estate, casinos and Bahamian properties. It is not known what grand pictures Osborne painted for the Benguet firm, but these offshore promoters obviously thought a bonanza was within their grasp. They engaged consultants who secretly surveyed the area and drew up plans for the Bowl that included a vast housing development with peripheral skiing facilities.

About this time, Ray—who had been a director of B.C. Hydro since 1961—began hearing rumours of a request for a substantial power feed into the Cypress Bowl area. It seems that Benguet's consultants had approached Hydro's engineers and, although insisting on confidentiality, had asked Hydro to begin planning for the future needs of their proposed development.

In due course the promoters were ready to show their hand and inform the government they had taken over the proposed development from Alpine Resources. They arrived with their consultants for an appointment with Ray, bearing detailed plans which showed condominiums, apartment buildings, retail establishments—everything needed for a major development in the mountains above West Vancouver. And although the rumours had prepared Ray to a certain degree, he sat astounded as the company's grandiose scheme was revealed. Finally he interrupted them. "Well, I've finally met the people who bought the Brooklyn Bridge."

"What do you mean?"

"Obviously you have negotiated in good faith with the Alpine group, but they had no rights whatsoever in their agreement with this government to do the things which you now propose. It won't be approved."

Mouths dropped open as the Benguet delegation slowly realized that all their planning, all their detailed engineering and surveys, not to mention the expense, had gone down the tube. They would sue Alpine Resources! But whether suit was ever brought is not known. What is known is that Osborne left for an extended visit to Australia at almost exactly that time. Since the mountain was now cleared of timber as well as woolly aphis and Osborne's development company was in receivership, the government decided to proceed on its own to put the road in, open the area as Cypress Provincial Park and establish public ski facilities.

One provincial park was to give trouble to Ray and to every government which followed W.A.C. Bennett's administration. The problems with the Skagit Valley Park had their roots in a 1924 treaty that gave Seattle Power and Light Ltd. the right to harness the Skagit River which rises in southern B.C. east of Hope and drains southwestward through Washington state. The agreement allowed the company to build a series of power-generating dams on the river as well as a storage dam about 20 miles south of the U.S./Canada border. The Ross Dam, as this storage dam was to be called, would initially back water up a mile into British Columbia, but the company had the option of increasing the height of the dam at such time as more power was needed, thus backing the water up an additional seven miles. In 1931 the B.C. government sold the company the 256 hectares (552.576 acres) of land on which the first part of this reservoir would be located. Seattle Power began clearing the area in 1936, cutting the trees off at the point where the taper began since it was anticipated that even stumps of this height would be completely submerged after the dam was raised.

By 1936 two generating dams—the Diablo and the Gorge—had been built on the American portion of the river. Then in 1941, Lot #2203, a 6,350-acre tract in Canada's portion of the Skagit Valley, was surveyed and leased to the Americans to provide an area for the full eight-mile-long Ross Lake reservoir. It was approved for clearing in 1946. Around this same time a provincial campsite and park was established at the eventual northern limit of this lake to make the most of its recreational potential. The first stage of the Ross Dam—an arch type structure 1300 feet long and 540 feet high—was completed in 1949.

Within five years Seattle Power was feeling the pinch for power again, and the company began making overtures to the B.C. government for permission to raise the dam's height by 125 feet. The International Joint Commission (IJC), however, was still studying the Columbia River, and W.A.C. Bennett stalled the Seattle company to await the results of that contest. The signing of the Columbia River Treaty, which established the principle of 50 percent of downstream benefits going to the country with the upstream source, cleared the way for B.C. to resume Skagit Valley negotiations in 1964. Since B.C. would gain additional, easily accessible electric power, Ray convinced the cabinet to come out in favour of issuing a permit for the dam's height to be increased. In addition, he pointed out that the extension of Ross Lake would provide southwestern B.C. with a much-needed recreational lake, taking the pressure off Cultus and

Harrison lakes. Seattle Power also expressed willingness to establish roads and trails around the Canadian portion of the lake, and agreed to maintain the lake's level high enough for all recreational purposes during the summer months. For these reasons, and knowing that in any event the IJC was going to insist on compliance with the terms of the 1924 treaty, in 1967 Ray signed an agreement-in-principle with the company that would allow them to flood B.C. land to the full extent outlined in the 1924 treaty in exchange for $5.50 per flooded acre per year, a total of $34,566(US) annually, plus 50 percent of the additional power generated downstream.

While the Seattle company and most of its customers were eager to complete negotiations and make a start on the project, people with summer homes around the American portion of Ross Lake objected because they would be flooded out if the High Ross was built. Gaining no sympathy for their plight in their own country, they looked for support in B.C. and found it in the Liberal MLA for North Vancouver, Dave Brousson. With an election looming, he launched a letter-writing campaign to force Ray not to proceed further with the agreement on the grounds that this was an invasion of Canadian soil. One of the few lighter moments during his attack occurred when Brousson's campaign manager sent one of her weekly reports on the progress of the letter-writing campaign to Ray instead of to her boss. Ray, vastly amused, tucked it into an envelope and sent it along to Brousson with a note of explanation. Meanwhile, the newspapers had taken up the refrain, with photographs and stories showing that the mile of lake on B.C.'s side of the line was "bordered by a revolting rim of blackened stumps scattered around the shores like tombstones in an abandoned cemetery." Opposition also began to mount from groups like Run Out Skagit Spoilers (ROSS) and the Society for Pollution and Environmental Control (SPEC).

After the Social Credit government lost the election of 1972, it was the NDP's turn to deal with Seattle Power. MLA and environmental advocate Dr. Tom Perry was adamantly opposed to further flooding, and he made enough noise to stall negotiations for a full three years. Jack Webster made several attempts to lure him to his radio talk show to debate the issue with Ray, but Perry avoided the showdown. Finally on November 10, 1975, Resources Minister Bob Williams made a proposal to Seattle Mayor Wes Uhlman. In exchange for no further flooding of the Skagit Valley and a "fairer rent" for existing flooding, B.C. would return all rents and taxes paid by Seattle Power on the land owned by them in B.C. and give possible "energy assistance" to Seattle at market prices.

One month after this overture to Seattle, the NDP was voted out of power, and the problem landed on Bill Bennett's desk. This time flooding was opposed by Vancouver South MLA Peter Hyndman who had jumped from the Conservative leadership to the Social Credit backbenches in 1974. An ardent Skagit River fisherman, he insisted that the river would be ruined by flooding the lower reaches, although in fact some of the best fishing is on the upper reaches in the vicinity of the Hope-Princeton Highway. Ray attempted to convince Bennett that the benefits of the original agreement would outweigh the value of potential fly-fishing, but Bennett was not about to take the advice of one of his father's former colleagues and he committed his government to a No-High-Ross-Dam policy. The Americans retaliated by demanding just compensation. They had a legal and binding treaty right to increase the dam's height, backed by both the IJC and a 1979 judgement by the U.S. federal Court of Appeals, and they had no intention of letting B.C. off the hook.

The province was forced back to the bargaining table and on March 30, 1983, the IJC announced an agreement on the Skagit. Seattle Power was to give back the land the company owned in B.C. and contribute toward an environmental endowment fund dedicated to "enhancing the recreational opportunities and protecting the environmental resources" of the Skagit Valley. In return, B.C. was to supply Seattle Power with the amount of power that would have been generated by all three dams—Ross, Diablo and Gorge—if the additional water storage had been allowed. The catch was that British Columbia must sell this power at the price it would have cost Seattle Power to generate it—that is, the price of raising the dam's height—and raising it would have been comparatively cheap since the original structure had been designed so that it could be merely capped in the future.

Under the final terms, Seattle Power was to receive up to 300 megawatts of power during periods of peak use for 80 years beginning in 1986 when the agreement was to come into effect. For this the company would pay the province $21.8 million annually for the first 35 years of the agreement—that is, to the year 2021. At that point, the payments having equalled the capital cost of capping the dam, Seattle Power would cease payments and get free power for the remaining 45 years of the agreement—to the year 2066. Should B.C. decide to pull out of the deal after 1996 but before 2021, the province would have to pay the lion's share of the cost of raising the Ross Dam; should B.C. pull out after 2021, the province would have to pay the full cost. Seattle Power, on the other hand, can terminate the agreement any time after 1996 on five years notice, but must give up all rights to flooding the Skagit Valley; there is, of course, absolutely no reason for Seattle to terminate a sweet deal like this.

Compensation for B.C. in this agreement came in two packages. First, the province was given the right to raise the height of the Seven Mile Dam on the Pend d'Oreille River near Trail, flooding 24 hectares (59.304 acres) of Washington state land owned by Seattle Power with no compensation to the company. Theoretically this would provide B.C. with the equivalent of the energy that would have been due to B.C. had the Ross Dam been raised. Second, Seattle Power was to donate $4 million to establish the environmental endowment fund, with B.C. donating another $1 million; after these initial donations the fund would be continued by a surcharge on power sales from the Seven Mile Dam.

To carry out the terms of the agreement, Premier Bill Bennett ordered B.C. Hydro to sign a contract with Seattle Power, but many of Hydro's board of directors—including Ray's old friend from Prince George, Harold Moffat—had done their homework. They knew, for example, that B.C. Hydro was going to be stuck for the "wheeling costs" of delivering the power to the border. And although Bennett was assuring the people of the province that the $21.8 million that Seattle would be paying annually was "found money" since B.C. Hydro had surplus power at that time, the board members knew that Hydro's surplus was rapidly dwindling. (In fact, within eight years there was no more surplus.) The board members knew that Hydro's generating costs were rising steadily. And they were also aware that the total cost of capping the dam had been assessed on the basis of 1982 dam construction costs with no allowance for inflation over the term of the agreement. All of these facts meant that the Americans would soon be paying far less than market price for the power. As a result, Moffat and the other board members who had done their homework refused to sanction such a contract. They knew it would commit the people of B.C. to subsidizing the hydro bills of Seattle residents for the next 80 years because someone would have to pay the difference between the cost of generating the extra power for Seattle and the price that Seattle would be paying for it. Bennett's response to their refusal was to dismiss them and replace them with more malleable directors. And the contract was signed.

The day after the IJC announced the agreement in 1983, a Vancouver *Sun* editorial announced that "the deal had not come cheap. . . . It has been an enormously expensive experience. Pray that our governments have learned from it." As far as Ray was concerned, the lesson the newspaper was advocating was the wrong one. Given the fact that the province was irrevocably bound by the 1924 treaty, simply by agreeing to the creation of an eight-mile-long reservoir, the province would have gained 50 percent of the additional electrical power generated by the three dams, the lower mainland would have benefited by the addition of a valuable recreational lake, and the people of the province would *not* have been saddled with 80 years of subsidizing Seattle's light bills. "In time," says Ray Williston, "the arithmetic in this lesson is going to become painfully obvious."

As well as pushing to set land aside for parks, Ray was largely responsible for establishing B.C.'s program of ecological reserves. His involvement began as the result of the "Resources for the Future Conference" that was held in Montreal in 1962 during John Diefenbaker's time as Canada's prime minister. Since the planners were the ten provincial resources ministers, Ray represented B.C.; Rene Levesque, Quebec's resources minister, became conference chairman.

The week-long affair wound up with a banquet in the Queen Elizabeth Hotel with 1500 people in attendance. Levesque presided at the head table at which were seated the provincial representatives in coast-to-coast formation, the Newfoundland minister at one end and Ray at the other. The featured speaker was Paul Hoffman, the authority on redevelopment in Europe under the Marshall Plan, and when he concluded his talk the audience rewarded him with a standing ovation. Then Levesque rose, speaking first in fluent English before switching to French. Ray, presuming Levesque to be thanking the speaker, was suddenly flabbergasted to hear, in English, "I now call upon Ray Williston to thank our guest speaker."

Fortunately Ray had listened intently to Hoffman and was able to conjure up some appropriate words. Finding an appropriate word for Rene was more difficult. "What's the big idea?" he demanded afterwards. Rene gave his particular brand of Gallic shrug and grinned. From his standpoint this had been a great little joke.

Before the banquet wound up that evening, Diefenbaker, carried away by the success of the meeting, stood up and declared there should be an extension of the conference. A round of applause heightened his euphoria, and he announced that the federal government would sponsor and provide financial support for a permanent resources organization. In the dispersing crowd Ray encountered a fuming Levesque, incensed that Diefenbaker had made his pronouncement without warning and without first consulting the provincial people. "What's his big idea?" stormed Levesque. Ray's response was a Rene Levesque-style shrug and a big grin.

Diefenbaker's declaration resulted in the formation of the Canadian Council of Resource Ministers, whose founding executive members were Ray Williston, Rene Levesque and Ontario's Wilf Spooner. It was determined that Rene would organize the administrative office for the Council, and he arranged for space in Hydro Quebec's recently acquired headquarters in Montreal where he had his own office. It was not long before directives began issuing from Council headquarters that did not reflect agreed policy. When he checked up on it, Ray discovered that Rene had staffed the office with separatists who refused to accept direction. It was left to Ray and Wilf Spooner to close the office and start again in another location with Christian de Lach taking on the administrative duties.

In May 1965 when Ray served as chairman, the council held its annual meeting in Victoria, and there the resources ministers approved in principle Canada's participation in the International Biological Program (IBP), a co-operative project set up between the International Council of Scientific Unions and 58 participating nations in order to preserve natural environments. For many years prior to the establishment of the IBP, British Columbia's biologists had been working out a plan for the preservation of certain small undisturbed areas in this most biologically diverse province to provide "outdoor laboratories" for future biological and environmental studies, and these scientists became active members of the Canadian Committee of the IBP. With Dr. V.J. Krajina of the University of B.C. spearheading the program, the biologists divided the province into 11 biogeoclimatic zones. Their aim was to reserve three sites in each zone where large, heterogeneous natural gene pools of a wide variety of organisms could be maintained so that the diversity of life there would remain available in a world where whole species are becoming extinct every day. These sample sites would serve as resources for biologists, foresters, wildlife specialists, microclimatologists, geomorphologists and other scientists. They could also be used as benchmarks against which land practices elsewhere could be gauged and as outdoor classrooms for education in the principles of ecology, primeval landscapes and their biota.

The scientists had made sufficient planning progress by April 1967 to arrange a meeting with Ray and Ken Kiernan to ask for the provincial government's support. Six scientists led by Dr. Ian McTaggart-Cowan of Simon Fraser University and Dr. Peter Larson of the Pacific Biological Station in Nanaimo explained the need for the reserves and asked that the land be set aside. Their request came after the fact, however, because Ray was already hooked on the idea. He had been under pressure from the growing environmental movement to dedicate large blocks of land for wilderness areas which would remain untouched by humans, but the scientists' approach seemed to him to have much greater merit because the reserves would provide learning situations.

The meeting provided the impetus for the organization of an inter-departmental committee to work with the scientists on a province-wide basis. Dave Borthwick, deputy minister of Lands, was made chairman of the committee since he could expedite the selection, surveying and mapping of proposed sites. Initially there was some confusion within the various government departments concerning the differences between parks and ecological reserves, but gradually a common understanding with the scientists developed, and on February 21, 1969, Ray reported to the legislature that the government was committed to establishing the reserves throughout the province. Almost exactly one year later, Borthwick was able to report that 16 reserves had been established, but he stressed the need for the government to take a bolder step in the recognition of the program and suggested that in 1971, when British Columbia celebrated its hundredth anniversary as a province of Canada, a target of 100 reserves should be set. The Ecological Reserves Act, formally recognizing the new goal, was duly passed on April 2, 1971. It became the major impetus for all the work which followed and received favourable publicity all over the continent. In part the program also earned honourary doctoral degrees at the University of B.C. for Ray Williston and Dr. V.J. Krajina who together provided the leadership for the continuing fieldwork.

Although the IBP in Canada was financially supported by the federal government through National Research Council grants, the scientists involved in the B.C. project volunteered their services and worked without any honouraria. Only the expenses of their actual field work were covered by government. At the end of April each year, workshops for up to 40 scientists were held in Victoria to prepare the necessary programs and maps for the coming summer's surveys of potential reserve areas. The summer field work was followed up with a meeting in early winter where applications for new reserves were discussed, then forwarded to the relevant ministries for comment and approval; no reserve was created without the agreement of all affected ministries.

(After the NDP became the government in 1972, the establishment of ecological reserves came under the Ministry of the Environment. By September 1978 there were 92 reserves covering 210,134.8 acres—0.09% of the total area of the province.)

At the same time as the ecological reserves program was getting underway, Ray was absorbed in developing a practical approach to environmental control. It was his view that since destruction and change in the environment could be affected for good or evil by the day-to-day operations in the field, environmental policy had to be incorporated into the agendas of every government department and carried out by every one of that department's workers. The operations of the Ministry of Forests provided him with a precedent. Forest rangers were already responsible for carrying out environmental policy in every forested acre of the province: if a logging road was poorly constructed or a logging site was suffering erosion, the ranger had the power to order the situation rectified immediately. It seemed to Ray, therefore, that all the people who were in charge of developments within the environment should become part of an environmental committee to control it, and from this concept the Environment and Land Use Committee was born. It was composed of all government ministers who had anything to do with the environment—Water, Lands, Forests, Mines, Agriculture and Health. Their job was to set environmental policy that would be interpreted and acted upon by an Action Committee composed of all the deputy ministers. The guidelines provided by the Action Committee then became the blueprint for the workers in the field.

The Environment and Land Use Act of 1971 gave Ray's new committee the strongest authority of any regulatory body to that time. It was set up so there was little room for disagreement between ministries since the prime function of each was the maintenance of the environment. Only one new employee— general administrator Axel Kinnear whose job it was to coordinate and oversee policies—was added to the government payroll on behalf of the new committee. Unfortunately, the end of the Social Credit regime in 1972 also saw the phasing out of the Environment and Land Use Committee before it was fully functioning.

CHAPTER NINE:
Life After Politics

RAY WILLISTON FOUGHT HIS LAST ELECTION CAMPAIGN IN AUGUST 1972. Only three years earlier the Social Credit party had won its seventh consecutive election victory with its largest majority ever—46.8 percent of the popular vote—and returned 38 members to the legislature. But circumstances changed between 1969 and 1972. Inflation rose, leading to unrest and strikes among workers. Industrial growth slowed for the first time since the mid-fifties, automation was being introduced in the resource industries, and by the beginning of 1971 unemployment had reached 9.4 percent.

In Ray's Fort George constituency, the northern extension of the railway and the generation of electric power on the Peace River had brought a new prosperity and thousands of new jobs, especially in the pulpmills. Ironically, it had also increased union membership and these workers put their money on the NDP. "Until the pulp workers came along, our campaigns were pretty homespun in the north," he recalls. "I lost the election by a few votes, but I think I was ready to leave politics by then, and in any case, I would have hated being in the Opposition."

After 19½ years, the route between his home and the legislative buildings had become as familiar to him as his own back yard. He would miss the challenges, the decision-making, his many happy relationships with co-workers and people outside the government—particularly those in the forest industry. Grey-haired now and 58 years old, he had been the hardest working minister in Bennett's cabinet.

While he was still clearing out his office, a visitor from New Brunswick phoned him. Would Ray come over to the Empress Hotel for a chat? Reg Tweeddale had just been commissioned to do a study of the forest industry in New Brunswick. Would Ray consider coming to New Brunswick to give a hand with the study?

"Sorry, Reg," he said. "I'm bushed. I need a holiday. I haven't taken more than three in the last twenty years." He and Gladys had arranged to go to Mexico for a month.

The vacation worked. He returned fully rested and ready for work. But doing what? Was that New Brunswick thing still open? He phoned Tweeddale to say he was available.

Tweeddale was surprised to hear from him. "You sounded so cold to my proposal that I didn't bother to mention it to anyone here. Let me nose around and I'll call you back." The next day, a Friday, Tweeddale phoned. Would Ray come to Fredericton to talk things over? Could he get there by Tuesday? Yes, he would and yes, he could.

Tweeddale spent the next two weeks with Ray in tow, explaining the nature of the study he was conducting and showing him various aspects of forestry in New Brunswick. The Irving family, owners of the largest forest holdings in the province, had spruced up Veneer Siding Limited, the most modern of their mills, for inspection, and after giving the two men a tour, Jim Irving turned proudly to Ray. "Well, what do you think of it?"

"It would have been a darned good mill 20 or 30 years ago, but it's really out of date now."

Irving was so obviously taken aback that Ray said, "Look, I'll be back in Victoria next week. If you want to send some of your people out, I'll drive them around and show them some modern sawmills."

The day after his return to Victoria, Ray received a phone call from Harry Boyle, an Irving engineer who was coming to B.C. to take him up on the offer. He was to be accompanied by another engineer, newly hired by Irving, who had at one time been employed by MacMillan Bloedel. Ray later learned that Irving had sounded this man out on the state of B.C.'s mills. "Williston says our mills are obsolete compared to B.C.'s. Is that right?" "No," said the new man, although he had not been back to British Columbia for many years. "Well," Irving had said, "I'm sending you to B.C. with Harry Boyle for a look."

Ray promised to meet the two engineers in Vancouver the following Monday morning. However, while driving towards the Bayshore where they were staying, his nearly new Mazda was struck broadside by another vehicle, and it was late in the day when Ray, carless, met the New Brunswick pair. Harry Boyle then rented a car and the three of them set off up the Fraser Valley, visiting mills in Boston Bar, Kamloops, the North Thompson, then on to various operations in the 100 Mile House area. By the end of the week they had also been to Williams Lake and Quesnel, completing their safari in Prince George before Boyle and his colleague flew back to New Brunswick.

On Ray's return to Victoria, there was a message from Reg Tweeddale asking him to come back for more talks. Once in New Brunswick again, Ray phoned Irving's office—a suite of rooms over a gas station in Saint John—but Irving was not there. He was in British Columbia, checking out the truth of his emissaries' report. As a result of his fact-finding mission, Irving ordered two complete Chip-n-Saw mill assemblies and constructed two new mills to handle small wood. The front ends of the mills were not designed to handle wood fast enough to keep the Chip-n-Saws supplied, however, and they had to be torn out and reconstructed.

Meanwhile, Ray had been invited to take part in the New Brunswick study, and he signed a contract that bought his services on a daily, rather than a fixed-period, basis so that he could take on other consulting jobs from time to time. Tweeddale and his colleagues offered to find a house in Fredericton for the Willistons who would settle there after Christmas.

They had barely arrived in their new home when Ray was phoned by an official in the United Nations Development Program (UNDP) in New York. Would he be interested in taking on a review of a forestry project in Nepal? Why him? he wondered, but he soon discovered that the Food and Agricultural Organization (FAO), headquartered in Rome, was dominated by Canadian foresters. As some were from British Columbia and knew that Ray was the most experienced senior government administrator then available, they had recommended him to the UNDP. (Under the UN hierarchy, the FAO, which was the technical branch, reported to UNDP; although the FAO had its own regular budget, the cost of FAO special projects was underwritten by the UNDP.) By 1973 the FAO and the UNDP had begun questioning forestry conditions in southeast Asia, and officials of the World Bank, which had been funding that area for some time, had become worried about its investments.

The assignment interested Ray and since he was consulting on a day-to-day basis in New Brunswick, he could take it on, but when he arrived in New York a senior official told him there had been a sudden change in plans. Instead of going to Nepal, Ray was to go to Indonesia to examine the state of forestry there and make recommendations. (The job in Nepal went to Alan Moss, the well-known Kelowna forester.) Although both the World Bank and the FAO had been concerned about the level of corruption and senior mismanagement there for a number of years, their officials had been denied entry to the country for first-hand examination until the World Bank cut off further credit pending independent assessment of forestry conditions. This changed the Indonesian government's tune, and the FAO immediately assembled a team of eight foresters to undertake the examination. Ray's job was to take charge of the group, with the senior FAO man on the team as second-in-command. When Ray met the team in Rome, he learned that, instead of going directly to

Jakarta, Indonesia's capital, they were to proceed to Bangkok to meet with a Mr. Joseph of Sri Lanka who was responsible for all UNDP projects in Indonesia. Although stationed in Jakarta, he happened to be at a regional meeting in Bangkok.

"The Indonesians will not meet with you or give you any co-operation," Joseph announced, and Ray realized that the man was afraid Ray's group would be wasting money from his budget. "Do not order the other members of your team to join you," he continued. "When you have carried out a preliminary investigation, wait there until I return to consult with you."

In Jakarta, Ray and his partner met friendly and very co-operative Indonesian forestry officials, and by the end of the first week, since Joseph had still not returned and they were wasting valuable time, Ray called the members of his team from various parts of the world to assemble in Jakarta. When Joseph finally appeared the following week, he was highly incensed that his orders had not been followed and refused to accept responsibility for the project, telling Ray that he held him personally accountable.

Ray's team began by focussing on an overview of the government's administration of the forest resource. Many of the bureaucrats were holdovers from the Dutch occupation of the territory, and while they had a remarkable knowledge of the botanical names and identifying features of all the islands' wood species—literally thousands of them—and passed this knowledge along to a new generation of employees, they had little or no concept of forest management. Over the years, various global companies had sent forest engineering consultants to Indonesia; some had actually carried out forestry projects, but the local forestry people had been unable to evaluate their reports or put them to good use.

The team found one example of this problem in a forest harvesting project on Java. The central part of this long narrow island is very fertile and intensively cultivated valley lowlands. Food production is the top priority here because of the dense population, yet foreign consultants had recommended clear-cutting the timber on the surrounding hills and extracting the logs for export via an access road carved out of the centre of the cultivated valley.

Ray's team recommended against continuing the project, not only because it was a waste of prime farm land, but also because some of the harvested areas already showed severe erosion. Indonesia's own foresters had earlier reached the same conclusion, but they had neither the authority nor backing from their Forest minister to reject the harvesting proposal. When Ray told the minister that it was obvious that kick-backs were involved, the minister countered by asking how he could be expected to cancel such a proposal from a recognized international corporation when it had been endorsed at the top level of his own government. Ray could only tell him to face the problem head on and not allow such practices to continue.

Indonesia's most serious negative forestry situation was rapidly developing in Kalimantan on the island of Borneo where the "close canopied" tropical forests represented one of the largest unlogged timber stands in the world. These forests contained an estimated 4,000 tree species, many with great commercial value, but no survey of them had ever been done. While the pyramid-shape of the trees in non-tropical forests allows inventories of species and wood volume to be made by aerial photography, such assessment was not possible in Indonesia because the leafy branches of the deciduous hardwood trees form a uniform blanket which even prevents sunlight from reaching the ground. As a result, the only maps for Kalimantan were rough sketches compiled for local areas.

In 1967 when Suharto became Indonesia's head of government, he found that his predecessor, Sukarno, had stripped the treasury. To get ready cash, therefore, Suharto had sold 20-year timber cutting licences in Kalimantan's forests. Boundaries for these cut-blocks were drawn in pencil on the sketch maps so that conflicts frequently arose over the extent of the leases, especially where valuable timber stands were located. No accurate estimate of the timber volume on these cut-blocks could be made because of the lack of topographic maps, hence there was no check on the operators' performance. To add to the problem on the ground, corruption pervaded the government at all levels. It was this grave situation that had made the World Bank push for an independent assessment.

Because of time restrictions and the large area of Kalimantan to be covered, Ray divided his team into smaller groups, assigning each group a different task. His own job took him north to Tarakan, just south of the border with Malaysia, from where he travelled by outrigger canoe westward up the river for several hours to a large logging camp that looked very similar to those of the Pacific Northwest. But although the foresters had been trained in Oregon and were using logging equipment similar to that used in Oregon, the company operating it was from the Philippines. Unfortunately, the ground here could barely support the heavy machines, and the hardwood logs were so dense they could not be floated downriver without buoyant support, usually bamboo, which was generally scarce. To make matters worse, the camp location was so remote that loggers had encountered naked "stone age" people who used poisoned blow-pipes for weapons, and many of the frightened workers had fled the camp. As a result, so little harvesting had been done that Ray was unable to make a proper assessment.

He returned to Samarinda and Balikpapan near the mid-point of the east coast where other team members had been at work on plans for a forestry training centre, recommending machinery for lumber and pulp production facilities and doing forest inventories. Using Samarinda as headquarters, Ray visited numerous logging sites close to the coast where major foreign companies were at work taking out hardwood for the manufacture of the thin veneer then in demand. He was appalled at the conditions and practices he discovered during his inspections. Logging roads were so poorly constructed that they caused almost immediate serious erosion, and there were trucks abandoned all along them. None of the companies were harvesting more than three or four species in their cut-blocks. When he asked why prized trees such as the ironwoods were not being cut, he was told that the fallers would not touch them because they dulled their chain saws. One Korean contractor had 20 large bulldozers at work cutting a single species—the most valuable in the forest. Although his lease was for 20 years, he would abandon the cut-block in 3, and it would be unprofitable for other contractors to harvest what was left because the most valuable timber had been removed. With this type of high-grading, the close canopy was not opened sufficiently to permit sunlight in to regenerate the forest. What was left would eventually die and rot, and only then would new trees take root.

There was very little manufacturing of lumber and no plywood plants or pulpmills in Kalimantan because most of the raw logs were sent to Japan, Korea and Singapore for manufacture. The government could not collect proper stumpage fees because the local Indonesian foresters did not scale the logs, accepting instead the volume figures given by company employees, and no accurate count was kept of the logs loaded onto ships. Government officials, meanwhile, had little knowledge of what was actually taking place because they sat in their offices in town, explaining they were not dressed to go out into the forest.

At the end of their Indonesian tour, Ray and his team made recommendations for the management of the forest, the expansion of timber manufacturing facilities, the training of forest workers and the organization of controls over timber scaling and revenue collection. A year later, he was invited by the Indonesian government to return to that country and take charge of developing a total forest management program based on the recommendations of his report, but he declined.

Back in New Brunswick, the forestry study had been completed and one of its recommendations was the establishment of a pilot project to demonstrate specific aspects of forestry including redevelopment of forest nurseries, planting, thinning, better utilization of the wood, and integration of sawmills with pulpmills. The pilot project's objective was not to compete with industry but to improve all aspects of forestry, including development of sawmills to harvest and utilize small wood. It had been decided that the project would be located near Bathurst where the New Brunswick government had crown forest lands. In the past, these lands had been administered almost entirely by the Consolidated Bathurst Company, the major operator in the region, but the company's management had been so inadequate that the government had taken the area back. Bathurst now chose not to co-operate with the pilot project, although its ancient pulpmill, which turned out the corrugating medium used in box manufacture, was badly in need of the project's advice on renovation.

Ray accepted the job of manager of the pilot project. He would be working closely with the Forestry Branch of the Department of Resources and with Ralph Redmond, senior official of the New Brunswick Management Authority. An advertisement for a practical person to organize the wood-lot and supervise the construction of roads and the cruising, harvest and separation of the timber brought a flood of applications. The job went to Barry Nelson, who had been working on small wood in B.C. Subsequently, an office was opened in Fredericton, and Ray induced Clear Lake Sawmills of Prince George to come to Bathurst to build a close-utilization sawmill on the project land. Since the mill had to be specifically designed for the wood it was to process as well as for the efficient handling of the waste, Clear Lake required an accurate estimate of the average waste or rot in the stands marked for cutting. The company was provided with a cruise of the area carried out some years previously under the supervision of Rudy Hanusak, who in the meantime had become deputy minister. With Hanusak's assurance that the survey was still valid, Clear Lake expected 8 or 10 percent rot and an average capacity of usable wood in each tree of approximately 6.8 cubic feet, but once the mill was in operation, they discovered that the waste was really between 20 and 22 percent and the average volume of each tree was only about 5.3 cubic feet. To overcome the problem, a sort table had to be devised so that logs with a high degree of rot could be channelled off to a chipper.

While that particular problem was solved, the management of Consolidated Bathurst, who seemed bent on having the project fail, continued to be thorns in Ray's side. Max Kator, the pulpmill manager, preferred to continue using round wood for his mill rather than take chips from the project at a fair price, and he flatly refused to take an increased quantity. Some of the company's obstruction was due to embarrassment at the way the pilot project had built roads and done a considerable amount of advanced forestry work on the lands the company had managed so poorly for so long. But there were definite political overtones to this obstruction; in fact, any decision made by Ray in Fredericton one night was known by the head of Consolidated Bathurst in Montreal by the next morning. And that head man happened to be Maurice Sauve, whose wife was Jeanne Sauve, at that time federal minister of Forests. Ray's relations with Mme Sauve were cordial—in fact, he served for a time on her advisory committee—but her husband had no intention that the pilot project should succeed, which it did not. A few years later, Clear Lake was forced to give up on the mill, at which point Consolidated Bathurst promptly took it over. On a visit to New Brunswick in 1991, Ray dropped by to see it and found it humming. Max Kator showed him around, and when they arrived in the planer mill at mid-morning coffee break, Kator called the staff over. "I think you better meet the godfather of all this operation," he said, without elaborating.

Ray's foreign travels resumed in the summer of 1973 when the Canadian International Development Agency (CIDA) asked him to head a team of technical forestry experts to Bangladesh. The team also included W. Locke, a pulpmill specialist, and the FAO's Dr.

LIFE AFTER POLITICS

George Nagle, a wildlife and forest expert who several years before had spent three years on inventory surveys in Bangladesh.

Bangladesh was still reeling from the devastating civil war of 1971 in which it won independence from Pakistan. The UN and many volunteer agencies had launched massive relief efforts, but much more than food and clothing was needed. The Bangladesh government had asked Canada to help finance a number of forestry projects and to lend technical assistance, particularly in developing timber tracts south and east of Chittagong. The principal mandate of Ray's team was to carry out a general overview of economic conditions and make recommendations.

Flying into Dacca, the capital, Ray could see the vast flatness of the lowlands intersected by watery highways connecting with the Bay of Bengal and understood why Canada was supplying river craft rather than trucks to Bangladesh. The Canadian team quickly confirmed that a steady supply of wood was vital to maintaining the economy of the country. Timber formed the primary base for all manufactured goods which were primarily lumber, pulp and furniture. Locally made wooden boats provided the means to move goods and people. Wood was also the prime material for housing, there being little rock or gravel, and the chief source of fuel, and trees such as the mango, banana and jack fruit provided food.

One of the first assignments for Ray's group was to check on a reforestation project in the highlands surrounding the deltas of the Ganges where most of the country's 75 million people lived. The difference in altitude between these so-called highlands and the lowlands of the delta is only three feet, but because the heavy rains of this region cause serious and continuous leaching of the high ground, Canada had earlier provided assistance for a highland reforestation program. This project, however, had not been in the best interests of the farmers in the lowlands where, because of the importance of food production, competition for fertile land is intense, and they counted on the continuous leaching to enrich their land. Ray's group found that in many instances recently planted seedlings had mysteriously died; on closer inspection they discovered that local farmers had pulled up the small trees, clipped the roots off and shoved the stems back in the ground to wither and die.

One of the more unusual proposals that the team was asked to report on was the planting of a forest barrier near the mouths of the Ganges to catch typhoon debris that would otherwise be washed out into the bay. These typhoons, spawned in the Bay of Bengal, move walls of water far up the delta; when they recede, entire houses and trees are carried out to sea and lost. A tree barrier, it was theorized, would catch much of the floating material and also provide another source of timber. The team decided it might work, but they could provide no assurance that it would.

Until the civil war, Bangladesh had grown half the world's supply of jute. Many of the mills had re-opened and were in production, but because of world-wide competition from synthetics, it was now necessary to find other uses for jute, such as pulp and paper-making.

When Ray's team examined pulpmills, however, they found major mechanical problems caused by the use of water which had not been properly treated to prevent corrosion in the steam boilers. Simple precautions, such as the regular tightening of machines on their bases, had not been carried out and the result was undue wear on movable parts and inevitable breakdown. They discovered that a number of European governments had financed pulpmills for which no fibre supply was available. In one case, sugar cane from which the sugar had been removed was to provide the raw fibre source, but that same cane had already been committed for fuel. In another, reeds had been identified as a fibre source, but the area where they had been grown in the past had now switched to more valuable products.

Up a river just east of Chittagong, the team visited a pulpmill located on a reservoir behind a hydro-electric generating station.

LIFE AFTER POLITICS

This poorly maintained mill had numerous problems, beginning with an infestation of an Australian water weed that was plugging up the reservoir, but its main problem was the fibre supply for its cellophane production. The principal source of local fibre was bamboo, but as bamboo alone cannot provide the quality required for making cellophane, the mill was importing high grade kraft pulp all the way from Sweden as an additive. However, during shipment to Chittagong, then trucking to the mill site, the pulp was improperly protected and the dirt it acquired spoiled much of it for use in cellophane manufacture. Ray's team was able to point out that the necessary additive could be manufactured cheaply from local fibre, thus giving additional employment to the people of Bangladesh.

Canada had been requested to finance the construction of a road from the mountainous area bordering Burma to a point on the coast just south of Chittagong, but when Ray asked for an inventory of the timber which would be made available for harvest if the road were built, he learned that no survey had ever been carried out. At the same time, he was told of a rumour that farmers from Burma had moved across the mountains and were practising slash-and-burn farming in that area.

Unless he could see the forests in the area himself, Ray told the local authorities, he could not make any recommendation about the road. A helicopter, he said, would do the job nicely, but the only helicopter known to be in the country was a huge Russian military unit designed to carry trucks and small tanks. The Russians had come to Bangladesh to clear the hulks of sunken World War II ships from Chittagong harbour after the UN had been unable to find the $6 million needed to do the salvage job.

Since there was no communication between the Russians and local government agencies, Ray appealed to the president of Bangladesh, and one of the president's assistants in Dacca made the arrangements. Before long, Ray and two government officials were sitting on the rear loading ramp of the helicopter, which remained open during the flight because of the heat. The three Russians operating the helicopter could communicate with neither Ray nor the Bengalis; however, as everyone aboard could read maps, pointing was the language used. Wherever Ray saw open areas on the ground, he would merely point down and the pilot responded. There were no signs of life until the helicopter began to descend; then streams of people would converge on the open area. By the time the helicopter touched down, it would be surrounded by at least a hundred forest dwellers, showing no fear of the aircraft or the moving rotor blades.

This reconnaissance showed that, although some of the slash-and-burn rumours were true, the forests were mainly intact and an access road would make timber available for manufacture. Ray recommended that Canada provide the technical assistance for road location and design and also support construction costs. He also emphasized that building the road was not enough; forest management and an infrastructure would be mandatory.

Ray's next CIDA assignment was in late 1973 in Peru where forestry was still in its infancy. There was no forest policy and no forest ministry, only a small branch within the Department of Agriculture. However, a request for a large forest harvesting contract had been submitted to the government by an American company which had a good reputation in land clearing but no experience in productive forestry, and the Peruvian government realized that before signing such a document—which would likely become the model for future contracts—they had better formulate a national forestry policy.

They turned to Canada for advice, and prior to sending a whole forestry team to Peru, CIDA asked Ray to go there to review the country's forest administration and make recommendations for ways in which Canada could assist. In Lima, he was met by the official who had arranged his itinerary. After a few days of briefing in the city, he set off in a Toyota—accompanied by a driver and two men from the Department of Agriculture—to drive to Huanuco, a large market centre high in the Andes to the northeast. The narrow road, though paved, twisted its way through mountainous terrain where thriving mines told of the country's mineral riches.

Near the top of the Andes, when Ray got out for a little exercise up the slope, he was quickly urged back into the car; the other passengers were familiar with the hazards of exercising in thin oxygen when you are unaccustomed to it. People who lived nearby, on the other hand, went about their chores normally, and in one village Ray even saw a soccer game going full tilt. At La Oroya a roadside sign announced the summit—4,843 metres—and it was here they spent the night in a farm workers' housing commune that had been jointly established by the government and a private company. There were 3,000 families subsistence farming on the dry and stoney soil of this area, although it could comfortably support only 450. Under a recently established land reform program, some of these families would be moved to the *selvas*, or lower slopes adjacent to the river, where the soil was more suitable for farming and grazing.

Back in Lima again, Ray sat in a disabled plane on the airport tarmac for three sweltering hours, waiting for it to be repaired sufficiently to fly him to Pucallpa. Near this town on the Ucayali River, a branch of the Amazon, 87,000 acres of forested land had been set aside, part of it to be cleared for agriculture and part earmarked for forestry. Here the logging companies floated their logs into lagoons when the river was high, then during the dry season when the river dropped as much as 40 feet, they winched them up to the mills. During visits to a pulpmill, a sawmill, a pole factory, a modern veneer/plywood plant and a parquet operation, he discovered that the supply of timber for all of these industries was haphazard, while transporting the finished products to Lima meant a week-long truck journey over the winding, hazardous road up one side of the Andes and down the other. Some years before, the German company that owned the plywood plant had experimented with a Canadian Caribou aircraft to transport its finished product from Pucallpa to Lima, but the cost had priced its plywood out of the market.

Ray was also bent on visiting the forest ranger station near Iparia, 40 miles south of Pucallpa. The trip took 3 ½ hours in a four-wheel-drive Toyota on the all-but-impassable road. Nearby, a Texan named Le Tourneau had cleared a large acreage for a cattle ranch, converting the logs from the clearing into lumber at a sawmill he had built for that purpose. He had already bought his cattle herds and hired his cowboys when the wet season arrived, turning the ranch into mud. After a few years he had cut his losses by giving both ranch and sawmill to the Peruvian government. However, the sawmill could be operated only 40 days a year because no provision had been made for a regular supply of logs. When Ray viewed Le Tourneau's cleared acreage, all that was left was the abandoned land-clearing equipment. The most interesting part about Le Tourneau's story was that he was the same man who had invented and constructed the Tree Crusher which had become irrevocably mired near Finlay Forks.

The government of Peru had been astute, Ray decided, to seek CIDA's assistance before signing the forest harvesting contract. Now they could start with a clean slate. His recommendations were wide-ranging, but were all ultimately based on adopting a national forest policy of sustained yield and selective cutting to replace the ongoing high-grading where only three or four species were being cut. Fast-growing varieties of the most desired species should be selected, he told them, and national forests established and directly managed by the government. The government would also need to build roads into promising forest areas and set up forestry schools to teach skills from technical to the professional level. He suggested establishing lines of credit through the Bank of Agricultural Promotion that would also enable small operators to take part in forest development. Finally, he told his hosts that they must actively seek foreign investment if they were ever going to establish secondary industries.

After Ray had given his report to CIDA, he returned to New Brunswick. It was now the fall of 1975. Back in British Columbia, Dave Barrett had just called an election for December 11, and Ray received a letter asking if he would come back and run for office again. The answer was no. He had put in his time and wanted no more of politics, but he did say that should Social Credit win the election and should he be needed in some capacity to help, he would come home. Social Credit did win, and in January 1976 Ray received another letter, this time from Don Phillips, the new minister of Transportation, asking if Ray would be interested in the job of chief executive officer of B.C. Rail. He was interested, but it was May before he was able to wind up his New Brunswick contracts and head for Victoria where he found that Premier Bill Bennett had other ideas. Would Ray take charge of British Columbia Cellulose Company instead?

B.C. Cellulose was the crown corporation which acted as the umbrella for four forest industry companies—Ocean Falls Corporation, Canadian Cellulose Corporation, Kootenay Forest Products Limited and Plateau Mills—all of which had been taken over by the NDP to save them from possible closure and prevent the resulting loss of jobs. The Social Credit government was determined to return these four companies to private ownership, and it would be Ray's job as chairman and president of the crown corporation to accomplish this.

To make sure that he was close to the day-to-day operation of the component companies, Ray also had himself made chairman of the board of Ocean Falls, Kootenay Forest Products and Plateau Mills. But when he approached the board of directors of Canadian Cellulose for a position on their board, he was turned down. The reason for their rejection went back to the end of the 1960s when it had become obvious to the board members—a strong international group—that Canadian Cellulose was failing, and they prepared to take over the company as it failed by buying up all available shares. To be certain that they had the inside track, they appointed a new CEO favourable to them, Ron Gross. About this time, the NDP's Bob Williams had decided that if his party became the government, it would take the company over when it failed. Ray had become aware of Williams' plans a day or two after the 1972 election when Williams, having heard a rumour that Canadian Cellulose had found a buyer, phoned to tell Ray that under no circumstances was he to approve such a sale. Ray, who was in the act of cleaning out his office, assured Williams that he had no such intention.

The NDP did take over the company, and Williams and his appointed representative, Ray Jones, immediately locked horns with Gross and the board of directors when the latter attempted unsuccessfully to get Jones to arrange for company shares to be released for sale so that they could buy them up. When Ray became head of B.C. Cellulose and the directors continued to stonewall him on the matter of a place on the board, he resolved the impasse by announcing that since he controlled the majority of the company shares, he would just have to vote himself onto the board at the annual general meeting. Shortly after this, they accepted him on the board, having that morning appointed Don Watson, formerly of Pacific Western Airlines, as their new board chairman.

The board members still hoped that since Ray's mandate was to return the company to the private sector, he could be persuaded to sell off some of the shares, but that was not what he had in mind. Within weeks after taking on responsibility for B.C. Cellulose, Ray had been approached by Pitt Desjardins of Weldwood and Bill Sloan of Pacific Logging who wanted to establish pulpmills so that waste chips from their lumber and logging operations could be utilized. They pointed out that when B.C. Forest Products Ltd. had entered into a joint venture with the eastern firm of St. Felicien to build a pulp mill in Quebec, 40 percent of the funding had been guaranteed by the federal and Quebec governments. Could the B.C. government take a similar minority position in a pulp venture to encourage the banks to lend the necessary additional capital?

It happened that at that time Ray was also trying to interest an Alberta firm, the Simpson Corporation, in a joint venture with Kootenay Forest Products—one of the companies under the B.C. Cellulose umbrella—and while exploring that avenue, he had become aware of the workings of the Alberta Energy Corporation. This enterprise, set up by the Alberta government, had been funded by the privatization of publicly owned assets in the petroleum industry; then once launched, the government sold shares to the people of Alberta. Profits for these shareholders were generated by assisting small ventures with their financing, either by undertaking development or taking a minority position, thereby increasing the corporation's holdings.

The success of the Alberta Energy Corporation gave Ray the idea that, if the four companies for which he was responsible banded together, a corporation similar to Alberta Energy could be formed and shares sold. This corporation would then have funds available not only to operate the four companies but also to take a minority position in new resource industries in the province. As in Alberta, it would then become attractive for financial institutions to provide the additional backing for such new enterprises.

Ray discussed his idea with Sloan and Desjardins who agreed that it would work. Next he took it to the cabinet to see if they would allow such a corporation to be formed. After lengthy deliberation, the cabinet told him to present his idea to a group of Vancouver financial experts to get their reaction. The meeting, held in Ray's Victoria office and chaired by financier Austin Taylor, concluded that the concept was feasible as long as Ocean Falls was not part of the package because they were convinced it would be a detriment to the sale of shares. They also decided that the three forest firms alone would not be "sexy" enough to attract investors. Other resources would have to be added.

In accepting the recommendations of this group, the government undertook to add certain oil and gas lands as well as the shares it owned in West Coast Transmission. The holding company formed was to be known as B.C. Resources Investment Corporation (BCRIC); subsequently, shares were sold to the public through the province's Department of Finance. Although the share price was set at $6, every citizen of the province was eligible for five free shares.

After the sale—one of the largest ever held for the sale of Canadian securities—Bill Bennett told Ray to stay clear of the new corporation, contending that he would give it the "smell of government." Bennett then appointed a board of directors from the private sector—all of them experienced in business and finance—but when Ray met with them, he found that none of them accepted the premise upon which BCRIC had been formed. They argued that investing only in the three major forestry firms making up the asset base and taking a minority partner position in new resource-based industries would not provide sufficient financial return. As a result, rather than sponsoring new developments (except for a few in oil and gas), BCRIC became associated with large enterprises such as Kaiser Coal and never fulfilled the purposes for which Ray had conceived it. BCRIC also became suspect in the public mind because of the scandal surrounding one of its directors, the president of Kaiser Coal, Edgar Kaiser. He was also the head the Bank of B.C., and as such, was largely responsible for the bank's policy of making major loans to real estate speculators. When the bank suffered enormous losses after the bottom fell out of the real estate markets, Kaiser was fired, and his fall blackened the already tarnished reputation of BCRIC.

With the establishment of BCRIC, Ray was no longer responsible for Canadian Cellulose, Kootenay Forest Products and Plateau Mills, but he had his hands full trying to find a solution for the problems of the pulpmill at Ocean Falls. Originally owned by Crown Zellerbach, it was hampered by an outdated pulpmill and a chronic shortage of available timber. Isolated some 350 miles north of Vancouver, the community could boast neither roads to the outside world nor a regular ferry service.

None of these problems were new. Towards the end of the 1960s, after worldwide efforts to find a buyer for the mill had proved unsuccessful, Crown Zellerbach had let it be known that it would be closing the mill. The government reacted by proposing to set up a ferry service connecting Port Hardy, Ocean Falls, Bella Coola and Bella Bella. Nothing, however, came of this proposal or any other government initiatives to improve Ocean Falls' circumstances. When Crown Zellerbach then restated its decision to close, Ray, who was minister of Forests at the time, had informed the company that by law the site would have to be left in its original condition. If instead the government decided to maintain the community there, Crown Zellerbach would be paid not more than one dollar for the site. He also reminded the company that it would lose the rights to the timber available for the mill, rights granted before World War I when the company had been established.

With these warnings in mind, Crown Zellerbach waited until after the NDP was elected in 1972 before again announcing plans to shut down the mill. This time the government decided to take over the plant and operate it. The two parties entered into an agreement—which was filed with neither the Forest Service nor Ocean Falls company headquarters, but came to light after Ray took on responsibility for Ocean Falls—that Crown Zellerbach would be paid almost $1 million for its holdings, most of which were housing mortgages, and that the company would be permitted to transfer its timber rights for use in its Elk Falls pulpmill. In return, Crown Zellerbach agreed to supply—should Ocean Falls require it—sufficient pulpwood at market price to maintain the operation for three years. The agreement also stipulated that if the document bore the authorized signature of the minister of Resources, Bob Williams, it would constitute a firm and binding agreement. The minister's signature was at the bottom.

It did not take long for Ray to discover that when the NDP took over the mill and provided loans to get it restarted, no capital improvements had been made to the plant or equipment. Instead, Acres Engineering had been hired to make a preliminary report on upgrading and expanding the newsprint mill, a losing proposition with its present capacity, but Acres found that the mill's hydro-electric plant could not provide enough power for an expanded plant. Next, Symonds Engineering was commissioned to do studies on converting the mill to the kraft process, but to be economically feasible, the mill—according to Symonds' estimates—would need to have a capacity in excess of 500 tons a day. The main problem in this scenario was that a chemical mill producing kraft pulp uses only the cellulose in the wood and therefore requires twice as much timber as a newsprint mill, and Ocean Falls was already suffering from a chronic shortage of available timber, made more acute by the re-routing of its timber supply to Elk Falls.

During the election campaign of 1975 the NDP was still promising that a new kraft pulpmill would be built in spite of the problematical timber supply, but the Social Credit government that was elected instead chose not to spend the $350 million which Symonds estimated would be necessary for the conversion. When in 1976 Ray distributed copies of the Symonds feasibility report to see if there was any private sector interest in establishing a kraft mill at Ocean Falls, there were no takers. There remained the possibility of interesting outside parties in taking over a newsprint plant that had the potential for expansion. In the meantime, in order to maintain production at about 300 tons a day, Ray instituted some improvements which could be tied into an eventual expansion.

During the next year the most serious contender for the purchase of Ocean Falls as a newsprint mill was the Kruger Company of

Montreal. When they backed off, realizing that it would be necessary to move the townsite and obtain additional power for the mill, Ray talked with the Aluminum Company of Canada at Kitimat about supplying sufficient power for an expanded mill, and he had Acres carry out a feasibility study to determine the cost of transmitting that power from Kitimat to Ocean Falls.

As for the proposed new community—necessary because the old town was in such a steep-sided fjord that no sun penetrated to it for five months of the year—a townsite on an attractive inlet ten miles from Ocean Falls had already been chosen by the NDP government. The Forest Service had been given the responsibility of planning the road to the new location, then contracting out the right-of-way clearing and preliminary construction work. Like all NDP projects, however, this job was completely unionized, and that fact plus the remoteness of the site made the costs exorbitant. Men and equipment had been moved in, but when Ray came on the scene, although most of the clearing had been completed, very little earth-moving had been done. He then gave the contract to a non-union company which built a tote road the entire distance at minimal cost. To provide a ferry dock, he arranged for the purchase of an old dock in Alaska and had it towed south and installed, also using non-union labour. While a design for the new community was taking shape, the Acres feasibility study was completed. The new transmission line would cost between $18 and $21 million, and as this was not unreasonable, Acres was authorized to proceed with the design and the necessary engineering so that contracts could be let.

All this positive activity persuaded Kruger early in 1978 to make a firm proposal to the government to purchase Ocean Falls, provided that there would be government assistance constructing the new community, that a transmission line would be constructed from Kitimat, and that there would be sufficient timber for an expanded mill. While there seemed to be no problems ahead regarding the first two provisos, Ray was having difficulty getting a commitment from the government on the matter of timber, although from information he had obtained on inventories and cut commitments already made on the coast, it seemed that it would be possible to arrange a tree farm licence or cutting rights for a mill of the capacity Kruger had in mind.

The government, however, sat on its hands for five or six months after Kruger's offer came in. Then, without consulting Ray, Bill Bennett contacted BCRIC's board of directors and tried to persuade them to operate Ocean Falls. Ray was astounded. Had Bennett forgotten that when BCRIC was founded the board had specifically rejected the Ocean Falls Corporation as a part of the package because they viewed it as a loser? BCRIC's answer was not long in coming: the board had not changed its collective mind. The corporation would not take on Ocean Falls.

And there the matter stood in the summer of 1978 when Ray and Gladys went on vacation to New Zealand. One night while there, Ray received a phone call from Don Phillips, his minister of report, who announced that Ray would have to come home immediately. "What for?" asked Ray.

"All crown corporations with surplus funds have to turn them over to the government. So you'll have to come home," Phillips explained.

"I can't do that, Don," Ray told him. "B.C. Cellulose is a legally constituted company. Only the board of directors could authorize that. Furthermore, we have obligations against a lot of the money on our books so it's not surplus. I'd have to assess our obligations before we turned any monies over to the government." In fact, those obligations included payment for the new ferry dock and the tote road.

"Well, I was told to tell you that you had to come home immediately and hand them over, Ray."

"And I'm telling you that I'm not coming home."

"Well," said Phillips, "don't forget I told you." And he rang off.

The reason for the order to turn over the funds was a financial crisis for Bill Bennett's government. It had been nearly three years in the making, but as far as Ray could see, it had been inevitable. During their term in office, the NDP had the benefit of the surplus that had been built up by W.A.C. Bennett, and they used it to initiate major changes in government policy—increasing social benefits, unionizing all construction projects, creating an Environment Department—but since most of these initiatives had only occurred in the final stages of the NDP mandate, no one had seen their costs translated into budget. As Bennett had come into office with many inexperienced ministers, he had made few immediate changes in policies or the bureaucracy that was handling them, and when Ray and other former ministers from his father's government had attempted to tell him what he was facing, he had ignored them. Ray, in fact, had read all the financial reports shortly after his return from New Brunswick and had gone to Bennett to plead with him to get his spending back under control. "For God's sake," he told him, "look what's happening!" On that occasion, an assistant to the premier, Norman Spector, was so pointedly rude to Ray that he never entered the premier's office again.

Now Barrett's chickens had come home to roost in Bill Bennett's barn, and with an election coming up the following year, Bennett needed to show a balanced budget or, better yet, a surplus. He hit on the idea of milking the crown corporation surpluses.

When Ray finished his holiday in New Zealand and returned to his office, no one mentioned the surplus funds. Fall came and as Christmas loomed, election talk grew and Bennett's chances for re-election began to look rather dim. In the midst of this, someone in government checked the books to see how they were faring financially and discovered that B.C. Cellulose had not turned over its surplus funds. Consequently, Ray received a letter signed by Bennett, his Finance minister and Don Phillips, ordering him to turn his surplus over to the Department of Finance immediately. He called a meeting of his board. The company had $10 million that was technically surplus, but there were obligations against nearly half of it, so the board reluctantly moved to give the government $5 million. If it wanted more, it could have the whole company because the board would resign. Accordingly, Ray wrote a cheque for $5 million and took it to the Department of Finance where the official who accepted it said, "Thank God! If you hadn't brought it in, I was told I had to come after you for it!" No one from Bennett on down ever mentioned the money again.

Meanwhile, Kruger's offer to buy the Ocean Falls mill was still open, but there had been no move by the government to make more timber available. It was, in fact, a continual battle for Ray to get enough timber to feed the mill as it was. Then to compound his anxieties, in the summer of 1979 the final engineering report for the transmission line came in: instead of the original estimate of $18 to $21 million, it was going to cost $55 million. Building it was now totally out of the question. Reluctantly, Ray advised Kruger that he could not fulfill their provisos and their offer was withdrawn.

At the beginning of December 1979, Ray came to the conclusion that there were no alternatives left. The mill was by this time losing $1.5 million per month. He would have to close it down, but with Christmas only weeks away he could not bring himself to announce the closure at that time. It would be less traumatic for everyone, he decided, if the mill were to close the following June when the children would be out of school and the shut-down could be made in an orderly manner. He arranged a meeting with Ian Barclay of B.C. Forest Products in which he pointed out that if it should become apparent that the major forest companies had wood lying around in storage that they refused to sell at a reasonable price to keep Ocean Falls operating, the public reaction to the companies and to the government would be harshly unfavourable. Barclay responded by assuring Ray that his company would supply wood for the operation of the mill until the following June. Ocean Falls was thus given the extra six months of life that Ray needed for it.

Under the union agreement, notice would have to be given to the employees by the end of March, after which time the closure would begin on a gradual scale. However, as the day the notices would have to be handed out grew closer, nobody in government had given Ray permission to close Ocean Falls. Ray demanded a meeting with the cabinet, and once it was set up, he had the lay-off notices printed and prepared to have them handed out on the day of the meeting on the four o'clock shift.

That morning, however, the *Province* newspaper carried a bold headline: OCEAN FALLS TO CLOSE. The story had been leaked to the press by Don Phillips who, knowing that Ray was going to have a hard time getting the approval of cabinet, had done it to force the government's hand. The cabinet would have to make a decision before the House began the afternoon sitting because the *Province* story would be the main subject of debate in the question period. Ray spent a frustrating two hours with the cabinet, explaining why the mill had to close, but even though he told them that he had made arrangements with the union and that he had his announcement ready, they continued to argue with him. Around 11:30 he was asked to leave the meeting and wait in Grace McCarthy's office until a decision had been made. An hour later they summoned him back. They had come to the conclusion, they said, that they guessed he'd have to close the mill, but he was not to announce it just yet. They would call in a public relations firm to gussie up the press release, and sometime the following week he could make the announcement.

Predictably, Ray blew his stack. The government could fire him, he told them, and do whatever they wished with Ocean Falls, but he was not going to have public relations people putting words in his mouth. By that time the cabinet had to leave for the daily caucus meeting, and Ray waited again in McCarthy's office. When it was over, Ray was told he could go ahead with the announcement but that the responsibility for shutting down the mill would rest on his shoulders. As soon as the House sitting began, Don Phillips would announce that Ray would be making a statement at four that afternoon in the legislature's press room. Ray was dismissed.

When four o'clock came, he announced that B.C. Cellulose was shutting down the Ocean Falls mill as of June 1980; at that same hour the workers received their lay-off notices. There was no negative reaction either in the media or the industry or in union circles, and within three days the closure was no longer news, much to the astonishment of Premier Bill Bennett who wanted to know how Ray had done it. Three months later the mill was silent.

As newsprint was in short supply at the time, Ray knew that closing Ocean Falls would affect several large contracts in the newspaper world, and he was not surprised when, shortly after the closure was announced, the Chandler family, publishers of the Los Angeles *Times* and Los Angeles *Mirror*, declared its intention to sue. The amount, however, was surprising: $30 million. Crown Zellerbach, the previous owner of the mill, was also affected by the closure because the company still owned the shipping line which held the contract to transport Ocean Falls' newsprint to Los Angeles. When the contract between the Times-Mirror Publishing Company and Ocean Falls was cancelled, the shipping contract was automatically cancelled, so Crown Zellerbach also announced its intention to sue.

When news of the forestry company's proposed suit got to Ray, he contacted the Attorney General's office to notify them he wanted to take counter action. "You can't do that," he was told. "Just drop it."

But Ray was not prepared to drop it. He phoned Tom Rust, president of Crown Zellerbach Canada. "Tom, you sue and on my own initiative I'll take you people to court."

"You'll take *us* to court?"

LIFE AFTER POLITICS

"That's right. For the improper transfer of the Ocean Falls timber licence to Elk Falls in 1973." Ray had already received assurance from lawyer Clarence Cooper, who had been with the Forestry Department before he retired and was familiar with the improper transfer, that he would take the case if Ray was prepared to pursue it. Which he was. He knew that if he made an issue of the timber licence transfer, it would be awkward for Crown Zellerbach officials because they were right in the middle of negotiating the sale of their Canadian company to Fletcher-Challenge of New Zealand. A court case would foul up the whole procedure. And so, like magic, within a few days of Ray's phone conversation with Rust, Crown Zellerbach dropped its threat to sue.

There remained the suit by the Chandler family. So far there had been no publicity about the case and Ray was grateful because the Times-Mirror contract was only one of several that had been cancelled. There were contracts around the world, including a very large one with Rupert Murdoch, the Australian newspaper tycoon, and a suit by Murdoch would have been far costlier and more difficult to fight than one by the Chandlers.

Ray was convinced that he could win the Chandler case as the reasons for closing the mill were legitimate, falling within the bounds of a *force majeure* clause in the contracts—in other words, conditions beyond the control of the company—but winning was not going to be easy. Fortunately, he had made many friends in the forest industry in the years that he held that portfolio, and one day he received a phone call from Seattle from one of them, a man who was now the forestry representative for a foreign government. "Ray, what's this I hear about Ocean Falls?"

Ray explained what had happened and his friend wished him luck and rang off.

By the spring of 1981 Times-Mirror Publishing was prepared to launch its lawsuit, although by now it had been reduced to a mere

$3.5 million, a sum closer to the company's real losses. At this point, the Attorney General's department advised Ray to negotiate a settlement. Ray refused.

"Well," said the Attorney General's representative, "if you want to fight them, it will be on your own responsibility!"

"So be it," said Ray.

It was about this time that he received another call from his friend in Seattle. "How are you making out with that lawsuit, Ray?"

"The examination for discovery is coming up, and Times-Mirror has lined up a battery of hot-shot lawyers to represent them, including former Chief Justice John Farris and some of his associates."

"It's really strange," said the Seattle friend, "that they would be suing when they have their own newsprint mill."

"What?"

"You didn't know? It's in Oregon."

Ray was incredulous. "Are you sure?"

"They've been in production since last November. Near Newberg, south of Portland." And he went on to explain the details.

If that's the case, why all the crying about no newsprint? Ray wondered. The next morning he and Gladys were on their way to Newberg. In the newspaper office there they went through the back issues and found an uncanny coincidence. For more than a year the paper had carried frequent articles on the progress of the newsprint mill's construction. Then at the end of March 1980—the very month when Ray had announced the Ocean Falls closure—all the newspaper publicity about it had stopped, and there were no further references to the mill in the local press.

Ray spoke to both the editor and the publisher. "Why was coverage of the newsprint mill cut off?" he asked. They seemed puzzled. "Listen," he went on, "that mill was finished ahead of schedule, and that's quite an accomplishment for the labour force. I'm surprised they weren't publicly commended."

"But the mill isn't finished," they insisted.

At the Chamber of Commerce, he asked again about the mill, but the staff there was also unaware that it had been completed. It was becoming clear that the Chandlers would go to unusual lengths to propound the myth that they did not have enough newsprint when they not only could get newsprint from Newberg but they actually owned the mill.

When Ray appeared before the examination for discovery, he was questioned for two or three days about the closure of the mill, but the prosecuting lawyers did not appear to know much about forestry or forest inventory. Afterwards, the frustrated lawyers announced that they would secure the services of forest consultants to challenge what he had said and that their testimony would be used in the trial. Later, Ray's lawyers discovered that several foresters in the province had been approached, but the prosecuting lawyers could not find one of sufficient standing who was willing to testify against Ray.

The case was assigned a date in court, but before that time came around, the files were removed from the court records. The Chandlers had quietly withdrawn their suit and gone home. Back in his office, Ray breathed a sigh of relief to be finally rid of the litigation. His phone rang. It was Deputy Attorney General Dick Vogel.

"You were right, Ray," he said graciously, "in sticking to your guns."

After the Ocean Falls pulpmill closed, Ray was pressured by the government for an early decision on the future of the town itself, but he was busy considering other industries which might move in to fill the gap and keep the town intact. He knew there was a large quantity of low-grade and decadent cedar in the forests neighbouring Ocean Falls because the mid-coast had been high-graded for many years and the profile of the forest—that is, the complete cross-section of species and grades—had never been cut. To Ray, it seemed possible that this cedar could be used to make oriented strandboard at the former pulpmill.

Particle board had been around for years as a substitute for plywood, as had strandboard, which is similar to particle board but with longer chips. Recent research showed that structural strengths comparable to plywood could be obtained if strands averaging three inches in length were laid down, somewhat like plywood, in three-layered sheets with the centre sheet of strands at right angles to the length-oriented outside sheets. This new product was known as oriented strandboard.

To find out if cedar would make a marketable product in competition with other strandboards and plywood, Ray initiated a series of experiments. Since the chippers used to form chips for pulp produced a fibre too short to provide the strength needed for strandboard sheets, Ray's first attempt involved the use of a flaker owned by MacMillan Bloedel and stored in the company's research building in Vancouver. When he asked to borrow it, however, he was told the company did not have such a machine. The person who had suggested it in the first place insisted that MacBlo did have it but guessed that nobody knew enough about it to understand what it was. When Ray went back, the machine was found and he was able to flake some maxi-chips to make the first board.

For the next experiment, which would have to be on a much larger scale, a maxi-chipper would be needed to cut strands of the right size. None were available in British Columbia, so Ray contracted a maxi-chipper operator in Wenatchee, Washington, to take his mobile chipper to Everett where he would cut chips from waste cedar trucked down from British Columbia. Next, a ring flaker to break the large chips into strands was located at the Weyerhaeuser Company which loaned it to B.C. Cellulose (which later purchased it). The next hitch occurred because it was discovered that cedar dulled the chipper's cutting edges very quickly; this was rectified by importing special steel blades from Sweden. Finally, when enough strands had been produced, they were sent to an experimental plant in Potlatch, Idaho, to be made into 4-foot by 8-foot sheets of oriented strandboard, after which they were tested at a U.S. government facility and certified as meeting construction standards.

In the course of this experiment, several German companies, who made most of the equipment used in the manufacture of particle boards and strandboards, became interested in how the cedar strands were being made, and subsequently a cooperative arrangement was made between B.C. Cellulose and a German company to fly six tons of maxi-chips to Germany. This resulted in ring flakers and maxi-chippers being incorporated into that company's new machinery—another step forward in the manufacture of oriented strandboard.

None of this benefited Ocean Falls because it had gradually become apparent to Ray that Ocean Falls would not be the appropriate site for an oriented strandboard plant. Converting part of the old pulpmill into such a plant was turning out to be impractical, and even had the required volume of waste cedar been readily available and assembled—which it was not—the cost of transporting a relatively heavy finished product of low value to market from the mid-coast would be uneconomical.

But by this time Ray was so caught up in the idea of using waste cedar for oriented strandboard that he began looking for an alternative site. The lower Fraser Valley seemed to be the most promising area because from the mouth of the Fraser to Chilliwack, on both sides of the river, there were at least 70 mills making cedar into shakes, shingles and lumber. Because cedar is toxic in land fills and few waste burners could meet smoke pollution standards, these mills traditionally used only high-grade logs with little waste, but if there was an industry nearby—such as an oriented strandboard plant—that could utilize waste cedar, these mills would be able to use lower grade logs. With this goal in mind, Ray secured a suitable site on the south shore of the Fraser near its mouth for a B.C. Cellulose mill, then carried out initial preparation of the property in order to proceed with the plant design.

Meanwhile, word about the potential of oriented strandboard had begun to circulate in B.C. Although it was being manufactured in central and eastern Canada and in the United States, there had been little interest in this province where plywood dominated the sheeting board market, and manufacturers were openly opposed to a competitive board made from waste. "If you make this work," a plywood official told Ray, "you know what it will do to the plywood industry!" And because that industry had powerful friends in government, it became impossible to secure government support for an oriented strandboard project on the lower mainland. Ironically, a similar plant proposed by an American company for Dawson Creek—but using aspen and poplar—was approved and underwritten by the government.

In recent years, oriented strandboard has come to dominate the sheeting market, but as Ray comments wistfully, "This is one wood product in which British Columbia does not provide leadership. Only recently has a modern plant been built at 100 Mile House by Ainsworth Lumber. Its owner, Dave Ainsworth, was one of the few who had encouraged the original experimentation. I think that if such a venture using waste had happened back when I was trying to push it, it could have benefited the whole coast wood industry in the same manner that pulp made from waste in the interior proved to be so successful. However, that opportunity was lost."

Although he had decided that Ocean Falls was not suitable for an oriented strandboard mill, for a number of reasons Ray was still convinced that it would be very useful to maintain a community there. The introduction of self-dumping log barges had practically wiped out the gyppo loggers in the mid-coast district because the gyppos, geared to production that could be boomed and towed out by tugs, could not collect enough logs to call in a barge. At the same time, rising costs meant that large companies could only afford to establish camps in selected areas where they could high-grade. Even then, it was too expensive for them to bring families into camp and provide the amenities for them, so they had to shoulder the cost of flying their workers in and out on rotation. It was Ray's theory, therefore, that Ocean Falls was in the right place to provide the kind of family community that all these companies required, a place where schools, hospital and medical care would be available. It could also provide the booming grounds needed for a wood-processing station where the gyppo outfits, which cut the whole profile of the forest, could tow their logs for sorting. Since the site had a good power source, the low grade timber could be chipped on site and sent on to pulpmills, while high grade logs could be sent down the coast from there by barge.

While engineering studies for this whole plan were being carried out, Ray began searching for a market for the small logs which came from the mid-coast. These logs, although valuable for lumber, had traditionally been chipped because there were no facilities for milling them on the coast. There was a possible market in China where the Chinese were already buying 40-foot, high-grade sawlogs from B.C., but it was not known what they were doing with them. Even Bill Bennett's group of business and industry people who had visited China in 1982 had not been allowed into the Chinese sawmills, only into furniture factories. Ray made contact with a man named Khoo, a Hong Kong medical doctor with special influence in Beijing, and suggested that the small logs he could provide would be a less expensive alternative to the high-grade logs China was importing. Was there perhaps an opportunity for a joint venture with the Chinese with B.C. supplying a small sawlog mill and showing the Chinese how to use it? Dr. Khoo agreed that it was worth investigating and arranged for Ray and several advisors to visit China.

In the meantime, Ray had been in touch with a gentleman in Vancouver named Paul Leung who, although raised in B.C. and apparently a UBC academic, actually vetted proposed business deals for the Beijing government. Leung agreed to investigate the response to Ray's concept during his next visit to Beijing, and in due course he presented a very substantial bill and a report which contained nothing Ray did not already know. Ray paid the bill but told Leung that his report was useless. Enraged, the man threatened to sue Ray and promised him that he would never do business in China.

In the fall of 1984 Ray took a team which included forester Ian Mahood to Hong Kong where Dr. Khoo had arranged everything for their trip to Beijing and the industrial city of Tientsin. At the Hong Kong airport the group was delayed for a long time before their flight to the mainland while the Chinese sorted out a mistake in the group's passenger list—Ian Mahood had been listed as Ma Hood, obviously a Chinese name, and Ian was obviously not Chinese. While they waited, Paul Leung showed up in the same departure lounge. He beckoned to one of the Chinese members of Ray's group, and having learned where they were headed, he again became enraged and threatened to have them thrown out of China. He almost succeeded: the next morning when the group wakened in the Tientsin Friendship Hotel, they discovered that Dr. Khoo had been up all night arguing with bureaucrats to prevent the group from being placed on the next Hong Kong-bound plane. Once this was cleared up, their hosts were most gracious, even putting on a huge banquet in their honour.

At Ray's insistence, the group was allowed into the sawmills of Tientsin, although they were required to put on jackets that were provided so that they would be dressed like the workers. They discovered that since the Chinese did not have long enough carriages in their mills to accommodate the 40-foot B.C. logs, they first had to cut them in half in the yard, destroying some of the lumber potential because the cuts they made were not at right angles. These mills cut lumber to order only for large contractors; then the huge amounts of waste produced were taken back to the yard where the small carpenters chose what they needed and hauled it away on their bicycles or donkey carts. Ray's team was subjected to a long harangue on the Chinese system by a commissar who actually knew very little about it, but the young engineers in the plant were very informative and very interested in what B.C. had to offer.

In the end, Ray was asked to make a joint-venture proposal for a sawmill, but in the meantime the commissar wanted a detailed report on the visit. It took Ray 18 hours to find a typewriter before he could prepare his report; the Chinese bureaucrats then copied it out almost word for word to make their own report on the visit. At the same time, Ray was busy trying to find more than $2000 to pay for the compulsory return banquet for their hosts. Since cheques and credit cards were not acceptable, it meant cleaning out the pockets of his entire team.

Although Ray returned home with the potential for a joint venture that would provide a market for mid-coast small logs, he learned that Don Phillips had become determined to close and dismantle Ocean Falls. To facilitate this, he installed Henry Wakabayashi over Ray to liquidate the assets of B.C. Cellulose. Ray now accepted the inevitability of the end of his great plan.

But the closure of Ocean Falls presented a new problem: the law required that if the hydro plant at Ocean Falls was dismantled, the dam also had to be destroyed, a demolition that would cost B.C.'s citizens at least $3 million. And if people stayed on in Ocean Falls, the government would have to install a diesel generator there. Ray therefore went to B.C. Hydro to ask them to take over the plant and put in a transmission line to Bella Bella. They refused, but one of their engineers, a young man named Tony Knott, proposed taking over the plant and the dam himself, providing Ocean Falls with power and running a transmission line to Bella Bella. Knott, however, needed a contract with B.C. Hydro in order to supply Bella Bella; fortunately for him, Hydro had acquired a new head about this time, Chester Johnson, who just happened to be the close friend of Henry Wakabayashi. As a result, Hydro suddenly became amenable to granting a contract and Knott took over the dam and power plant at Ocean Falls.

As liquidation of B.C. Cellulose's assets continued, Ray's job slowly disappeared. He had no regrets for himself, but he was worried for his secretary-cum-accountant-cum-assistant, Debra Ainsworth, whom Ray admits "did everything I didn't do." But the government also recognized her outstanding abilities and agreed to hire her for Economic Development, transferring her pension benefits as well. Ray was out of a job by March 1986, but by this time Jack Heinrich had become minister of Forests, and he asked Ray if he would act as his consultant. Ray agreed, but his services were seldom needed and he terminated the arrangement a year later.

On a personal level, the mid-1980s had been very difficult for Ray and his family. In January 1984 in the midst of plans to travel to Oberammergau in Bavaria for the Passion Play Festival, Gladys complained of tiredness and abdominal trouble. Within days it was diagnosed as a malignant pancreatic tumour, and although immediate surgery was scheduled, it was cancelled when her doctors realized that her condition was too advanced. With the help of the hospice society and dedicated friends, Ray made her as comfortable as possible at their Victoria home for the next four months. In June she was admitted to the hospice where her family visited and made their good-byes. She died ten days later. Gladys had been the major focus of her three children's lives as Ray's attentions had been fully absorbed first with education, then the airforce, then politics. Although she and Ray had found little time for holidays until 1975 when he left politics, they had made up for lost time after that with travel to Mexico, New Zealand, Spain and Australia and explorations of Canada and the U.S. Ray and Gladys had been married for 45 years.

In 1985, Ray renewed his acquaintance with Eileen Thumm, the widow of Walter Thumm who had been one of the first teachers he had hired when he became principal in Prince George. Walt had been on a sabbatical in Germany from his teaching position at Queens University when he died, and Eileen had returned to B.C. where she bought a retirement home in Gibsons on the Sunshine Coast. Ray and Eileen were married later that year and settled in Gibsons where they both became busy and popular members of the community. Eileen had surgery for breast cancer in 1986; the cancer recurred in 1995 and she died on April 3, 1996.

CHAPTER TEN:
Retirement

IN 1997, RAY GILLIS WILLISTON CELEBRATED his eighty-third birthday, but the milestone marked no diminishment in his activities. He still sails, still takes part in alpine hiking and still gardens with enthusiasm. More importantly, this milestone has also not diminished his interest and involvement in the government of this province, the forest industry and ecological concerns.

Ray has some regrets, but they have less to do with things he hoped to achieve than with the dismemberment by subsequent governments of initiatives begun during his term in office, in particular, forest and environmental policies. As soon as the Barrett administration took over, Dr. Peter Pearse, a professor of forest policy at the University of B.C., was commissioned to complete a report on forest administration and make recommendations for improved legislation. Pearse's report was not submitted until the dying days of the NDP's term of office, so it was the new Social Credit Forests minister, Tom Waterland, who had to interpret and translate it into legislation. Having come from a mining background, he had no forestry expertise, and he turned to a three-man committee of specialists for help. John Stokes, the highly respected deputy minister, represented the Forest Service on this committee, but he did not control the process because the other two members had ties to the Council of Forest Industries. It was therefore the Council's slant on forestry which was reflected in the new policies.

Ray was well aware of Pearse's views since he had been arguing with him for much of the 16 years he held the post of minister of Forests, and he was not surprised that in spite of the hearings that Pearse held across the province, the report he submitted sounded much like the policies he had been expounding all that time, with a strong emphasis on professionalism. In particular, he was offended that Ray's forest rangers were not professionals and that they wielded powers of administration beyond their capabilities. In contrast, Ray believed—and continues to believe to this day—that it was important to have forest rangers in the field with personal jurisdiction over every forested acre in the province, backing them up with professionals at headquarters who could provide them with expert advice. When a query or complaint came in about forest practices in any particular district, a radio-phone call from Victoria to the local forest ranger could provide headquarters with information about what was actually happening there.

Even before the new forest legislation inspired by Pearse's report was passed, the rangers, who had refused unionization when attempts had been made to organize them during Ray's tenure, were legislated into the government employees union and re-classified as "forest technicians." They were required to check into their offices at eight in the morning and five at night, somehow sandwiching hours of bush travel and minutes of inspection into the period between office appearances. As a consequence, they were soon out of touch with day-to-day logging operations. Unionization of the forest rangers also meant that the service's marine division could no longer operate efficiently, since in the past its crews had operated in the same autonomous manner as the rangers. This division was disbanded and all the forestry patrol boats sold; some of their work was taken over by aircraft, but the upshot of this change was that much of the coast industry was no longer subject to close supervision.

Unaware how the rules had changed, in 1976 after he took over management of B.C. Cellulose, Ray had called on the services of a forest ranger in the Kootenays. As he had to make a reconnaissance of his company's timber stands, he asked the ranger to meet him at six in the morning and take him by truck to the various sites which he wanted to inspect. The trip took all day and well into the evening, and when the ranger dropped him off at the motel where he was staying, the last thing he asked was that Ray not mention the length of the day they had put in or he would have to deal with the union representative. Had he followed the rules, the inspections would have taken days—and cost the province considerably more.

Looking back, Ray agrees that a new Forest Act was probably more than due. "I had worked through regulations and not through legislation," he explains, "because regulations could be changed in light of changing circumstances and conditions. Once you cemented something into legislation, it was very, very difficult to make adjustments, so it's true that I had made few changes to the administration of forests through legislation."

The new act, however, set up an entirely new forest system—guided by the key phrase "decentralization of administrative control." In place of the six forest districts that had existed—based in Prince Rupert, Prince George, Williams Lake, Kamloops, Vancouver and Nelson—dozens of new forest administration areas were established throughout the province. The old forestry stations were sold and construction of more grandiose headquarters for each administration area begun. But the cost of these changes had not been considered, and it soon became apparent that they were neither affordable nor necessary. In Bella Coola, for example, the cost of constructing and operating new offices actually exceeded the stumpage revenue coming from that entire district. The staff has since operated out of a few rooms in this large complex.

It wasn't until 1978 that Premier Bill Bennett began to understand what the full cost of completely reorganizing the forest administration was going to be, and he called a halt, with the result that the Forest Service had—in Ray's words—"done away with the administration of yesterday and hadn't replaced it with the administration of tomorrow." Instead, it was the views of the forest industry which influenced the remaining years of Social Credit forest policy. In the meantime, the environmental lobby had begun to catch the media headlines, but while many of these people had a sincere interest, they had no practical experience in guiding the administration of the forests. When they expressed their concerns to the Ministry of Forests, they could not get answers because Victoria no longer knew what was happening in the forests. And since the industry was no longer properly policed, the environmentalists' concerns increased and the industry became the direct target for their escalating criticism.

"I remember attending a public meeting in 1976 on the future use of the forests of the northwest coast," Ray recalls, "where all of the companies logging in that area were asked their intentions for the next decade or two. In every instance they indicated that they planned to carry on as they had in the past—high-grading the forest. Not cutting the profile—the average stand of timber that should have been harvested—but just taking out the quality timber. And this policy was allowed even though it was making it more difficult to harvest those lands that were both more expensive and less productive, but unless they were harvested they would never produce crops of quality timber. I argued with the bureaucrats at the time. I said that operators should have to take a percentage of the bad with the good, but my presentation was given no serious consideration. I was fairly depressed with what was happening.

"But I'll give this present [NDP] government credit," comments Ray, "with their forest codes and other new legislation, they're just beginning to get the damn thing back into some kind of control again. But the basic administrative structure is still not reacting to take advantage of opportunities. There are complaints everywhere about delays in timber sales and about the fact that foresters in both government and industry are spending more time in their offices wrestling with paper than they are in the forests bettering the standards of utilization. The fact that the Forest Renewal Fund has been allowed to build to such proportions without plans for using it is just a symptom of the larger problem."

Perhaps Ray's greatest regret lies in government's abandonment of his Environment and Land Use Committee model in favour of a Ministry of Environment. When the NDP government took office in 1972 a new Department of the Environment was set up under Bob Williams' Ministry of Resources with more than 170 people suddenly in control of all environmental matters, removing that responsibility from foresters, mine inspectors, water resources engineers and the other government workers in the field. "My philosophy is that looking after the environment should not be a bureaucratic thing but a practical application of firm policies. There is absolutely no way that people in offices writing each other messages can know exactly what is going wrong out in the field and do anything about it as it is occurring. The environmentalists that the NDP brought in were dedicated people but they had no practical experience with the administration of the other departments. They didn't know how to get to these people, nor did they have any power to make the bureaucrats of other departments carry out their policies. They could issue orders, but it was difficult for them to have them enacted or to police them if they did. You couldn't put enough watchdogs over the whole province to police all the civil servants who worked for the six or seven departments who could really influence what was happening in the environment. And that's the way it has remained—regulations and legislation after the damage has been done."

Since Ray's retirement, the Columbia River Treaty has also come back into his life through Dr. Neil Swainson of Victoria who wrote his doctoral thesis on the treaty in 1979 and has remained in close touch with officials in both Bonneville and B.C. Hydro. As a result of this connection, in 1994 when B.C. Hydro began experiencing difficulty in its attempts to open negotiations on the second 30-year term of the treaty, due to commence in 1996, the company bought up all the remaining copies of Swainson's thesis, *Conflict Over the Columbia*, as resource material for its negotiators. No one at Hydro, apparently, thought of speaking to the members of the team who had negotiated the first 30-year term.

In this second round of talks, the Americans began by claiming that an under-the-table agreement had been concluded during the first round to the effect that capacity benefits would no longer exist after 1996, thus greatly reducing the value of benefits after that date. After they produced papers to "prove" that this agreement had taken place, a Hydro official told Swainson of the problem, and Swainson responded by phoning Ray. Would Ray contact Hydro, Swainson asked, to supply them with information and/or advice? Ray obligingly phoned the head of Hydro and was told that if he wished to make a statement to be placed on the record, he could contact the Vancouver legal firm of Lawson Lundell Lawson & McIntosh in whose hands the investigation of the Americans' claim now rested. End of conversation. Since Hydro seemed very little interested in what he had to offer and Ray had no idea of the exact nature of the problem, it was unclear what he should make a statement about. As a result, he did nothing more.

Time passed while a member of Lawson Lundell criss-crossed Canada contacting everyone who might have information about the original agreement in order to counter the Americans' position. The results of her interviews were negative, and as Hydro would soon have to face the international tribunal set up by the terms of the treaty to resolve such disputes, the lawyers were getting edgy. Then one day a member of the firm chanced to meet former Attorney General Robert Bonner on the street, and recalling that he had "had something to do with" the original negotiations, asked if he could shed some light on their problem. Bonner, explaining that he could remember little of the details, asked what Ray Williston had to say about it. After all, he had been chairman of the negotiations.

RETIREMENT

Thus the lawyers finally called to enlist Rays's help nearly a year after he had offered his services. They had copies, they explained, of the irrefutable evidence that the Americans were holding to back their position, and Ray invited them to bring this evidence to his home in Gibsons. On the appointed day, a young woman lawyer appeared at his home and spread the documents out before him—and Ray began to laugh. She was not amused. What was he laughing about?

In the 1960s, after every negotiation session on downstream benefits, the American team had prepared a written report of the proceedings which they would submit at the next meeting. In each report—which they stated was an accurate report of what had gone on—they inserted the statement that the capacity benefits on the river would disappear at the end of the first 30 years because by that time enough nuclear power plants would have been constructed on their side of the border to handle the total base load for their system. Since their hydro plants would only be used to provide peaking requirements, they would no longer be run at full capacity and would not require specific regulation of the water supply from Canada. Having presented their reports, the American negotiators would then ask that they be adopted as the official accounts of the proceedings, at which time Ray would routinely refuse to allow a vote to be taken for their adoption, using a variety of pretexts for his refusal. In retrospect, he feels he should have stated clearly that the capacity benefits would only lessen if the nuclear plants were actually built—and he was firmly convinced they would not be—but at the time it was undiplomatic to say so because all of the American plants were either in an advanced planning stage or under construction. So the routine continued at each meeting with the Americans asking for their report's official adoption and Ray refusing to allow a vote. At the final meeting they spent several hours trying to force adoption, but at last they ran out of time without getting what they wanted.

Now the Americans—none of whom had been involved in the original negotiations—were contending that since this statement was in all of these reports, there must have been general agreement by both parties that this was in fact the case. The lawyers for B.C. Hydro had not understood that the real reason it was in all the reports was that there had been *no* agreement, and the Americans had returned again and again to the topic in an attempt to push it through. When Ray pointed out to the lawyer that the reports had never been adopted as official documents and showed her how the refrain had been re-phrased and repeated in all of them, she understood and asked if he would appear as a witness before the international tribunal. He agreed and promised to enlist the services of Gordon Kidd, one of his consulting engineers at the negotiations, to appear as well. Together the two men prepared for the tribunal, but three weeks later Ray received a letter from Lawson Lundell explaining that it would not be necessary for them to testify. It seems that when the Americans had been informed that the former head of B.C.'s negotiating team and one of his principal advisors would be appearing on behalf of the provincial government and B.C. Hydro, they had decided to drop their case.

Unfortunately for Premier Clark who then jumped in to take over the negotiations, he never asked Ray about the pleasures of dealing with the officials at Bonneville Power. If he had, he would have understood that Bonneville and the American Corps of Army Engineers had never wanted a treaty, believing that if they waited, sooner or later Canada would build dams on the river which would automatically regulate the flow on the U.S. side of the border at no cost to them. He would have known that they are still trying to get the regulation of the river for nothing. And he would also have known that officials at Bonneville are adept at finding loopholes and re-interpreting the wording of agreements. Not being informed, he charged into the negotiations, demanding a $250 million advance payment and annual payments for the next 30 years, and came out with what appeared to be an agreement. Bonneville, however, has suffered serious financial setbacks since the 1960s, having paid out millions for nuclear plants that were aborted before they began producing and been forced to take up the slack in the power supply which would have come from those plants. Therefore, while Finance Minister Elizabeth Cull was in the act of writing the $250 million advance payment into her budget, Bonneville Power was re-interpreting the agreement and cancelling the payment. What the annual payments will eventually amount to is anybody's guess, but no one has lately had the temerity to take pokes at the negotiating abilities of Ray's original team.

Unlike the many politicians who serve a term or two, then disappear into the boardrooms of industry or into retirement and are forgotten, Ray Williston continues to be recognized for his contributions to British Columbia, most recently in the form of an honourary doctorate at the University of Northern British Columbia. Much of this recognition has to do with the "hands-on" style in which he served this province, getting out into the field to find out for himself, really listening to his staff and giving them a free hand, and always avoiding new legislation in favour of regulations which could be adapted as conditions changed. "If you are willing to work by regulations," he says, "you are willing to take a chance." He took his chances, and as a result, the province is heir to a remarkable legacy.

Index

100 Mile House 148, 249, 280
Abbotsford 47
Acres Engineering 268-269
Acres (H.G.) and Co. 187
Acts, see BC Ecological Reserves Act; BC Environment and Land Use Act; BC Forest Act; BC Power Development Act; BC Water Resources Act
Adelphi 31
Agricultural Hall (Cloverdale) 36
Agriculture, see BC Agriculture (Dept./Ministry)
Ainsworth, Dave 280
Ainsworth, Debra 284
Ainsworth Lumber 280
Air Force, Canadian (RCAF) 44-50, 208, 284
Airlines, see Canadian Pacific; Pacific Western; Tyee
Airplanes, Caribou 262; DC-6 112; Elizabethan 209; flight training 46-49; Grumman Goose 112; Grumman Mallard 105
Airports, 224-225; Hong Kong 282; Lima 261; Tokyo 165; Victoria 85
Akihito, Prince 164-165
Alaska 46, 104, 159, 174, 197, 213, 269
Alaska Highway 46, 174
Alberni 233
Alberta 11-12, 15, 37, 74, 104-106, 138, 156-157, 265; see also Calgary; Edmonton; Lethbridge
Alberta Energy Corp. 265
Alcan (Aluminum Company of Canada) 99-100, 172, 269
Alexandra Forest Industries 212-213
Alexandra Forest Products 154
Aleza Lake 135
Allen family 29
Allenby 39
Allison Pass 44
Alpine Outdoor Recreation Resources Ltd. 233-235
Aluminum Company of Canada, see Alcan
Amazon River 261
Amber Ski Club (Princeton) 41
Amber tobacco 41
American, see United States
Andes Mountains 261
Andrews, Gerry 174
Anglicans 24
Archives, provincial 92, 221
Arctic Ocean 216
Army, American 23; see also United States Corps of Army Engineers; World War
Army, Canadian 14; Prince George barracks 61-62; Victoria huts and land 84-86; see also Air Force; World War
Arrow dam (High Arrow dam;

Keenleyside) 192-193, 202, 219
Arrow Lakes 171, 184, 186, 190, 219
Ashcroft 26, 160
Asia 250; see also Bangladesh; Burma; China; India; Indonesia; Japan; Korea; Nepal; Pakistan; Phillippines; Singapore; Sri Lanka
Aspen 145, 211, 280
Atlantic Ocean 140
Atlin 65
Attorney General, see BC Attorney General
Australia 125-126, 235, 259, 275, 284
Australian water weed 259
Austria 138
Automobiles, see Chevrolet; Mazda; Mercury; Pontiac; Toyota

Bahamas 234
Bailey, Harry 57, 60-61, 64
Balikpapan 253
Balsam 211, 234
Bands, see Music
Bangkok 251
Bangladesh 256-260
Bank of Agricultural Promotion 262
Bank of British Columbia 266
Bank of Montreal 98, 133
Bank of Nova Scotia 198-199
Banks, see also Canadian Bank of Commerce; Royal Bank; World Bank
Barclay, Ian 218, 272
Baron Byng Elementary School (Prince George) 58
Barrett, Dave 263, 271, 287
Basketball, in Princeton 42
Bassett, E.W. 184, 191
Bathurst (N.B.) 255
Bavaria 284
Bay du Vin 23

Bay of Bengal 257-258
Bayshore Inn (Vancouver) 249
BC Agriculture (Dept./Ministry) 92
BC Archives 92, 211
BC Attorney General 77, 89-90, 117, 120, 184, 188, 197, 274, 276-277, 292
BC Building Code 225
BC Cellulose Co. 263-265, 270-271, 274, 278-279, 283-284, 288
BC Centennial 92-93 (in 1958); 93, 243-244 (in 1971)
BC College of Education 82, 84-85
BCE, see BC Electric
BC Ecological Reserves Act 244
BC Economic Development (Dept.) 284
BC Education (Dept./Ministry) 11, 13-14, 16-17, 60-63, 65, 75-113, 117, 118-120, 128
BC Electric (BCE) 38, 92-93, 169-170, 178-181, 183, 187, 193-197, 202, 204-205, 231
BC Energy Board 183, 189, 192-193
BC Engineering Ltd. 172
BC Environment (Dept./Ministry) 244, 271, 291
BC Environment and Land Use Act 245
BC Environment and Land Use Committee 245, 291
BC Ferry Corp. 93, 199
BC Finance (Dept./Ministry) 75, 86-87, 94, 129, 188-189, 202, 208, 266, 271-272, 295
BC Forest Act 131, 150, 289
BC Forest Code 290
BC Forest Products Ltd. 115-116, 118, 120, 144, 154-156, 166, 213, 218, 264, 272
BC Forest Renewal Fund 291

INDEX

BC Forest Service (Forestry Service) 115, 135, 210-212, 228, 234, 267, 269, 287, 289
BC Forests/Forestry (Branch/Dept./Ministry) 117, 122, 129-130, 141-142, 145-146, 157, 217, 275, 284, 288, 290; see also BC Forest Service; BC Lands and Forests; BC Lands, Forests and Mines; Forest Management Licenses; Pulp Harvesting Area licenses; Tree Farm Licenses
BC Health and Welfare (Dept./Ministry) 90-91, 226-227
BC Highways (Dept.) 100
BC House (London) 174
BC Hydro and Power Authority 9, 153, 197-199, 202, 204, 210, 215, 217, 220, 234, 240, 283-284, 291-292, 294
BC Interior Forest Products 151
BC Lands (Branch/Dept./Ministry) 184, 191, 217, 223-245
BC Lands and Forests (Ministry) 94, 115, 117, 119-245, 284, 288, 290
BC Lands and Municipal Affairs (Dept.) 123
BC Lands, Forests and Mines (Dept./Ministry) 116-117, 170
BC Lieutenant Governor 217
BC Liquor Control Board 102-103
BC Mines (Dept.) 117, 121; see also BC Lands, Forests and Mines
BC Municipal Affairs (Ministry) 225-227; see also BC Lands and Municipal Affairs
BC Parks Branch 228
BCPC, see BC Power Commission
BC Power Commission (BCPC) 169-170, 179-182, 184, 186, 188, 191, 197, 199

BC Power Corp. 204
BC Power Development Act 197
BC Public Works (Dept.) 85
BC Rail 214, 263
BC Resources (Ministry) 268, 291
BC Resources Investment Corp. (BCRIC) 266, 270
BCRIC, see BC Resources Investment Corp.
BC Royal Commissions, see Royal Commissions
BC Supreme Court 131, 204
BC Surveyor General 174
BC Surveys & Mapping Branch 223-225
BC Teachers' Federation 53
BC Tel 39
BC Transportation (Ministry) 263
BC Utilities Commission 196
BC Water Resources Act 225
BC Water Resources Branch 225-226
BC Water Rights Branch 171-172, 176-177, 184, 215-216
BC Welfare, see BC Health and Welfare
Beech, Alan (Dr.) 27
Beech, Jack 30-31, 34, 55
Beech, Stuart (Dr.) 27
Beer, see Breweries
Beijing 281-282
Beirut 227
Belgian Congo 176
Bella Bella 267, 283
Bella Coola 127, 267, 289
Bellingham (Wash.) 36, 119
Bellos, Bill 59
Benguet Consolidated 234-235
Bennett, Bill (Premier) 238-240, 263, 266, 270-272, 274, 281, 289
Bennett Dam 218-219; see also Peace River
Bennett, W.A.C. (William Andrew

299

Cecil; Premier) 11-12, 15-18, 73-80, 86, 90-95, 109, 113, 117, 119-121, 126-127, 129, 143, 163-165, 169, 171-172, 178-179, 181-184, 187-189, 191-199, 201-208, 210, 216-219, 231, 235-236, 248, 271
Bentley, L.L.G. "Poldi" 138, 143
Beny, Roloff 164
Bessette, C.J. "Phos" 151
Bircher, Alan 98
Bjorne, Premier 11
Blackburn, Agnes 26
Blaine (Wash.) 37
Blair House (Washington, DC) 173
Blakeburn 39-40
Boards of Trade, see Chambers of Commerce
Bond, Mr. 21
Bonner, Robert 77-80, 89, 117, 120, 184, 188, 193, 197-198, 208, 292
Bonneville Power 194, 201, 203, 291, 294-295
Bonney, Parker 229
Borneo 252
Borthwick, Dave 243
Boston Bar 149, 249
Boyle, Harry 248-249
Breweries 24, 100-105
Bridgeman, Mr. 13
Briggs, H. Lee 181-183
Britain, British, English 14, 23, 66, 83, 139-140, 174, 178, 223; see also London; Scotland
British Columbia, see BC
British Thompson Houston Ltd. 175
Brooklyn Bridge 235
Brousson, Dave 237
Brown, Vic 161-163
Brynelson, Bernard O. 141
Building Code, BC 225

Bulkley Valley Pulp and Timber Co. 153-157
Burma 259
Burnaby 38
Burns Fry Ltd. 198
Burrard Inlet 181
Burrard Motel (Vancouver) 75
Busing, school 61, 87-88
Butchart, Mrs. Bert 30-32
Butchart, Shirley 32
Butchart, Stanley 32
Bute Inlet 130, 181

Cadet Corps (Princeton) 40
Calgary 46, 49
California 161, 234
Calvert, Phil 27
Camera 164
Cameron Commission, see Royal Commission on Education
Cameron, Max 53
Campbell, Harold 79-80, 84, 94-95
Campbell, Reverend 27
Canada-Alaska Railway 174
Canada Dept. of External Affairs 184, 191, 201
Canada Dept. of Finance 184, 202
Canada Dept. of Justice 184
Canada Dept. of National Defence 85; see also Air Force; Army
Canada Dept. of Northern Affairs and Natural Resources 171-173, 184, 186, 191, 207, 256 (Forests)
Canada Exchequer Court, see Exchequer Court of Canada
Canada Hotel (Prince George) 102-103
Canada National Energy Board 183, 189
Canada National Research Council 244
Canadian Armed Forces, see Air Force; Army

INDEX

Canadian Bank of Commerce 29, 98
Canadian Car and Foundry Ltd. 148-149
Canadian Cellulose Corp. 263-264, 266
Canadian Council of Resource Ministers 242
Canadian Customs, US border 35, 37
Canadian Embassy, Beirut 227; Japan 166
Canadian Forest Products (CanFor) 9, 129-131, 133-134, 138-141, 144, 149
Canadian International Development Agency (CIDA) 256, 260, 262-263
Canadian National Exhibition (Toronto) 45
Canadian National Railway (CNR) 16, 118
Canadian Pacific Airlines 56, 66-67
Canadian Pacific Railway (CPR) 23, 26, 28, 37, 43, 54, 118, 169, 226
Canadian Pacific Railway Hotel (Sicamous) 28
Canal Development Ltd. 161-163
Canal Flats 185
CanFor, see Canadian Forest Products
Canon (camera) 164
Cape Flattery 167
Carbon River 176-177
Caribou aircraft 262
Caribou Pulp and Paper Ltd. 159-161
Carney, Pat 156
Cars, see Automobiles
Cass-Beggs, David 220
Castlegar 170-171, 184
Catholics 68
Cattermole, Bob 213
Cattermole Logging 212
Cattermole Timber 154-156, 211
CCF Hall (Prince George) 17
CCF Party 12, 17, 19-22, 73, 79, 120, 195, 197
Cedar 277-279
Cedar Hill Crossroad (Victoria) 97-98
Celista 228
Centennial, BC, 92-93 (in 1958); 93, 243-244 (in 1971)
Centennial, Canadian, 93 (in 1967)
Chambers of Commerce (Boards of Trade), Newberg, Oregon 277; Prince George 12, 135-136; Victoria 85
Champion Papers Inc. 159-160
Chandler family 274-275, 277
Chant, William 85
Chantrill, Ralph 176, 178-180
Chase 33
Chave, Cyril 36
Cheakamus power house 179
Chetwynd 149
Chevrolet (car) 46
Chilliwack 88, 279
China, Chinese 281-283
Chip-n-Saw 148-150, 249
Chittagong 257-259
Christianson, Jack 232-233
Chuckanut Drive (Wash.) 34
Church Brothers 218
Churches, see Religion
CIDA, see Canadian International Development Agency
Citizen, see Prince George Citizen
Clark, Premier 294
Clarkson, John A. 91
Clayoquot Sound 115-117
Clear Lake Sawmills 255-256
Clearihue Building (Victoria) 95
Clearihue, Joseph B. (Judge) 84, 94
Clippers (logging machines) 146
Clotworthy, Alfred J. 76
Cloverdale 35-36, 43
Cloverdale United Church 43

Clowhom power house 179
Clyne, J.V. 128-129, 133, 154-155, 157
CNR, see Canadian National Railway
College of Education, BC 82, 84-85
College of Heralds (London) 93
Colleges, see College of Education; College of Heralds; Vancouver Normal School; Victoria College; Victoria Normal School; Universities
Collier, Andy 26, 30
Columbia Cellulose 153-156, 158
Columbia River Engineering Board, see International Columbia River Engineering Board
Columbia River power development and dams 161, 170-174, 178-179, 182-185, 187-189, 192-196, 199-205, 208, 210, 214, 219, 220, 222, 236, 291-292
Columbia River Treaty 184, 191-193, 195-196, 200-210, 214, 220-222 (book), 291-295; see also International Joint Commission
Columbia Storage Power Exchange 205, 210
Cominco Mining and Smelting 169
Condel Hotel (Fort St. John) 65
Conflict Over the Columbia (thesis) 292
Congo, Belgian 176
Connaught Elementary School (Prince George) 7
Conservative Party and government 11, 21, 75, 169, 173-174, 178-179, 186, 198, 202, 205, 238
Consolidated Bathurst Co. 157, 255-256
Cooper, Clarence 275
Copper Creek 184-185, 191
Copper Mountain 39
Corps of Army Engineers, see United States Corps of Army Engineers

Council of Forest Industries 128, 287
Council of Resource Ministers, Canadian 242
Courts, see BC Supreme Court; Exchequer Court of Canada; United States Court of Appeals
Craigdarroch Castle (Victoria) 83
Craigflower Elementary School (Victoria) 25
Cram, Jack 227-228
Cranbrook 118, 161, 163, 168
Cranbrook High School 163
Crescent Spur 16, 146
Crestbrook Pulp and Paper 163
Crippen, Glen 172
Crippen-Wright Engineering 172, 187, 185, 191
Crow's Nest Coal 161-162
Crown Zellerbach 118, 127, 138, 147, 151, 154, 158, 166, 229, 267, 274-275
Cull, Elizabeth 295
Cultus Lake 236-237
Customs, Canadian/US border 35, 37
Cutt, Bill and Mrs. 102-104
Cypress Bowl 233-235
Cypress Mines 161
Cypress Provincial Park 235

Dacca 257, 259
Dahl, John 211, 213
Daishowa Paper Manufacturing Ltd. 159-161
Dams, see Arrow; Bennett; Columbia River; Diablo; Duncan; Gorge; Keenleyside; Kootenay River; Libby; Mica; Peace River; Portage Mountain; Revelstoke; Ross; Seven Mile
Davis, Jack 209
Dawson Creek 280

INDEX

DC, see Washington (DC)
DC-6 (plane) 112
Decker, Garth 9
DeGrace, Larry 135-136, 139, 142
DeLach, Christian 242
Deluka, Geneen 158
Depression 33, 88
Desjardins, Pitt 160, 264-265
DeWolf, John 198
Dezell, Cliff 21
Dezell, Denise 21
Dezell, Garvin 21-22, 101
Diablo dam 236, 238
Didsbury (Alta.) 37
Diefenbaker, John 193, 200-201, 241-242
Diptheria 46
Disneyland 174
Doctorate, Honourary 295
Dogwood trees 93, 164-166
Doman, Herb 150
Dominion Construction Co. Ltd. 166
Dormitories, school (in Prince George) 7, 61-64
Dorr Diversion 185
Douglas, C.H. (Major) 11-12
Douglas Channel 158
Douglas firs 166-168, 229
Douglas Lake Cattle Ranch 112
Doukhobors 88-92
Downie Creek 184, 219
Drama, theatre 36-37, 40
Drumheller 46
Duchess Park area/school (Prince George) 58-59
Duncan dam 192-193, 202, 219
Duncan Lake 184-186, 190
Duncan River 219
Dunsmuir, Robert 83
Dunster 19
Dutch 251

East, Charlie 61
East Kootenay Power and Light 169, 195-196
East Kootenay region, see Kootenay
Eburne Sawmill 149
Ecological Reserves Act, BC 244
Ecological reserves and parks 228-245
Economic Development (BC Dept.) 284
Eddy (E.B.) Company 23
Edmonton 15, 47, 106, 182, 226
Edmonton Journal newspaper 69
Education 24-25, 28-29; busing 61, 87-88; Dept./Ministry of Education 11, 13-14, 16-17, 60-63, 65, 78-113, 117-120, 128; dormitories 7, 61-64; inspector 65-71; principal/district administrator 53-65; teaching 30-34, 49-53; textbook rentals 60-61; see also Colleges; Schools; Universities
Egypt 176
Eisenhower, President 171, 192-193
Elbow Park (Calgary) 46
Elizabethan (plane) 209
Elk Falls 267-268, 275
Elk's Hall (Princeton) 39
Elmwood Cemetery (Winnipeg) 23
Embassy, Canadian, in Beirut 227; Japan 166
Empress Hotel (Victoria) 139, 248
Emsley Cove 158
Enderby 34
Enemark, Spike 21
Enemark, Tex 21
Energy Board, BC 183, 189, 192-193; National 183, 189
Engineering Record (publication) 200
England, see Britain
English Bay (Vancouver) 38
Enso-Gutzeit Oy 158

303

Environment, see BC Environment (Dept./Ministry)
Environment and Land Use Act, BC 245
Environment and Land Use Committee, BC 245, 291
Environmental Endowment Fund (Ross dam) 238-239
Ernest, John 149
Espley, Ed 92
Essondale 227
Eurocan Pulp and Paper Ltd. 157-159
Europe 46, 50, 93, 138, 140, 158-159, 241, 258; see also Austria; Britain; Dutch; Finland; Germany; Italy; Poland; Russia; Scandinavia; Scotland; Spain; Sweden; Switzerland
Evans, Magistrate 92
Everett (Wash.) 278
Evergreen Lumber Sales 116, 120
Ewing Building (Victoria) 84-85
Exchequer Court of Canada 125, 208
Exhibitions, see Canadian National Exhibition; Centennial; Expo
Experimental Station (Aleza Lake) 135
Expo 70 (Osaka) 163, 166-168
External Affairs, see Canada Dept. of External Affairs

Fadear Creek Lumber 151
Fairey, Francis T. (Frank; Dr.) 14, 16-17, 62, 71, 78-79
Fairs, see Canadian National Exhibition; Expo
FAO, see United Nations
Farquhar, Hugh 94-96
Farris, John 276
Farstad, Al 161-163
Feldmuehle Pulp and Paper Co. 139, 144

Feller-bunchers 146
Ferguson, Doc 28
Ferguson, Noel 122-124
Ferries, see BC Ferry Corp.
Fiji 24
Finance, see Banks; BC Finance (Dept./Ministry); Canada Dept. of Finance
Finland, Finns 158-159
Finlay Forks 211-212, 217, 262
Finlay River 174, 176-177, 211
Fisher, J.V. (Dr.) 184
Fisher, Johnny 20-21
Fisher, Rosabelle (Williston) 20, 24, 37, 39
Flag, provincial 93
Fleming, Donald 202
Fletcher-Challenge 275
Floen, Alex 11
Flying school, see Air Force
FML, see Forest Management Licenses
Foley, Joe 133
Food and Agricultural Organization, see United Nations
Ford Motor Co. 133
Forest fires 94, 136
Forest Management Licenses (FML) 77, 115-116, 119, 122; see also Pulp Harvesting Area licenses; Tree Farm Licenses
Forests and forestry, in Bangladesh 256-260; BC 115-284; Indonesia 250-254; New Brunswick 248-250, 254-256; Peru 260-263
Fort George riding 15-16, 18, 21, 73, 97, 99-100, 105, 108, 247
Fort Nelson 67
Fort Nelson Indian School 67
Fort St. James 214
Fort St. John 65, 108-109, 176
Fortin, J.M.E. 211-212

INDEX

Fox, Ted 92
Fraser Canyon 34
Fraser River 25, 38, 172-173, 183, 279
Fraser Valley 74, 95, 249, 279
Frazer Co. 144
Fredericton (N.B.) 248, 250, 255-256
French 112, 241
Fulton, E. Davie 184, 186-188, 191-192, 205

Gabriel, Elizabeth Anne, see McCalman
Gabrielle, Chuck 11-12
Gaglardi, Phil 94
Ganges River 257-258
Georgia Strait 181
Germany, Germans 102, 139, 174-175, 261, 279, 285; see also Bavaria
Gibb, Cliff 37-39, 49
Gibb, Lizzy 23
Gibson, Gordon (Sr.) 115-117
Gibsons (BC) 285, 293
Gilliland, Harry 94
Gillis, Jack 24
Ginter, Ben 99-102, 104-105, 158-159
Glade (BC) 90
Goodfellow, J.C. (Rev.) 43-44
Gordon Head (Victoria) 84-85, 94
Gore, Bernard 174-175
Gorge Dam 236, 238
Goulding, Bill and family 46
Government, see BC; Canada; Canadian; Political parties
Grand Forks 90
Grandview Heights School (Surrey) 35
Grant, Bill 65, 70
Grauer, Dal 180
Gray, Arthur Wellesley 123-124
Gray, H. Wilson "Wick" 116, 120
Gray, Percy 174-175
Great West Life Insurance Co. 26

Greater Victoria Teachers' Association 16-17
Green, Howard 184
Greenwich (England) 223
Gross, Ron 264
Grosvenor Hotel (Vancouver) 43
Grumman Goose plane 112
Grumman Mallard plane 105
Gunderson, Einar 75

Hall, T.R. 32
Halle, Pentii 158-159
Hamilton, Alvin 184
Hammond, Terry 13
Hamre, Ed 35-36
Hanusak, Rudy 255
Harding, Randolph 198
Harrison Lake 237
Hart, John 169
Harvard University 126
Hawaii 207
Hayashi, Yoshio 9, 166
Haymore, Eddie 226-228
Health, see BC Health & Welfare; Hospitals
Hearn, Mrs. C. 63
Hebrides 24
Heinrich, Jack 284
Hendon 30-33
Heraldry 93
Herbert Spencer Elementary School (New Westminster) 50
Hermes (typewriter) 124-125
Hickman, Harold (Harry; Dr.) 83, 94
Higgins, Larratt 200
High Arrow dam, see Arrow
Highway 2 (US) 34
Highway 99 (US) 34
Highway Garage (Cloverdale) 35-36
Highways, see Alaska; BC Highways (Dept.); Highway 2; Highway 99;

Hope-Princeton; Pacific;
Trans-Canada
Ho-O Maru (ship) 167-168
Hodson, Stuart 199
Hoffman, Paul 241
Hoffmeister, Bert 129
Holding, Art 151
Holding Lumber Co. 151
Homathco River 181
Hong Kong 281-282
Honshu Pulp and Paper 161, 163, 168
Hope 44, 74, 107, 235, 238
Hope-Princeton Highway 238
Hope-Princeton Trail 44
Hospitals 225; Nanaimo 230; Ocean Falls 280; Prince George 64-65; Vancouver 20
Hotel Georgia (Vancouver) 108
Hotel Vancouver 53, 179
Houston 153
Howard, Frank 121
Howard, Ron 131-132
Huanuco (Peru) 261
Hudson's Bay property (Victoria) 84-85
Hudson's Hope 176-177, 219
Huff, Walter and family 35
Hull (Quebec) 23
Hume Hotel (Nelson) 90
Hydro-electric power, see BC Hydro; Dams; Hydro Quebec; Manitoba Hydro; Ontario Hydro
Hydro Quebec 242
Hyndman, Peter 238

IBP, see International Biological Program
ICREB, see International Columbia River Engineering Board
Idaho 278
Idians (Charles) & Sons 24-25
IJC, see International Joint Commission

Imperial Hotel (Tokyo) 164
Imperial Tobacco 200
India 176
Indians, see Native
Indonesia 250-254
Industrial Forest Service Ltd. 135
Ingersoll (Ont.) 140
Ingledow, Tom 179-180
Intercontinental Pulp and Paper 144-145
International Biological Program (IBP) 242, 244
International Columbia River Engineering Board (ICREB) 170, 184-185
International Council of Scientific Unions 242
International Joint Commission (IJC) 170-173, 183-184, 190, 200-201, 203, 236-238, 240
International Utilities 182
Invermere 185
Iparia (Peru) 262
Ireland, Willard 92
Irving, Jim and family 248-249
Irwin, Bert (Pop) 41
Irwin, Bertie 41
Irwin, Billy 41
Irwin, Maisie 41
Irwin, Myrtle 36
Irwin, Tom 73
Isle of Islay 24
Israel 175
Italy 217; see also Rome
Izowski, Nestor 12-13

Jackson, Nina 41
Jackson, "Scoop" 206
Jakarta (Indonesia) 251
Jake 32-33
Japan, Japanese 159, 161-168, 174, 254

INDEX

Japanese Consulate (Vancouver) 165
Jasper 54, 105, 118
Java 251
Johnson, Byron "Boss" 11, 79
Johnson, Chester 283
Johnson, Lyndon (President) 210
Jones, Ray 264
Joseph, Mr. 251
Juneau (Alaska) 197
Justice, see Canada Dept. of Justice; Law

Kaiser Aluminum Corp. 170-171
Kaiser Coal 266
Kaiser, Edgar 266
Kalamalka Lake 113
Kalimantan 252-254
Kamloops 34, 105-107, 151-152, 249, 289
Kamloops Lumber 151
Kamloops Pulp and Paper 151, 153
Kator, Max 256
Keenleyside Dam 219
Keenleyside, Hugh (Dr.) 182, 184, 187, 191, 199, 206, 208, 219-220
Keller, Betty 8-9
Keller, John 60
Kellogg Foundation 15
Kelowna 113, 196, 226-227, 250
Kemano 99
Kennedy, President 192, 202
Kennedy Siding 211
Kennedy stop 38
Kettle Valley railway 118
Khoo, Dr. 281-282
Kickinghorse Timber Products Ltd. 161-162
Kidd, Gordon 172-173, 191, 294
Kiernan, Kenneth (Ken) 92, 117, 199, 243
Killy, Ivor 145

Kinbasket Lake 220
King, Lou 16-18
Kinnear, Axel 245
Kirk, Jack 36-37, 43
Kirk, Ray 36
Kitimat 153, 157-158, 172, 269
Klagges, Hans (Dr.) 139-140, 144-145
Knight Inlet 130
Knott, Tony 283-284
Kobe (Japan) 167
Kochum 149
Kootenay Forest Products Ltd. 263, 265-266
Kootenay Lake 90, 170, 184, 219
Kootenay River 170, 184-185
Kootenay River dams 170
Kootenay Valley, region 88, 161, 163, 169, 185-187, 190, 288
Korea 254
Krajina, V.J. (Dr.) 242, 244
Krestova 90
Kruger Co. 268-270, 272
Krutilla, John (Dr.) 221

La Oroya (Peru) 261
Labatt's Brewery, Prince George 100-102; Victoria, 24
Ladner 24-25
Laing, Arthur 207
Lajoie power house 179
Lakes, see Aleza; Arrow; Clear; Cultus; Douglas; Duncan; Harrison; Kalamalka; Kinbasket; Kootenay; McNaughton; Moberley; Moose; Okanagan; Ross; Shuswap; Slocan; Summit; Takla; Williams; Williston
Lancaster, Jake 39
Lands, see BC Lands (Depts/Ministries)
Langley 37
Lansdowne campus (Victoria) 83, 85, 95

Larson, Peter (Dr.) 243
Lash, A.W. 191
Latchford River 172
Law, see Acts; BC Attorney General; Canada Dept. of Justice; Courts
Lawson Lundell Lawson and McIntosh 292, 294
Lebanon 227
Leboe, Bert 16, 22, 146
LeClair, Spike 27
Lee, F. Arthur 182
Legion (Prince George) 98-99, 102
Legislation, see BC Ecological Reserves Act; BC Environment and Land Use Act; BC Forest Act; BC Power Development Act; BC Water Resources Act; and entries under Government
Lesage, Jean 171-173
Lethbridge 118
LeTourneau (R.G.) Tree Crusher 211-213, 262
Lett, Sherwood (Chief Justice) 204
Leung, Paul 281-282
Levesque, Father 68-69
Levesque, Rene 241-242
Lewis, Dean 54
Lewis family 33
Lewis, Slim 39
Libby 170, 189
Libby Dam 170-171, 184-186, 189, 191
Liberal Party and government 11-14, 21-22, 99, 115, 169, 172-173, 201-203, 207, 209, 233, 237
Licenses, see Forest Management Licenses; Pulp Harvesting Area licenses; Tree Farm licenses
Liersch, John 133, 140-142, 149
Lieutenant Governor, BC 217
Lillooet 115

Lima (Peru) 260-262
Liquor Control Board, BC 102-103
Lloyd, Donna 9
Locke, W. 256
Lodgepole pine 142, 145
London (England) 93, 140, 174
Lone Butte 148
Long, Ken 151-152
Lord, Arthur (Judge) 116
Los Angeles 274
Los Angeles Mirror newspaper 274
Los Angeles Times newspaper 274
Lost Lagoon (Stanley Park) 38
Lower Arrow Lake, see Arrow Lakes
Lower Mainland 170, 202, 217; see also Fraser Valley; Vancouver
Loyalists, United Empire 23
Lucas, Bill 38-39, 42
Luce, Charlie 201, 203, 206
Lulu Island 25-26
Luxor (BC) 185

MacBlo, see Macmillan Bloedel
Macfarlane, Alan 233
MacGregor, Malcolm (Dr.) 92
Mackenzie (BC) 154, 213
Mackenzie, Alexander 213
Macmillan brothers 148
Macmillan Bloedel Ltd. (MacBlo) 118, 128-134, 138, 140-141, 144, 153-158, 166, 249, 278
Macmillan, H.R. 128, 130-132, 141
Magee High School (Vancouver) 79
Magnuson, Warren 206
Mahood, Ian 141-142, 144, 282
Maillardville 24
Mainwaring, William C. (Bill) 178, 195
Malaysia 253
Manilla (Phillipines) 234
Manitoba 99, 104, 181, 196; see also Winnipeg

INDEX

Manitoba Hydro 196
Maps, for schools 224; see also BC Surveyor; BC Surveys and Mapping Branch
Marpole (Vancouver) 25
Marriage 43, 285
Marriott, Earl 65
Marshall Plan (Europe) 241
Martin, Jack 41
Martin, Paul 201-202, 204, 206-208, 210
Mather, Barry 122
Mazda (car) 249
McBride 16, 18-19, 22, 61, 74, 105, 146
McCalman, Elizabeth Anne (Gabriel) 23-25
McCalman, Islay, see Williston
McCalman, Peter 23-25, 27-28
McCance, Larry H. 93
McCarthy, Grace 273
McDonald family 56
McDonald, John (Dr.) 95
McGugan, Colonel 103-104
McInnes, Doris 42
McInnes, Gladys, see Williston
McInnes, May 42-44
McInnes, Neil 42
McInnes, Rhea 47
McInnes, Roberta 43, 56
McKee, Gerry 125-126
McKenzie, Norman A.M. (Dr.) 82-84, 86, 95
McKinnon, F.S. "Finn" 126
McKinnon Gymnasium (Victoria) 96
McMahon, Frank 109
McNaughton, A.G.L. (General) 173, 183-186, 190-191, 200-201, 220
McNaughton Lake 220
McNeil, Fred 132-133
McNeil, Jack 105-107
McTaggart-Cowan, Ian (Dr.) 243

Melody Four/Five/Six (band) 28-29
Mercury (car) 66
Merritt 107
Mexico 248, 284
Mica Creek 184-186, 220
Mica Dam 192-193, 202, 220
Michiko, Princess 164-165
Milburn, George 59
Miles-Pickup, H. 212
Miller, Ellen 122-123
Mining, see Alcan; Allenby; BC Lands, Forests and Mines; BC Mines; Blakeburn; Cominco; Copper Mountain; Crow's Nest; Cypress Mines; Kaiser; Nickelplate; Nine-Mile; Noranda; Waite Amulet Mines
Miramichi 23
Mitsubishi Co. 161, 163
Moberley Lake 66-67
Moberley Lake School 66-67
Mobraaten, Tom 42
Moffat, Alex 18, 111
Moffat, Harold 18-19, 55, 57-58, 61-62, 135, 230, 240
Moffat, Helen 19, 230
Molson's 104
Mongolia 7
Montana 170
Montreal 241-242, 256, 269
Montreal Engineering Ltd. 173, 186-188
Moose Lake 105-106
Mortimer, G.E. 79
Moss, Alan 250
Moss family 37
Mount Bruce 77
Mount Robson Park 105
Mountains, see Andes; Copper; Mount Bruce; Mount Robson; Portage; Rocky

Mountainview (Ont.) 45
Municipal Affairs, see BC Lands and Municipal Affairs; BC Municipal Affairs
Murdoch, Rupert 275
Murdoch, Sally 9
Murphy Creek 184
Museums 92
Music, bands, in Penticton 41; Salmon Arm 28-29

Nagle, George (Dr.) 256-257
Nanaimo 230, 243
Nanaimo Hospital 230
National Energy Board 183, 189
National Exhibition, Canadian 45
National Forest Products 141-142, 144
National Research Council 244
Native people 67-70, 175
Nazi Party 138, 175
NDP, see New Democratic Party
Nechako [River] lake system 99
Nelson (BC) 90-92, 289
Nelson, Barry 255
Nelson, Elmer 11
Nepal 250
Nesbitt, James K. 119, 165
New Brunswick 23, 157, 166, 220-221, 248-250, 254-256, 263, 271
New Democratic Party (NDP) and government 205, 220, 227, 233, 237-238, 244, 247, 263-264, 267-269, 271, 287, 290-291
New Denver 90-92
New Westminster 38, 49-50, 54, 102
New York 171, 199, 250
New Zealand 64, 270-271, 275, 284
Newberg (Oregon) 276
Newfoundland 241

Newspapers, see Edmonton Journal; Los Angeles Mirror; Los Angeles Times; Murdoch, Rupert; Paris Match; Prince George Citizen; Southam; Times-Mirror; Vancouver Province; Vancouver Sun; Victoria Colonist; Victoria Times
Niagara Falls 179, 216
Nickelplate Mine 40
Nicks, William F. 198-199, 204
Nicola Valley Sawmills 151
Nimpkish Valley 130
Nine-Mile Coal mine 44
Noranda 141-142, 144
Normal School, see Vancouver Normal School; Victoria Normal School
Norris cartoon 231
North America 140, 158-159, 180
North Okanagan Regional District 227
North Thompson, see Thompson River
North Vancouver 131, 209, 237
Northern Affairs, see Canada Dept. of Northern Affairs and Natural Resources
Northern Hardware Store (Prince George) 18, 55, 57-58, 111
Northwest Territories 65
Northwood Mills Ltd. 134, 141
Northwood Pulp and Timber Ltd. 142-144

O'Brien, Jerry 157
Oberammergau (Bavaria) 284
Ocean Falls 154, 277, 279-284
Ocean Falls Corp. 263, 265, 267-270, 272-277
Ogilvie, Lady 111
Oil (Alberta) 12
Oji Paper 9
Okanagan 28, 34, 42, 169, 226, 228
Okanagan Lake 226, 228

INDEX

Ontario 45, 140, 149, 196, 200, 242; see also Ottawa; Toronto
Ontario Hydro 196, 200
Ootsa Forest District 153
Orchard, C.D. 125-126, 130, 134
Orchestras, see Music
Oregon 148, 253, 276; see also Portland
Orr, Bill 92
Osaka (Japan) 163, 167
Osborne, E.E. "Ted" 233-235
Ottawa 50, 84-85, 171-173, 186-188, 190, 202-203, 206-207, 210

Pacific Biological Station (Nanaimo) 243
Pacific Club (Victoria) 73
Pacific Coast Services 120
Pacific Command (army) 84
Pacific Fort St. John No. 4 gas well 109
Pacific Great Eastern Railway (PGE) 74, 111, 118, 174-175
Pacific Highway 35
Pacific Logging 264
Pacific Northwest 213, 253
Pacific Rim 159
Pacific Western Airlines 264
Paget, Arthur F. 172-173, 177, 184, 191, 214-216, 221
Pakistan 257
Paris Match newspaper 109, 113
Parks and reserves 228-245; see also Elbow Park; Jasper; Mount Robson; Portland Island; Stanley Park
Parksville 229
Parsnip River 174, 176-177, 210, 212, 217
Particle board 278-279
Paul (E.B.) Building (Victoria) 85, 95
Peace Arch 210
Peace Power, see Peace River Power Development Co.
Peace River area and power projects 11, 15, 65-66, 70, 74, 108, 156, 161, 174, 176, 178, 180-181, 183, 189, 192, 195, 199, 202, 210, 212-214, 216-218, 220, 247
Peace River Canyon Dam 219
Peace River Power Development Co. (Peace Power) 178-181, 189, 195-197, 202, 210, 213-214, 231
Peak, Mary 111
Pearkes, George (General) 84-85, 94, 217
Pearse, Peter (Dr.) 287-288
Pearson, Lester B. 183, 204, 210
Pend d'Oreille River 239
Penticton 34, 53-54, 112, 224
Perepelkin, John 89
Perry, Frank 99
Perry, Tom (Dr.) 237-238
Peru 260-262
Petch, Earl 42
Peterson, Les 94, 120
PGE, see Pacific Great Eastern Railway
PHA, see Pulp Harvesting Area
Phillippines 199, 234, 253
Phillips, Don 263, 270-271, 273-274, 283
Pine 142, 145
Pine Manor (Prince George) 7, 65
Planes, see Airplanes
Plateau Mills 263, 266
Plumtree, A.F.W. 184
Plywood 118, 159, 278, 280
Point Grey (Vancouver) 24
Poland 99
Police (RCMP) 91, 103, 109-110, 112-113, 117
Political parties, see CCF; Conservative; Liberal; Nazi; New Democratic; Republican; Social Credit

311

Pontiac (car) 30-31, 34-36, 39
Poplar 280
Port Alberni 155
Port Coquitlam 50, 54
Port Hardy 267
Portage Mountain and dam 176-178, 180, 210, 213-218
Portland (Ore.) 209-210, 276
Portland Island 109, 113
Potlatch (Idaho) 278
Powell River 38
Powell River Co. 118, 127, 130-133, 153
Power Commission, see BC Power Commission
Power Corp., see BC Power Corp.
Power Development Act, BC 197
Prairies 88, 118
Prentice, John G. 138
Presbyterians 24
Prescott, Jack 138
Prince Akihito 164-165
Prince George 7, 11-13, 15-17, 21, 53-56, 59, 61, 63-65, 70, 73-74, 79, 81, 87, 91, 97-102, 104-106, 111, 118, 126, 134-142, 144-145, 155, 158, 174, 213-214, 217, 230, 240, 249, 255, 285, 289
Prince George Brewery 100-102, 104
Prince George Cafe 12
Prince George Citizen newspaper 12-13, 21
Prince George Hotel 54
Prince George Junior-Senior Secondary School (High School) 54, 61-62
Prince George Pulp and Paper Co. Ltd. 139, 141-144, 153
Prince Rupert 118, 153-154, 158, 289
Princess Margaret 108-113
Princess Margaret Island 109, 113
Princess Michiko 164-165

Princeton 38-44, 169, 238
Province, see Vancouver Province
Prudential Insurance 159
Public Works (BC Dept.) 85
Pucallpa (Peru) 261-262
Pulp Harvesting Area (PHA) licenses 142-143, 145, 151-157, 159, 161-163
Pulp mills and pulpwood 118, 134-157, 247, 255-256, 258-259, 261, 263-284
Pulpmill Road (Prince George) 99

Quebec 23, 141, 210-211, 241-242, 265; see also Montreal
Queen Charlotte Islands 125
Queen Elizabeth Hotel (Montreal) 241
Queen Mary Elementary School (Vancouver) 25
Queen's University 285
Quesnel 15, 97, 111, 149, 159-160, 249
Quick, Dad 27

Railways 16, 27, 39, 46, 50, 54-55, 97, 111-112, 118, 149, 169, 247; see also BC Rail; Canada-Alaska Railway; Canadian National; Canadian Pacific; Kettle Valley; Pacific Great Eastern; Wenner-Gren
Ranch, Douglas Lake 112
Rasmussen (flight instructor) 47-49
Rath, George and family 229-233
Rathtrevor Provincial Park 229-233
Rattlesnake Island 226
Rauvsep, Walter 221
Rayonnier (forestry company) 118
RCAF, see Air Force
RCMP, see Royal Canadian Mounted Police
Redmond, Ralph 255

INDEX

Reed Paper Co. 139-141, 144
Regional districts 225-227
Reid, J. Alan 76
Reid, Miss 30
Religion, churches, see Anglicans; Catholics; Doukhobors; United; Presbyterians
Republican Party (US) 192
Reserves and parks 228-245
Resources, see BC Resources (Ministry); BC Resources Investment Corp.; Canada Dept. of Northern Affairs and Natural Resources; Canadian Council of Resource Ministers
Resources for the Future Conference (Montreal) 241
Resources for the Future Inc. 221
Revelstoke 172, 184-185, 219-220
Revelstoke Canyon 184
Revelstoke dam 172, 219-220
Rhodesia 175
Rhododendron Flats 44
Ritchie, A.E. 191
Ritchie, Cec 42
Rivers, see Amazon; Carbon; Columbia; Duncan; Finlay; Fraser; Ganges; Homathco; Kootenay; Latchford; Nechako; Parsnip; Peace; Pend d'Oreille; Powell; Salmon; Saskatchewan; Skagit; Thompson; Ucayali; Wicked
Roads, see Highways
Robertson, R. Gordon 191
Robson Junior High School (Lower Mainland) 50-51
Rockcliffe air station 208
Rocky Mountains 174, 210, 212, 220
Rogers, Will 84
Rolston, Tilly 75-78, 80
Rome 158, 250
Rose, Bert 41

Ross dam 235-236, 238-239
Ross, Frank 108, 112
Ross Lake 236-237
Rossland 116, 120, 170
Royal Bank of Canada 204
Royal Canadian Air Force, see Air Force
Royal Canadian Mounted Police (RCMP; police) 91, 103, 109-110, 112-113, 117
Royal Commission on Education (Cameron Commission; Cameron Report) 53, 78
Royal Commission on Forestry, see Sloan Royal Commission
Royal Commission on power projects 189
Run Out Skagit Spoilers (group) 237
Runyon, Ernie 148-149
Rusk, Dean 210
Russia, Russians 46-47, 88-89, 180, 259-260
Rust, Tom 274

Saanich 84-85, 109
SAFE store (Salmon Arm) 26-31
Saint Felicien, see St. Felicien
Saint John (N.B.) 23, 249
Saint Laurent, see St. Laurent
Salmon 173
Salmon Arm 25, 28-30, 32, 34-35, 37-38, 55, 76
Salmon Arm Farmers' Exchange 25-26
Salmon Arm United Church 25
Salmon River Valley 30
Salt Spring Island 77
Samarinda 253
San Francisco 151
Sardis 87-88
Saskatchewan Power and Light 220
Saskatchewan River 220
Sauve, Jeanne 256

313

Sauve, Maurice 256
Scandinavia 140, 149
Schools, see Baron Byng; Connaught; Craigflower; Cranbrook; Duchess Park; Fort Nelson Indian School; Grandview Heights; Herbert Spencer; Magee; Moberley Lake; Prince George Junior-Senior; Queen Mary; Robson; Silver Creek; Strawberry Hill; see also Colleges; Education; Universities
Schultz (C.D.) and Co. 120
Schultz, Charles 120, 122
Scotland, Scottish 12, 83, 91, 122
Scott Road (Surrey) 37
Seattle 15, 152, 165, 178, 235-241, 275-276
Seattle Power and Light Ltd. 235-241
Sechelt 233
Senior citizens residence (Prince George) 64
Seven Mile Dam 239
Sherman, Paddy 200
Shields, Roy 49
Shimizu Construction Co. 168
Shirley, Mrs. 28-29
Shorter, Ernie 132
Shortreed, Mr. 132
Shrum, Gordon (Dr.) 153, 183, 189, 192, 195, 197, 199, 215-218
Shuswap Lake 172, 228
Sicamous 28
Silver Creek School (Salmon Arm Valley) 33
Simon Fraser University 220-221, 243
Simpson Corp. 265
Sinclair Spruce Mills 141
Singapore 254
Singh, Dagwinder 123
Skagit Bluffs 44
Skagit River 235, 238

Skagit Valley 235-236, 238-239
Skagit Valley Park 235
Ski clubs, Princeton 41
Ski resort, Cypress Bowl 233-235
Skogster, Mauri 9, 158
Skookumchuck 163, 168
Sladen, Cec 28-29
Sladen, Lilian 30
Sloan, Bill 264-265
Sloan, Gordon 117, 131
Sloan Royal Commission and forestry commissions 115, 117, 121, 127-129, 134, 156
Slocan Lake 90
Slocan Valley 90
Slumber Lodge Inns and Motels Ltd. (Prince George) 99
Smith, F.A. 182
Smithers 157
Social Credit Party (Alberta) 11
Social Credit Party and government (BC) 11, 15, 17-18, 21, 70, 76-77, 88, 100, 116, 166, 169, 176, 178, 195, 197, 202, 220, 227, 230, 237-238, 245, 247, 263, 268, 287, 290
Socialists 12, 20, 76
Society for Pollution and Environmental Control 237
Solomon 156
Sommers, Robert 115-117, 119-123, 127, 130, 170-171
Sons of Freedom, see Doukhobors
Sorrento 228
South America, see Peru
South Thompson River, see Thompson River
Southam Press 200
Spain 284
Spector, Norman 271
Spooner, Wilf 242

INDEX

Sprague, Lillian 45
Spruce 74, 140, 145, 211
Squamish 74, 131
Squire, Jack 233
Sri Lanka 251
St. Felicien (company) 264
St. Laurent, Prime Minister 171
Stafford, Harold 61
Stanley Park (Vancouver) 38
Steele, Bill 50
Stevens, Jack 178-179
Stokes, John 287
Stonehill, Harry 199
Strachan, Robert 205
Straith, W.T. 14, 62
Strandboard 278-280
Strathcona 232-233
Strathcona Park 233
Strawberry Flats 44
Strawberry Hill School (Surrey) 37-38
Strid, Berger 174-175
Strike, brewery workers 104
Sturdy, David 117
Stymiest, Phoebe, see Williston
Suharto, President 252
Sukarno, President 252
Sumas 48
Summerland 226, 228
Summit Lake 213
Sun, see Vancouver Sun
Sunshine Coast 285
Sunshine Coast Regional District 226
Supreme Court, see BC Supreme Court
Surrey 33, 35-37, 42
Surrey Teachers' Dramatic Club 36
Surveying, see BC Surveyor General;
    BC Surveys & Mapping Branch
Swainson, Neil (Dr.) 9, 291-292
Swanson, Cornelius "Blondie" 131
Sweden, Swedish 174, 259, 278
Swift Canadian Co. 23-24

Switzerland 124
Symonds Engineering 159, 268

Tacoma (Wash.) 152
Tahsis Co. 232
Takla Lake 156
Tarakan 253
Taylor, Austin 265
Taylor, E.P. 116
Taylor Flats 108-109
Teachers' Association, Greater
    Vancouver 16-17
Teachers' Federation, BC 53
Teaching, see Education
Telegraph Creek 65
Telephone, see BC Tel
Tennant, Walt 26
Terrace 61, 153
Texas 262
TFL, see Tree Farm Licenses
Theatre, see Drama, theatre
Thermal plant, Burrard Inlet 181;
    Williams Lake 161
Thompson River 34, 152, 226, 249
Thompson River Valley 152
Thorstenson, Roy 39, 41, 229
Thow, Jimmy 98
Thumm, Eileen, see Williston
Thumm, Walter Dolf 7, 65, 284-285
Thurso (Quebec) 211
Tickle Toes (band) 29-30
Tientsin (China) 282
Timber (magazine) 136-138
Times-Mirror Publishing Co. 274-276
Tokyo 164-165
Toney, John 18
Toronto 45, 54, 93, 198-199
Tory 179; see also Conservative Party
Toyota (car) 260, 262
Tractau Lectric Co. 211-212
Trail 39, 116, 120, 169-171, 239

Trans-Canada Highway 34, 88
Transportation (BC Ministry) 263
Treaties, see Columbia River Treaty
Tree crusher, see Le Tourneau
Tree Farm Licenses (TFL) 127, 130-132, 153; see also Forest Management Licenses; Pulp Harvesting Area licenses
Trees, see Aspen; Balsam; Cedar; Dogwood; Douglas fir; Poplar; Spruce; Pine
Tweeddale, Ed 28
Tweeddale, Mrs. 28-29
Tweeddale, Reg 248-249
Twist, Bert 98
"Two Rivers Policy" 8, 169-222
Tyee Airlines 233

Ucayali River 261
Uhlman, Wes 238
Uncle Ben's beer 102; breweries 104; see also Ginter
Union Club 182
Union Station (Toronto) 54
Union Steamships 21
Unions 104, 124, 247, 273-274, 288-289
United Church, Cloverdale 43; Princeton 43; Salmon Arm 25
United Empire Loyalists 23
United Nations (and FAO Food and Agricultural Organization) 158, 182, 250-251, 256-257, 259
United States, Americans 23, 34-35, 37, 47, 64, 104, 118, 138, 147, 149, 158-159, 170-173, 178-179, 181, 183-187, 189-195, 200-207, 209-210, 213, 219, 221-222, 224, 228, 236-238, 240, 260, 279-280, 284, 292-294; see also Alaska; California; Hawaii; Idaho; Los Angeles; Montana; New York; Oregon; San Francisco; Texas; Washington (DC); Washington (State)
United States Corps of Army Engineers 183, 203, 294
United States Court of Appeals 238
United States Plywood Ltd. 159
Universities, see Colleges; Harvard; Queen's; Simon Fraser; University
University of Alberta 15, 47
University of British Columbia 7, 33, 35, 43, 81-84, 92, 95, 132-134, 148, 183, 217, 221, 242-244, 281, 287
University of Northern British Columbia 295
University of Toronto 53-54
University of Victoria 94-96, 291; see also Victoria College
University of Washington 15
Upper Fraser Lumber Mills 141
US, see United States
Utilities Commission, BC 196

Vancouver 7, 20, 24-25, 27, 34, 38-39, 43-44, 50, 74-75, 79, 81-83, 92-93, 95, 107-108, 115, 119, 122, 131, 149, 156, 165-167, 172-173, 187, 198, 200-201, 209, 231-235, 237-238, 240, 249, 265, 267, 273, 278, 281, 289, 292; see also Lower Mainland
Vancouver General Hospital 20, 108
Vancouver Island 130, 166, 170, 181, 229, 232
Vancouver Normal School 81-83
Vancouver Province newspaper 27, 115, 122, 156, 198, 200-201, 273
Vancouver Sun newspaper 38, 115, 119, 156, 165, 231, 240

INDEX

Veneer Siding Ltd. 248
Vernon 34, 113
Victoria 13-17, 23-25, 29-31, 35, 62, 73-74, 79-85, 88-89, 93, 95, 97, 99, 109, 116, 119, 123, 130-131, 135, 138, 148, 151, 161, 165, 171, 175, 193, 207, 209-210, 224-225, 229, 231, 234, 242, 244, 248-249, 263, 265, 284, 288, 290
Victoria College 82-85, 94; see also Victoria Normal School; University of Victoria
Victoria Colonist newspaper 79
Victoria Feed Co. 24
Victoria Lumber Co. 138
Victoria Normal School 29-31, 35, 80-83; see also Victoria College
Victoria Times newspaper 95, 119
View Royal 224
Vogel, Dick 277

WAC Bennett Dam, see Bennett Dam
Waite Amulet Mine (Quebec) 141
Wakabayashi, Henry 283-284
Wallace, Laurie 92-93
War, cold war 215; War Assets Corp. 61; see also World War
Washington (DC) 23, 173, 193, 207, 210
Washington (State) 34, 152, 171, 193-194, 205-206, 210, 235, 239, 278; see also Bellingham; Blaine; Everett; Seattle; Tacoma; Wenatchee
Wasyluk, John 62
Water Resources, see BC Water Resources Branch; BC Water Rights Branch
Water Resources Act, BC 225
Water Resources of the Columbia River Basin (report) 184
Waterland, Tom 287

Watson, Don 264
Weatherby, Hugh 136
Webb, Arnold 85
Webber, General 201, 206
Webster, Arnold 79
Webster, Jack 238
Weldwood of Canada Ltd. 21, 159, 264
Weller Building (Victoria) 93
Wells Gray Park 233
Wenatchee (Wash.) 26, 205, 278
Wenner-Gren, Axel and company 154, 174-178, 182, 210, 213
West Fraser Mills 159
West Kootenay Power and Light 169, 182, 185, 189, 195-196
West Vancouver 233-235
Westcoast Transmission 108-109, 266
Western Canada Ski Championships (Princeton) 41-42
Western Forest Management Association 131-132
Weyerhaeuser Co. 152, 278
White House (Washington, DC) 173, 210
White Rock Players 36
White Sulphur Springs (N.Y.) 171
Wicked River 176-177
Williams, Bob 232, 238, 264, 268, 291
Williams Lake 111-112, 161, 249, 289
Williams, Ted 97
Williston, Dianne 49
Williston, Eileen (Thumm) 7-8, 284-285
Williston, Gladys (McInnes) 19, 36-37, 42-47, 49, 53, 56, 124, 231, 248, 270, 276, 284
Williston, Hubert (father) 23-26, 46
Williston, Hubert (son) 46, 49, 217, 219
Williston, Islay (McCalman) 23-27, 37, 39

Williston, John Bailey 23
Williston Lake 219
Williston, Norman 24-26, 28, 37
Williston, Phoebe (Stymiest) 23
Williston, Ray Gillis, see references throughout
Williston, Rosabelle, see Fisher
Williston, Sandra 65
Williston, Verna 24, 37
Wills, Mr. 95
Wilson, George 33
Winch, Ernie 73
Winnipeg (Man.) 23-24
Wood, C.B. 35
Wood, Freddie 28
World Bank 250, 253
World Fairs, see Expo
World War I, 14, 179, 267
World War II, 44-50, 61, 82, 84, 99, 170, 174, 241 (Marshall Plan), 259; see also Air Force; Army
Worley, Ron 17
Wright, see Crippen-Wright Engineering
Wright, Percy 73
Wright, Tom 134-135, 138

Yarrow Building (Victoria) 73
Yost, Evelyn 63
Young Building (Victoria) 83, 85
Yukon 65, 174, 197, 213

Zimmerman, Adam 144